Research

As

Resistance

Research

As

Resistance

Critical, Indigenous, and Anti-oppressive Approaches

Edited by
Leslie Brown and Susan Strega

Canadian Scholars' Press
Toronto

Research As Resistance: Critical, Indigenous, and Anti-oppressive Approaches
Edited by Leslie Brown and Susan Strega

First published in 2005 by
Canadian Scholars' Press/Women's Press
180 Bloor Street West, Suite 801
Toronto, Ontario
M5S 2V6

www.cspi.org
www.womenspress.ca

Canadian Scholars' Press/Women's Press gratefully acknowledges financial support for our publishing activities from the Ontario the Government of Canada through the Book Publishing Industry Development Program (BPIDP) and the Government of Ontario through the Ontario Book Publishing Tax Credit Program.

Library and Archives Canada Cataloguing in Publication

Research as resistance : critical, indigenous and anti-oppressive approaches / edited by Leslie Brown and Susan Strega.

ISBN 1-55130-275-6

1. Native peoples--Research--Canada--Methodology. 2. Oppression (Psychology) I. Brown, Leslie Allison, date. II. Strega, Susan

H62.R42 2005   305.897'071'072   C2005-901871-2

Cover design by George Kirkpatrick
Text design and layout by Brad Horning

05 06 07 08 09   5 4 3 2

Printed and bound in Canada by AGMV Marquis Imprimeur Inc.

Canadä

Dedication

In memory of Tanis Doe,
activist, teacher, researcher, scholar, comedian,
ballroom dancer, mother, colleague, and friend,
who lived her life without complaining,
but never without critique.

TABLE OF CONTENTS

◆

TRANSGRESSIVE POSSIBILITIES

Leslie Brown and Susan Strega

The phone rang and it was Susan, calling from Britain where she was working on her doctoral dissertation. She had been searching the library stacks for a radical and progressive research text. Knowing that I taught research, she thought I might make a recommendation. I confessed that I couldn't make a recommendation, and reminded her that I had been complaining that I couldn't find a research text to teach from that reflects the different realities of students and offers them possibilities for new ways of thinking. Since I had worked with several graduate students and practitioners who are doing innovative, transformative research, Susan wanted to know why I didn't write the book I wanted. Okay, I said. Want to do it with me?

This book is a collection of original pieces by practitioners and researchers from diverse locations who position social justice as necessary for research processes as well as for research outcomes. Many of these chapters were originally presented for commentary and critique at a series of symposia sponsored by the Research Initiatives for Social Change (RISC) Unit at the School of Social Work, University of Victoria. Thus, although this is a diverse collection, certain themes and issues recur throughout the chapters, resulting in an innovative book that we hope will provoke discussion and further understanding for senior undergraduates, graduate students, and experienced researchers in various fields.

One of these common themes is a willingness to explore the emancipatory possibilities of new approaches to research, even when these transgress the boundaries of traditional research and scholarship. While such explorations can be exciting, violating research and academic norms is also difficult and challenging given the extent to which we have all internalized dominant ideas about what constitutes "good" research and "acceptable" research practices. At one of the last symposia in the RISC series, Indigenous scholar Gale Cyr[1] was enthusiastically describing, in words and writing, her notion of research from the four directions. Running out of room on the whiteboard, she simply continued writing on the wall with her black marker, eliciting first a gasp of surprise and then silence from the participants. For many of us who are represented in this book, editors and writers alike, Gale's transgressive act has come to symbolize what we intend with this work: to make space and take space for marginalized researchers and ideas. We push the edges of academic acceptability not because we want to be accepted within the academy but in order to transform it.

Though as editors we share commitments to transforming and transgressing research practices, we come to this work from much different locations. Susan is an activist and practitioner whose sojourn in academia began relatively recently. She had a long and uncomfortable relationship with research through her membership in various exhaustively researched marginalized groups. Her commitment to ensure that her own research endeavours were politically progressive has led her through various methodologies (discourse analysis, grounded theory, feminist poststructuralism) to a focus on questions of ontology and epistemology: What is knowledge, and who has the right to determine what is or is not knowledge? Leslie came to the academy 15 years ago to teach research to social workers. A feminist, she was committed to applied research that would effect change and so developed research curricula grounded in social work practice, particularly community development. With a long history of working with Aboriginal communities and the completion of doctoral studies in Aboriginal governance and administration, her appreciation of the political nature of research and the duty to decolonize continues to push her to understand different ways of knowing, being, and doing.

It might be said that we are part of the challenge posed by the "crisis of representation" that has confronted social science research over the last quarter century. We stand in a line of feminists, critical race theorists, and postmodernists who have all problematized the Enlightenment paradigm that shapes both quantitative and qualitative approaches to research, and which gives rise to concepts such as "objectivity" and "neutrality" (Burt and Code, 1994; Featherstone and Fawcett, 2000; Hill Collins, 2000). They have questioned and politicized research processes such as fieldwork and data analysis and foregrounded the subjectivity of the researcher as a salient, if not determining, factor in research design and results. The principles of anti-oppressive practice, once restricted to the direct practice dimension, have begun to influence research practices and have contributed to these critiques by highlighting the relationship between the researcher and the "researched" (Kirby and McKenna, 1989; Lather, 1991; Ristock and Pennell, 1996).

Though these and other writers have made significant contributions to reframing research practices, several factors set this book apart. While each of the authors describe, in different ways, their encounters with and journeys through the boundaries of mainstream research, most also consider how their journeys have been shaped not only by their commitment to emancipatory goals but also by their location on the margins. This collection extends the range of many other "postpositivist" (Lather, 1991) works by featuring three Indigenous perspectives on knowledge creation. These chapters, and others in this volume, problematize, explore, and offer solutions for working with power relations between researchers and communities. Finally, this collection extends other theoretical and practical discussions of research methodologies by continuously bringing questions of ontology and epistemology into play, and by positioning them as necessary for any researcher seeking to work anti-oppressively.

Why Another Research Book?

Our intention is to enhance and continue the work of other theorists and researchers who have been asking critical questions about the purposes and processes of social science research. Like Ristock and Pennell (1996), writers in this volume have been influenced by postmodernism's challenge to the notion of epistemological guarantees, and are similarly concerned by questions about our relationship with those we "research." Some of the writers in this volume explore an explicitly anti-oppressive orientation to researching individual as well as community concerns. The researcher's use of self and the processes of reflexivity are taken up in new ways, with Indigenous ideas set alongside those of other marginalized researchers. Like works by Kirby and McKenna (1989), Lather (1991), and Weiss and Fine (2000), this volume integrates political and ethical reflections on research with concrete and practical suggestions for enacting political and ethical commitments, but takes as its starting point the necessity of reflecting not just on processes but on the philosophical underpinnings of research. Indigenous and non-Indigenous authors in this volume alike take up Tuhiwai Smith's (1999) call for the decolonization of knowledge and the processes of knowledge acquisition. Questions about who knowledge is created for, how it is created, and for what purposes are interwoven with concrete descriptions of how politically committed researchers can address these concerns in their work.

Despite the emergence of critical, feminist, and Indigenous approaches to research, anti-oppressive and critical research methodologies still rate little more than a mention in most research methods textbooks (see, for example, Neuman and Krueger, 2003; Salahu-Din, 2003). Ensuring that these approaches are not well articulated or well understood has contributed to their marginalization, as has the institutionalization of positivist research frameworks in mandatory ethical review procedures. In Canada, all universities and major funding bodies currently refer to the *Tri-Council Policy Statement: Ethical Conduct for Research Involving Humans* for ethical guidance. As other critiques have noted (van den Hoonard, 2002), the *Statement* and the ethical standards derived from it reflect both quantitative and Eurocentric biases. Principles related to protecting research "subjects" often conflict with non-Eurocentric understandings of relationship and community. By configuring research "subjects" in particular and limited ways, ethical review procedures are not only often problematic for social justice researchers but fail to consider ethical questions that are vitally important to them, such as voice, representation, and collaboration. Further, these standards are being applied not just to researcher conduct but also to research design in ways that are inimical to non-quantitative approaches.

This has constrained both the creation of knowledge and participation in the creation of knowledge. We contend that these constraints have maintained rather than challenged existing power relations—what Dorothy Smith (1987) called "relations of ruling"—and structural inequalities. Exemplars of anti-oppressive research that have been published often have a paucity of detail about how one might actually go about doing it (see, for example, Shera, 2003). Texts with considerable detail about methods sometimes omit any detailed discussion of the ontology and epistemology underpinning the methods (see, for example, Kirby and McKenna, 1989). Concerns about research with marginalized populations are sometimes interpreted as technical rather than political challenges (see, for example, Potocky and Rodgers-Farmer, 1998). Without the ability to understand anti-oppressive approaches at the level of praxis, it is difficult to know how they apply or how they may be applied and whether and to what extent they might contribute to social justice.

This book has been produced, in part, to provide accessible theoretical and practical explanations of critical, Indigenous, and anti-oppressive research. It seeks to make clear the theoretical foundations and practical processes of anti-oppressive approaches to knowledge creation, while at the same time acknowledging the breadth and possibility of these innovative research methodologies. Most of the authors in this volume, all of whom exist in one way or another on "the margins," experienced difficulties as they searched for research methodologies that were congruent with their commitments to social justice and anti-oppressive practice, and to their cultural traditions and life experiences. All methodologies carry within them underlying assumptions that shape both how information—"data"—is gathered and the kinds of knowledges that are constructed by and through information gathering and analysis. The marginalized and those who are committed to social justice at all levels of the research process want and need different kinds of knowledge and different and more congruent means by which to create it, or to allow previously subjugated knowledges to emerge.

We note that this book is written at a time of positivist resurgence in the academy in general and in the "practice professions" (social work, nursing, education) in particular (Leonard, 2001; Rose, 1998). Neo-liberal economic ideologies and their spawn, managerialism, have demanded that practice and policy be assessed in terms of fiscal accountability and little else. Such demands have nurtured a movement toward "evidence-based practice" and "outcome measurement" with the usefulness of evidence for practice based in a methodological hierarchy in which quantitative methodologies stand at the apex (Trinder with Reynolds, 2000). For example, Royse's recent (2004) text, *Research Methods in Social Work*, positions quantitative research as "legitimate" research and qualitative research as "popular." Faced with this hierarchy, qualitative researchers in the practice professions have often responded by accepting this arrangement but striving to prove the usefulness of their methodologies in two ways. One has been to suggest that a "natural" alliance exists between practice and qualitative research methods and data. The second has been an attempt to propose

5

and prove that qualitative markers of validity and reliability are as rigorous as those employed by quantitative researchers.

Framing the discussion about what constitutes knowledge within the discourse of positivism obscures important questions about how the development of knowledge is socially constructed and controlled, how knowledge is used, and whose interests knowledge serves. For both qualitative and quantitative research, it fosters an illusion of neutrality or objectivity that has come to be institutionalized within academia as the standard by which truth claims are assessed. The racialized and gendered foundation of the Enlightenment epistemology that quantitative and qualitative approaches share is rendered invisible, and truth claims are sequestered from questions of power, politics, and survival. In this approach, notions of anti-oppression become distorted and relegated to discussions of ethical treatment but otherwise kept separate from research "realities."

This book stands in opposition to those who would retrench positivism as the basis of research and practice in social work and other practice professions. Instead, we hope to assist in exploring the transgressive possibilities of centring critical, Indigenous, and anti-oppressive approaches to research. We want to contextualize these approaches in terms of the social justice world views they embody and express. At the same time, we want to make clear that we are not, by what has been included or excluded here, constraining or excluding other ways of theorizing or researching that contribute to social justice initiatives. These pieces are collected in part to argue against any one research methodology assuming the status of "truth"—indeed, these approaches are all about a challenge to the notion that there is a "truth" to be "discovered" or a "true path" to follow in creating, constructing, or uncovering knowledge. Rather, our intention is to contribute to the project of having research reflect, both in terms of its processes and in terms of the knowledge it constructs, the experience, expertise, and concerns of those who have traditionally been marginalized in the research process and by widely held beliefs about what "counts" as knowledge.

Research from, by, and with the Margins

Marginalization refers to the context in which those who routinely experience inequality, injustice, and exploitation live their lives. Being marginalized refers not just to experiences of injustice or discrimination or lack of access to resources. In the research context, it acknowledges that knowledge production has long been organized, as have assessments of the ways producing knowledge can be "legitimate," so that only certain information, generated by certain people in certain ways, is accepted or can qualify as "truth." Historically, this has meant that those on the margins have been the objects but rarely the authors of research, and the discomfort that those on the margins feel about adopting traditional research processes and knowledge creation has been interpreted as their personal inability or failings.

A number of events have contributed to the current challenge to this marginalization. Deconstructionist practices associated with postmodernism and poststructuralism have forced a reconsideration of "subject," "object," and "author" in research. Critical approaches such as critical race theory and feminism have foregrounded the political nature of all research, even that which most strongly insists on illusions of neutrality and objectivity. Further, critical approaches have pushed us to ask questions about who interprets, prioritizes, and owns research and research products. In Canada, Indigenous peoples' commitment to reclaiming traditional ways of knowing has also led to questions and critiques of research practices. Social justice approaches to research, such as participatory action research, have attempted to position those who might have traditionally been the objects or respondents of research as equal collaborators or co-researchers. All of these have contributed to a nascent interest in the relationship between research and margin.

Research from the margins is not research on the marginalized but research by, for, and with them/us. It is research that takes seriously and seeks to trouble the connections between how knowledge is created, what knowledge is produced, and who is entitled to engage in these processes. It seeks to reclaim and incorporate the personal and political context of knowledge construction. It attempts to foster oppositional discourses, ways of talking about research, and research processes that explicitly and implicitly challenge relations of domination and subordination. It is grassroots in the sense of considering as "legitimate" what we have to say about our own lives and the lives of others, and how the conditions of those lives might be transformed.

Although the landscape of inquiry may be undergoing a process of transformation, practices of marginalization continue alongside these changes. All of the writers in this volume discuss to some extent their own experiences of being silenced and/or being told that their methods of creating, constructing, or understanding knowledge are not legitimate. This volume has been created in response to these experiences and to the needs of others seeking to engage in critical, Indigenous, and anti-oppressive research. The theoretical discussions and the exemplars provided by the various authors are intended to demystify the research process, provide some guideposts to researchers, and contribute to making these innovative approaches more accessible. We hope that this book will also provide support to all who are questioning and problematizing what it means to do research, and most especially to those engaged in the project of centring subjugated knowledge(s).

Talking Back and Making Space

Postmodernism, critical race theory, and feminism's attempts to construct anti-oppressive theory have created important political openings for new ways of looking at research processes. At the same time, it is necessary to acknowledge that this space is small and continually under threat from those who seek to reinscribe the hegemony of traditional research methodologies. So what is this hegemony?

Positivist or quantitative research (the two terms are often conflated) continues to be the gold standard for social science research, and in the practice professions, this research is disproportionately favoured in funding, publication, and social policy decisions. Social science positivists take the view that information about social reality is objective and can be "discovered" through the same means by which "facts" about the natural world are determined. Unbiased observation and rigorous measurement by an allegedly neutral observer ostensibly produce neutral information on which all rational individuals can agree. While acknowledging the existence of other research approaches, most positivists position quantitative methodologies as superior. For example, Cournoyer and Klein (2000), in their review of research methods for social work, advocate the scientific method because it "has evolved to avoid most of the common fallacies of human reasoning to which most of the other ways of understanding reality succumb" (p. 3).

Interpretivist or qualitative social science, which encompasses hermeneutics, ethnomethodology, phenomenology, and other qualitative methodologies, is generally positioned as positivism's binary (though less valued) opposite. Qualitative researchers see social reality as subjective, and their research practices involve observing and interpreting the meanings of social reality as various groups and individuals experience them. Rather than challenging positivist ideas about neutrality and objectivity in research, interpretivists have contributed to their instantiation by utilizing alternative measures of rigour and validity, and insisting that researcher bias can be "bracketed" so as not to influence research results.

Although both quantitative and qualitative research has been used for progressive political and social purposes, both methodologies are positioned as separate from such concerns. For those hoping to align their research practices with social justice commitments, the development of critical research methodology offered an alternative. Critical research rejects the ideas of value-free science that underpin both quantitative and qualitative approaches to research. Instead, it positions itself as about critiquing and transforming existing social relations. Critical researchers view reality as both objective and subjective: objective in terms of the real forces that impinge on the lives of groups and individuals, and subjective in terms of the various individual and group interpretations of these forces and the experiences they engender. Feminist research has contributed the notion that research is gendered, and critical race theory has foregrounded issues of race. Where critical methodologies have been most challenged — by feminists, critical race theorists, and postmodernists — is in their failure to problematize research relationships. Critical research's concern with "false consciousness" reinscribed, however unintentionally, the traditional relationship between an informed and aware researcher and an "unconscious" research participant. Historically, the knowledge creation process has been separated from concerns about praxis: theorizing about the political nature of knowledge creation has rarely been translated into transforming our research practices. This book is deeply concerned with research as praxis, so the authors in this volume move continually between theory and practice, reflecting on how innovative and critical research theories might be applied, and then modifying theories as a result of their practice experience.

Critical, Indigenous, and anti-oppressive approaches to research see research as part of an emancipatory commitment, and seek to move beyond a critical social science to establish a position of resistance (Ristock and Pennell, 1996; Tuhiwai Smith, 1999). This book is concerned with the development of research approaches that empower resistance. This is not empowerment as it is popularly understood as an essentially private activity, as in individual assertiveness or the psychological experience of feeling powerful, but empowerment that is tied to an analysis of power relations and a recognition of systemic oppressions. Research that empowers resistance makes a contribution to individually and collectively changing the conditions of our lives and the lives of those on the margins. By centring questions of whose interests are served not only by research products but also in research processes, it challenges existing relations of dominance and subordination and offers a basis for political action.

As part of the project of noticing and reclaiming the personal and political context of all knowledge creation, this book challenges a broad range of currently popular research methodologies, across the range of positivism to postmodernism, by noticing that they all draw from a narrow foundation of knowledge based in the social, historical, and cultural experiences of White men: the dominant and hegemonic ideology under which we all live, and in whose image the academy is constructed. We take the position that research cannot challenge relations of dominance and subordination unless it also challenges the hegemony of current research paradigms. In order to make overt how power relations permeate the construction and legitimation of knowledge, the question of the researcher's location and political commitments, which are obscured by methodological claims to objectivity, neutrality, and gender and race-blindness, must be taken up. Thus, many of these chapters centre processes of reflexivity or self-reflexivity—the need and necessity for researchers to not only acknowledge but also examine their location and how that location permeates their inquiry at every level. These authors both acknowledge and show us how to acknowledge how our "invested positionality" (Lather, 1991, p. xvii) shapes our research approaches and understandings.

We believe that multiple paradigms are an evolutionary necessity and part of a commitment to social justice, and thus it is not our intention to be definitive about what constitutes a critical or anti-oppressive methodology. We have no desire to inscribe a new hegemony in which margin moves to centre and centre to margin. At the same time, we (and the authors featured in this volume) believe that modifying traditional methodologies through sensitizing their methods and procedures to diversity and difference is far from enough. Rather, we hope this collection contributes to disrupting the centre/margin relationship and other binary hierarchies in their entirety. It is an introduction, a starting point to encourage further exploration of alternative, critical, and anti-oppressive methodologies.

Who This Book Is For

This book is offered to those who are interested in social science research that is expressly concerned with redressing oppression and committed to social justice—those who, because of their location on the margins, the marginalized locations of those with whom they are conducting research, and/or their own commitments to anti-oppressive practice, want to learn more about how to go about conducting this research. In particular it is aimed at final-year undergraduates, beginning graduate students, and practitioners dissatisfied with their experiences with "traditional" research methodologies.

Traditional social science research, whatever its intentions, has silenced and distorted the experiences of those on the margins, taking a deficit-informed approach to explaining their lives and experiences. The histories, experiences, cultures, and languages (the "ways of knowing") of those on the margins have historically been devalued, misinterpreted, and omitted in the academy, where, as noted, only certain conceptualizations of information are counted as "valid" (objective and therefore authoritative) knowledge. In this process, many ways of knowing, which Foucault referred to as "subjugated knowledges" (1980), have been excluded or trivialized. The search for research methodologies that are capable of grasping the messy complexities of people's lives, especially the lives of those on the margins, involves reclaiming these knowledges while simultaneously moving away from the binary conceptualizations fostered under existing research paradigms. The theoretical pieces and exemplars in this book focus on racialized, gendered, differently abled, and classed experiences from a strengths-based focus and as sources of strength. Thus, it offers support for marginalized researchers attempting to cleave to the truth of their own experience. It also offers research ideas for those who are not from the margins, or who occupy both marginal and privileged spaces, but who want to engage in research practices from a position of solidarity with the marginalized.

This book is particularly relevant for those engaged in the practice professions, such as social work, nursing, education, and child and youth care. Of all the social science-based professions, it is the practice professions that have been most pushed toward postpositivist methodologies. This has occurred in part because of the dissatisfaction that those with whom they work have expressed with the absence of their experience and world views in the theoretical models that guide practice and policy. In part, it is related to the recent history of struggle around what constitutes legitimate or acceptable conceptual frameworks and methodologies by which we practice, develop policy, and conduct research.

Practitioners are being encouraged to embrace research as a core feature of practice. As previously noted, in social work at least there is strong support in many quarters for a move to "evidence-based practice" that reinscribes traditional positivist notions of how knowledge should be created and assessed, in which what constitutes "evidence" is understood securely within a positivist/Enlightenment (White, heterosexual, patriarchal) framework. We suggest that it is no accident that it is particularly the practice professions that are being pushed in this direction. As professions historically and currently dominated by women, they have long struggled with and for issues of legitimacy. As female-dominated professions and as professions that work with those on the margins, we have been tempted (and have at times in the past) taken the position of "proving" ourselves by subjecting ourselves as well as our research methodologies and processes to standards of legitimacy that are ultimately not in our own interests. Now we have a chance to step into the research space that has been opened up by those on the margins. In acknowledging that previous efforts to develop a critical social science have largely failed to contribute to anti-oppressive practice or policy making, we must ask different questions about how to construct and conduct our inquiries. This book is therefore for research practitioners in search of transgressive possibilities.

How the Book Has Been Organized

The chapters in this book address a variety of methodological, epistemological, and practice issues in critical, Indigenous, and anti-oppressive approaches to research: What they are, why they are needed, how they might be done, and what lies ahead. Each engages, in one way or another, with the challenges of linking research methodologies with commitments to anti-oppressive practice and social justice. The authors in this book refuse to be complicit in the illusory disconnect between ideology and methodology and instead attempt to delineate how these are linked.

We have chosen not to separate the more theoretical chapters in this book from those with more of a practice focus, but instead have interspersed them; this reflects our understanding of research as praxis. To start us off, Maggie Kovach invites us to accompany her as she explores Indigenous research paradigms and methodologies while resisting the imposition of dominant ideas about who can do research, and how. She offers some thoughts on what Indigenous epistemology is, the role of an Indigenous theoretical framework in research, and how these link with methodology. Through highlighting key themes in Indigenous methodologies, she proposes some principles that can guide researchers interested in Indigenous and other emancipatory approaches to research.

In the next chapter, Mehmoona Moosa-Mitha situates anti-oppressive theories in relation to critical and other difference-centred perspectives such as White feminism, Marxism, and postmodernism. Starting from the fundamental premise that knowledge and the processes by which we come to know are situated in the experiences of those who make knowledge claims and exist in a social relationship with others who make contesting knowledge claims, Mehmoona defines and clarifies the theoretical assumptions of anti-oppressive theories, showing how these theories contest the ontological and epistemological assumptions of other theories. She argues that anti-oppressive theories are distinguishable from others by being both difference-centred and critical in their orientation, and thus perhaps particularly useful for emancipatory research endeavours.

As a beginning researcher and a disabled woman, Sally Kimpson struggled with issues of power and representation in her use of a critical autobiographical narrative methodology in her research. Among her many significant contributions to this collection is her inclusion of the body as a source of knowledge. She allows us to view her struggle to resist the academy's privileging of the idealized graduate student: male, able-bodied, White, heterosexual, and middle class. Thus, Sally calls into question dominant understandings of research and research processes, while offering insights into how one might "step off the road" into transformative practice.

For Kathy Absolon and Cam Willett, the researcher's location is a central and fundamental principle of Aboriginal research methodology. Their call for a declaration of positionality, from Indigenous voices to Indigenous researchers and students, speaks to all researchers seeking to work anti-oppressively. They open with a dialogue about location *as* research methodology and continue with a theoretical discussion of the purposes and processes of locating oneself. In this they offer research principles central to Aboriginal methodology and, perhaps, to all researchers seeking to work in marginalized communities: respectful representation, revising, reclaiming, renaming, remembering, reconnecting, and recovering. Implicit in all of these principles are strategies for resisting dominant norms in research.

Location is also a central concern for Fairn herising, who explores and rethinks the politics of location between researchers and the communities they wish to enter through the lens of queer flexibilities. Fairn draws our attention to how the context of history, colonization, discipline, and research and academic institutions shape research relationships. She proposes a politics of accountability that encourages researchers to attend to these relationships in new ways. Such concerns are also central to the chapter by Deborah Rutman, Carol Hubberstey, April Barlow, and Erinn Brown who share critical reflections and lessons learned from their experiences of conducting participatory action research (PAR). They discuss the challenges, opportunities, contradictions, and rewards of creating a research project that was not just about, but also with and for, marginalized youth, and delve into the complexities of roles, relationships, and power relations between differently located research team members. They provide an overview of PAR principles, relate PAR to anti-oppressive research, and provide insights into how research principles are affected by institutional requirements that often confound emancipatory researchers.

In "Wife Rena Teary," we journey with Rena Miller, a practitioner who did not, at the outset of her project, imagine herself as a researcher. Noticing a gap between her lived experience as the wife of a dying person and her experience as a recipient of palliative care, she sets out to explore the "line of fault" between these two experiences using institutional ethnography. Her detailed account of her research process provides guideposts for other researchers appropriating critical methodologies. This chapter concludes with some important insights into the relationship between research and the everyday world of practice.

Susan Strega's view from the margins begins with an examination and critique of the ontological and epistemological foundations of traditional social science. She ventures into feminist poststructuralism, offering an accessible description of this perspective and an exploration of its potential as an emancipatory research methodology. This chapter concludes with some useful proposals for how such research projects might be evaluated. In "Honouring the Oral Traditions of My Ancestors through Storytelling," Robina Thomas also takes up a particular research methodology, that of storytelling. This choice honours her Aboriginal heritage and resists historical and contemporary practices of colonization. Her description of her struggles offers insights for all researchers concerned with questions of voice and representation. The question of "how to do this work right" was central for Robina, and her adoption of uy'skwuluwun as a guiding ethical principle suggests transformations in how research ethics might be constituted.

The chapter "Becoming an Anti-Oppressive Researcher" by Karen Potts and Leslie Brown is a fitting way to conclude this collection. Starting with a discussion of what they consider to be the key principles of anti-oppressive research, the authors offer a detailed description of how being anti-oppressive looks throughout the process of inquiry. Their theoretical excursions are illuminated by foregrounding one student's experience with putting anti-oppressive principles to work.

T.S. Elliott once wrote, "Do I dare disturb the universe?" This book takes up that dare and, hopefully, provides bridges to other researchers who want to question taken-for-granted ideas about what research is, who is entitled to engage in it, and how it ought to be done.

Note

1.   Professeure, Université du Québec en Abitibi-Témiscamingue.

References

Burt, S., and Code, L. (1995). *Changing methods: Feminists transforming practice.* Toronto: Broadview.

Cournoyer, D., and Klein, W. (2000). *Research methods for social work.* Boston: Allyn and Bacon.

Fawcett, B., Featherstone, B., Fook, J., and Rossiter, A. (1999). *Practice and research in social work: Postmodern feminist perspectives.* London: Routledge.

Featherstone, B., and Fawcett, B. (2000). Setting the scene: An appraisal of postmodernism, postmodernity, and postmodern feminism. In Fawcett, B., Featherstone, B., Fook, J. and Rossiter, A. (Eds.), *Practice and research in social work: Postmodern Feminist Perspectives*, pp. 5–23. New York: Routledge.

Foucault, M. (1980). *The history of sexuality.* New York: Vintage Books.

Hill Collins, P. (2000). *Black feminist thought* (2nd edition). New York: Routledge.

Kirby, S., and McKenna, K. (1989). *Experience, research, social change: Methods from the margins.* Toronto: Garamond.

Lather, P. (1991). *Getting smart: Feminist research and pedagogy with/in the postmodern.* New York: Routledge.

Leonard, P. (2001). The future of critical social work in uncertain conditions. *Critical Social Work* 2 (1), http://www.criticalsocialwork.com/01.

Neuman, W., and Kreuger, L. (2003). *Social work research methods: Qualitative and quantitative approaches.* Boston: Allyn and Bacon.

Potocky, M., and Rodgers-Farmer, A. (Eds.). (1998). *Social work research with minority and oppressed populations: Methodological issues and innovations.* New York: Haworth.

Ristock, J., and Pennell, J. (1996). *Community research as empowerment.* Toronto: Oxford University Press.

Rose, N. (1998). Governing risky individuals: The role of psychiatry in new regimes of social control. *Psychiatry, Psychology and the Law* 5 (2), 177–195.

Royse, D. (2004). *Research methods in social work* (4th edition). Toronto: Thomson and Brooks/Cole.

Salahu-Din, S. (2003). *Social work research: An applied approach.* Boston: Allyn and Bacon.

Shera, W. (Ed.). (2003). *Emerging perspectives on anti-oppressive practice.* Toronto: Canadian Scholars' Press.

Smith, D. (1987). *The everyday world as problematic: A feminist sociology.* Toronto: University of Toronto Press.

Trinder, L., with S. Reynolds (Eds.). (2000). *Evidence-based practice: A critical appraisal.* Oxford: Blackwell Science.

Tuhiwai Smith, L. (1999). *Decolonizing methodologies: Research and Indigenous peoples.* London: Zed.

van den Hoonard, W. (2002). *Walking the tightrope: Ethical issues for qualitative researchers*. Toronto: University of Toronto Press.

Weiss, L., and Fine, M. (2000). *Speed bumps: A student-friendly guide to qualitative research*. New York: Teachers' College Press.

CHAPTER ONE

EMERGING FROM THE MARGINS:
INDIGENOUS METHODOLOGIES

Margaret Kovach[1]

Venturing into a graduate course, I was feeling anxious because I was presenting on my graduate research.[2] I was the second presenter of the day after the instructor led a seminar on Indigenous knowledge. Knowing beforehand of Indigenous content, I would usually brace myself for students' reactions, but I was preoccupied with my own presentation and didn't emotionally prepare. The seminar and the atmosphere it provoked were not unfamiliar. A tension entered the room with the usual remarks prefaced with qualifying apologies (e.g., "I am sorry, but I think Natives ....") by some students while others students were quietly uneasy with eyes downcast. And still other students offered comments in an attempt to neutralize the anxiety in the room. I was silently listening to the conversation unfold and sensed people were wondering about my reaction. What would she say? Would she inflict guilt, anger, absolution? In similar instances I would offer comments inevitably igniting a range of responses, my words poignant because I, an Indigenous woman, uttered them. Afterward, I would judge myself for not being clear, gentle, or educative enough—that I did not do justice to the Indigenous cause. However, I was tired and saving my energy for my presentation. All I could think of was, oh, great, the class is already stressed about Indigenous issues and I have to talk about Indigenous research—wonderful timing.

I did not speak during the class discussion, but was likely grimacing. The seminar was winding down, and I was presenting in five minutes. I discreetly slipped out of the classroom to use the washroom. As I re-entered the room, I noticed a hush among the students and the instructor was talking. I slid quietly into my chair, feeling eyes on me. I noticed a familiar gnawing sensation in the pit of my stomach that my bathroom break was interpreted as a political act, a walking out, as it were. I was up next and did not have time to deconstruct what happened, so I just grabbed my overheads and walked to the front of the room. I quickly pushed forward with my seminar. The goal was to introduce my research and its purpose. My research is of deep personal interest to me: social work education with Indigenous students. Excited about generating dialogue on my research, I planned to use liberatory language, stressing the social justice possibilities for Indigenous peoples inherent in this project. I did not.

In a blink of an eye I chose to talk about methodology. I rushed quickly through the topic of my research and inquiry question, then pulled out my methodology overheads. I focused on three common methodological paradigms (critical, interpretative, positivist), identified each, and explained that I was drawing from both critical and interpretative (I did not even mention Indigenous methodologies or conflicts arising from using "mainstream" methodologies in Indigenous research). Using the vernacular of academic research language, I skirted around social change, dodged upsetting the status quo, and was as apolitical as possible. People started to relax. Though I was talking the language of theory, of definitional criteria, of epistemologies fitting with methodology, I could have been handing out muscle relaxants. The tension dissipated. (To be fair, there was probably a lot of introspection because of the earlier conversation, but the classroom mood became considerably less edgy.) At this point some may wonder—didn't the methodology discussion delve into the political? It could have, but I made a choice to use language to deflect rather than engage. My only defence is that I didn't have the energy to go to contentious places (and I offer this writing as a makeup assignment).

There were two significant teachings arising from this experience. What I learned, through the acuteness of personal choice and action, is that critical research can be emancipatory—*or not*—depending on where you want to take it (either way it's political). What was the second insight? For many Indigenous peoples in contemporary academic classrooms in this country, going to the washroom can be interpreted as a stance. By merely walking through (or out of) mainstream doors, we tend to make spaces alive with a politicality that creates both tension and possibility. Indigenous researchers (and by that I mean Indigenous peoples) make research political simply by being who we are. Value-neutral research methodologies are not likely to be a part of the Indigenous researcher's experience and as such we have a natural allegiance with emancipatory research approaches. An anti-oppressive research anthology, such as this book, is a natural place to explore Indigenous methodologies, many aspects of which are shared by the other methodologies from the margins. The challenge for Indigenous research will be to stay true to its own respective theoretical roots of what counts as emancipatory as it ventures into mainstream academia. The goal of this chapter is to explore emerging writing, conversations, and thinking within Indigenous research and its role within the production of knowledge. It is from my perspective as an Indigenous person and emerges from that personal interpretation. However, before launching into a discussion of Indigenous research, I start this voyage with a brief review of emancipatory research.

Emancipatory Methodologies

Emancipatory research is inclusive of a variety of research methodologies. Humphries, Mertens, and Truman (2000) list several research approaches arising from epistemologies in feminism, critical hermeneutics, postmodern, and critical theory, all of which share an emancipatory objective. An Indigenous framework can be added to this list. The epistemological assumptions of these varied methodologies contend that that those who live their lives in marginal places of society experience silencing and injustice. Within the realm of research and its relationship to the production of knowledge, this absence of voice is significant and disturbing. To discuss liberating research methodologies without critical reflection on the university's role in research and producing knowledge is impossible. Universities have long claimed a monopoly in defining what counts as knowledge (Hall, 1998). As conservatism is recharging itself in the academy, it is an arduous (though not unfamiliar) struggle for intellectuals engaged in critical discourse to procure a slice of the epistemic pie. Carving space for emancipatory research in the academy, particularly for "new" methodologies, like Indigenous research, is exhausting. Questioning established views about what counts as meaning, knowledge, and truth provokes defensiveness.

Clearly, emancipatory research seeks to counter the epistemic privilege of the scientific paradigm, but when did it emerge and how does it connect with Indigenous research? The Enlightenment era was marked by the celebration of science and a perception that through scientific reasoning man could understand, control, and shape the natural, social, political, and economic world. Inherent in this method is the belief in a universal truth applicable to all people and cultures (Dockery, 2000). The emergence of modernity in the early 1920s with its mantra of *knowledge for progress* further entrenched the scientific model in both physical and social sciences, particularly in North America. Positivism was the answer for an individualist, industrial-centric society that was feverishly focused on production outcomes and profit. Universities became think-tanks for knowledge production culminating in research methodologies, extractive in nature, which served industry and business. While the scientific method was producing knowledge benefiting society, the problem was that it was becoming privileged. As positivism took increasingly more space to serve science, it squeezed out alternative forms of knowledge. Tandon points out: "The rise of the knowledge industry in the twentieth century has narrowed and limited epistemological options" (1988, p. 9). The exclusion of ways of knowing from the perspective of marginal groups (e.g., Indigenous peoples) thwarted the abundant possibilities of what knowledge could encompass.

The overwhelming presence of positivism in knowledge production, coupled with emerging questions about the exploitive nature of research, created an opportunity to challenge the established research paradigm. The 1950–1970s was a time when emancipatory epistemologies were both fermenting and surfacing in North America. And there was an increased number of researchers "exploring new methods" that were alternatives to the scientific model (Hall, 1982, p. 14). By the late 1970s there were at least three distinct groupings of research paradigms on the radar screen, including the *empirical* (positivist), *interpretative*, and *critical* approaches (Kemmis, 2001). Of these three categories, critical research incorporated emancipatory methodologies such as feminist research and participatory research (Indigenous methodologies could fall into this category as well).

While emancipatory methodologies are distinct from each other and stem from different epistemologies, they share similar principles. For example, Indigenous methodology flows from Indigenous ways of knowing (epistemology), incorporating an Indigenous theoretical perspective and using aligned methods (e.g., qualitative interviews, storytelling). Both the research process and product of emancipatory research is political (Humphries, Mertens, and Truman, 2000; Stringer, 1999). In an interview with Battiste, Bell, and Findlay, Linda Tuhiwai

Smith summarizes the purpose of critical research: "So it is really about focusing, about thinking critically, about reflecting on things, about being strategic. It is not simply about thinking yourself into a stationary position which often happens in the academy"(2002, p. 184).

Many Canadians would concur that Indigenous peoples of Canada have faced social injustices by the state. Yet in a developed, pluralistic country the relations of oppression are less glaringly oppositional, awash with pastel hues rather than primary colours. It can be argued that broader issues of Indigenous politics, such as self-determination, are carried out within the parameters of the larger Canadian state. On a smaller scale, social inequities are being challenged one community at a time. Research, and the control of research findings, has been critical in pushing forward community-based goals of self-determination. As has been the process of taking control of education, health, and social welfare, taking control of Indigenous research has been a long, arduous struggle with Indigenous peoples acutely aware of the power politics of knowledge. As Hoare, Levy, and Robinson point out: "If knowledge is fundamental to understanding, interpreting and establishing values within a society, then control over its production becomes an integral component of cultural survival" (1993, p. 46).

Gaining control of the research process has been pivotal for Indigenous peoples in decolonization. One methodology from the margins — participatory research — has been an ally. The critical, collective, and participatory principles of participatory research has made it a popular methodology for many Indigenous projects in Canada. Over the past 20 years, participatory research projects with Indigenous communities include the 1977 MacKenzie Valley pipeline inquiry; the Big Trout Lake project (1971–1982); the Dene mapping project that took place between 1972 and 1989; Abele's 1986 study of northern Native employment programs, and so forth (Hoare, Levy, and Robinson, 1993; Jackson and McKay, 1982). While an Indigenous research model and participatory research use distinct methodologies, they both share some common language. For example, in Canada the Royal Commission on Aboriginal Peoples developed one of the earliest documented protocols on Indigenous research for current times. In this protocol collaborative research is emphasized, and the Indigenous community's participation in the development and design of the research model is expected (RCAP, 1996). A more recent protocol developed by the Indigenous Governance program at the University of Victoria highlights the need for participation in all levels of research by the Indigenous participants and that the research benefit the community in some manner (2003). The language of participation and community benefit show evidence of a shared goal—that research should be respectful and honour relationships in addition to research outcomes. Challenges to the principles of both participatory research and an Indigenous research model can occur either at the community or institutional level. However, both will require a special vigilance within the politicality of the academic environment. This is of particular relevance with Indigenous research coming into its own in the academy. So what is all the buzz about Indigenous methodologies?

Indigenous Research

When I returned to university to complete my Ph.D. coursework, I knew I needed a refresher research course to sharpen my skills and to reorient myself to new thinking in research. When I was a student several years ago, the heated debate centred on qualitative versus quantitative methodological approaches. Feminism and participatory research were the new "methodologies from the margins" within the academy. They broadened epistemological choices, allowing for experience and action to enter into research discourse and practice. I don't remember if postmodernism was on the radar screen yet. At that time research *objectivity* and *subjectivity* was a hot debate and the "radical" research approaches were branded as "soft"—new methods raising eyebrows about scientific rigour and validity. There were few qualitative research books on the market and mostly one had to scan the recent left-of-centre journals to seek out these "subversive" methodologies. When I returned to school in 2003, the first place I went to was the campus bookstore. (I find that checking shelves is a quick and easy way to scope out the current buzz.) As I approached the general reference research section, I was truly awed by what I saw. There were at least 30 books on the shelf relating to "marginal methodologies" with a number of the books bearing the title of qualitative research approaches. Mixed in with the selection was Linda Tuhiwai Smith's book, *Decolonizing Methodologies*. Seeing the words *Decolonizing Methodologies* on a book jacket on the shelf was a rush, an external validation that Indigenous research counted. I swiftly put the book into my shopping cart. I smugly thought this is excellent, there's going to be a choice of books with chapters on Indigenous methodologies. Maybe I will even find a how-to chapter on

24

writing a comprehensive Indigenous research proposal with suggested font size, etc. No doubt I would have criticized a check-box approach to Indigenous research for a plethora of reasons—but to have the choice! Eagerly, I started to browse through the selection searching the table of contents of various books for the Indigenous methodologies chapter that I knew must be there. After a thorough scan, I left the bookstore with one book and considerably less enthusiasm. Though I knew I was guilty of high expectations, I really wanted to see my experience as an Indigenous researcher reflected in that row of glossy books. I left the bookstore and went to the library where my spirit was slightly lifted. Indigenous research may not have endemic status on general reference shelves in campus bookstores, but it is creating a small stir in a range of academic journals on library shelves (for example, see Battiste, Bell, and Findlay, 2002; Deloria, 1991; Wilson, 2001).

Epistemology and the Difficulty of Language

The ferment of the last 15 years has given rise to alternative research methodologies and Indigenous research seems to be boiling rapidly, ready to break surface. Before exploring the history, ways of knowing, methodology, and ethical dilemmas integral to Indigenous research, it is critical to preface this discussion with a caution about language. The language that we use shapes the way we think. Postmodern deconstructivists have illuminated the link between the dominant society's usage of language to silence the voices of those who are marginally located. It is the tool by which a meta-narrative of "truth" and "normalcy" is perpetually reproduced. In centres of knowledge production like universities, the language of research becomes powerful and pervasive. The marginal methodologies (e.g., Indigenous, participatory research), in stretching the parameters of what counts as legitimate research, has either absorbed some of its vernacular or experienced the academy's cold shoulder. It is no surprise that in reviewing textbooks of research from the margins, readers are still likely to find the standard vocabulary (epistemology, methodology, methods, qualitative, quantitative). For Indigenous research there are two difficulties here. One difficulty arises from indigenizing a Western concept such as research, which is rigid with definitional categories, evaluative criteria, outcomes, and goals. The second relates to language and epistemology—how it influences how we think, feel, and act.

The first issue is not new to research. Does putting the word "Indigenous" in front of a non-Indigenous concept like research, child welfare, or education make a difference? Indigenizing a Western model of research without critical reflection can result in the individualistic approach of a principle investigator determining the question, methodology, and methods and asking an Indigenous person to act as the "front." Tuhiwai Smith shares her experience with this type of research: "I was a researcher in those types of projects and that is why I don't want to go back to those types of projects ever again because, to put it crudely, you get set up as an Indigenous researcher"(Battiste, Bell, and Findlay, 2002, p. 183). Yet, many Indigenous researchers may still be approached to be involved in such projects. It is their task then to use their own personal/cultural knowledge to assess this type of "Indigenous research" and ask critical, difficult questions. Is the research goal manipulative or helpful for my community? Is the methodology respectful to culture and community? Do the methods meet cultural protocols? What are collectivist ethical considerations? Who is driving the research and what is the purpose? The usual yes/no binaries are not helpful here. For those who are non-Indigenous, the questions perhaps are more challenging: Am I creating space *or* taking space?

Manu Aluli Meyer identifies epistemology as "the philosophy of knowledge" with language as the means for interpreting and communicating ideas. He underscores the difficulty of using language that is not of one's own in constructing knowledge. In relating his own experience with the vernacular of knowledge making, he says: "I understand the tenuous line I walk between 10-dollar words and my Hawaiian people who say in exasperation 'Don't throw that word at us'"(Meyer, 2001, p. 101). Further, the stronghold of language, writing, and world view in generating "truth" creates difficulties for Indigenous peoples whose traditional philosophies are held deep within constructs that are neither written nor consistent with the patterns of dominant language. Most Indigenous languages are verb-based and tell of the world in motion interacting with humans and nature (Cajete, 1999). This is in contrast to the noun-based nature of the English language, which accentuates an outcome orientation to the world. Language is a central system of how cultures code, create, and transmit meaning. While many Indigenous peoples may not speak their language, cultural values remain alive and reflect a world view found in their native language. Values that honour relationships are important for cultures that value the journey as much as the destination.

Written language adds additional complexity in transmitting Indigenous ways of knowing, given that most Indigenous cultures are oral. Even storytelling, an important research method used in Indigenous research, loses a level of meaning in the translation into written script. Russell Means puts the dilemma squarely on the table: "I detest writing. The process itself epitomizes the European concept of 'legitimate' thinking; what is written has an importance that is denied the spoken." He goes on to say that traditional ways of knowing must come from the teaching of the "hoop, the four directions, the relations" (1989, p. 19). Indigenous epistemology is fluid, non-linear, and relational. Knowledge is transmitted through stories that shape shift in relation to the wisdom of the storyteller at the time of the telling. The additional task of delivering knowledge in 12-point font, cerlox-bound, written research reports is a little difficult, not the least of which are the frequent pauses from literature reviews, coding, and analysis to ask: What *exactly* am I doing? Why do I feel so antsy? Am I helping? For the Indigenous researcher, incorporating Indigenous epistemology into a non-Indigenous language with all that it implies is complex. It is a troublesome task of criss-crossing cultural epistemologies.

Yet, I feel the need to outline here, in English text, an epistemological positioning based on Indigenous ways of knowing. At this point I prefer not to delve into a critical analysis of how it differs from other epistemologies, but rather I will focus on my understanding of what it is and how it guides the research that I do. Epistemology, as Manu Aluli Meyer states, is huge in identifying how we know our world. "Every little thing. I mean, I can see a dead frog on the road, and it relates to epistemology" (2001, p. 192). An Indigenous epistemology is a significant aspect of Indigenous methodology and suggests an Indigenous way of functioning in the world.

So what is an Indigenous epistemology? Here are some thoughts. It includes a way of knowing that is fluid (Little Bear, 2000) and experiential, derived from teachings transmitted from generation to generation by storytelling; each story is alive with the nuances and wisdom of the storyteller (King, 2003). It emerges from traditional languages emphasizing verbs, not nouns (Cajete, 1999). It involves a knowing within the subconscious that is garnered through dreams and vision (Castellano, 2000). It is a knowledge that is both intuitive and quiet. Indigenous ways of knowing arise from interrelationships with the human world, the spirit, and the inanimate entities of the ecosystem (Battiste and Henderson, 2000). Indigenous ways of knowing encompass the spirit of collectivity, reciprocity, and respect (Wilson, 2001). It is born of the land and locality of the tribe. Indigenous knowledge ought to be purposeful and practical. It is born of the necessity to feed, clothe, and transmit values. As such the method of knowing must be practical and purposeful. Indigenous ways of knowing are organic with emphasis on reciprocity and humour. These ways of knowing are both cerebral and heartfelt. As the elders say, "If you have important things to say, speak from the heart."

From an Indigenous epistemology, I draw several key assertions that can guide research: (a) experience as a legitimate way of knowing; (b) Indigenous methods, such as storytelling, as a legitimate way of sharing knowledge; (c) receptivity and relationship between researcher and participants as a natural part of the research "methodology"; and (d) collectivity as a way of knowing that assumes reciprocity to the community (meaning both two-legged and four-legged creatures). An Indigenous epistemology within Indigenous research projects is important because Indigenous peoples will likely understand and share their experience from this perspective.

Linked with epistemology is the role of an Indigenous theoretical framework in research. Theory is inextricable from methodology. Theory is also referred to as a perspective, lens, or framework such as feminist lens, emancipatory framework, or Indigenous perspective. Creswell (2003) outlines the function of theory (or theoretical lens) as integral to the entire qualitative research process. He indicates that the researcher's theoretical lens will guide her or him in determining which issues are important to study (e.g., Indigenous decolonization); the participants that one ought to include in the study (e.g., Indigenous peoples); the role of the research in relation to the research participants (e.g., subjectivity acknowledged and honoured); and, finally, theory will determine how research is presented and written (e.g., co-writing). I would add to this list the rationale for choice of methods used within research. An Indigenous perspective/theory encompasses an Indigenous way of knowing (e.g., Indigenous epistemology previously defined); it incorporates what Tuhiwai Smith refers to as "researching back," indicating a decolonization objective (1999, p. 7); it is founded on collectivist research principles (and respects the inherent ethics and protocols associated); it has an ecological basis that is respectful of the natural world; and, finally, an Indigenous perspective values authentic/organic techniques in data collection.[3]

So how do epistemology and theory link with methodology? To understand this link, I had to grapple with what research methodology itself means. It appears that it can be either broadly or narrowly defined depending upon the perspective of the individual and the type of research (qualitative or quantitative). Methodology seems entwined with methods. It is a planning process that guides the choice of methods (Creswell, 2003) and is the foundational element of "science" within social science research (Neuman, 1997). A narrow definition of methodology focuses primarily on the methods (interviews, survey, coding) of research without acknowledging theoretical assumptions implicit in the work (Alford, 1998). In qualitative research, feminist scholars and critical researchers have illuminated the importance of both theory and method in methodological considerations. Feminist scholars have argued that one's theoretical lens ought to guide the research methods and, as such, methodology encompasses not only the mechanisms of research, but "how research does or should proceed" (Harding, 1987, p. 3). Also, feminist scholars have challenged the long-held methodological assumption of scientific objectivity that is deeply ingrained in positivism and hence what constitutes scientific research (Harding, 1987; Stringer, 1999). To ensure that methodology does not focus solely on methods of research, writers have placed each in separate categories — *methodology* being theory that guides method, and *methods* the techniques that a researcher uses (Esterberg, 2002; Harding, 1987; Van Manen, 2001). In the social sciences methodologies are categorized according to purpose of research (e.g., *positivist, interpretative, critical/emancipatory*) (Kemmis, 2001; Neuman, 1997). More recently Indigenous methodology, though nascent in a formal academic sense, has emerged as a research process with its own methodology (Battiste, Bell, and Findlay, 2002; Wilson, 2001) and while it can draw from both *interpretative* and *critical/emancipatory* theories, it does not easily fit into a pre-existing Western category.

In the last few years there has been a surfacing of Indigenous peoples writing about Indigenous research. In conjunction with previous work, Indigenous research is fast becoming a methodology of its own. Shawn Wilson defines methodology: "when we talk about methodology, we are talking about how you are going to use your ways of thinking (epistemology) to gain more knowledge about your reality" (2001, p. 175). From this perspective, methodology is about process.

There are three key themes of Indigenous methodology (all grounded in Indigenous epistemology and theory) that I would like to briefly highlight: (a) the relational; (b) the collective; (c) and methods.

The Relational: Indigenous ways of knowing have a basis in the relationships that are inclusive of all life forms. The philosophical premise of take what you need (and only what you need), give back, and offer thanks suggests a deep respect for other living beings. Integral in Indigenous methodologies is this foundational philosophy. A relationship-based model of research is critical for carrying out research with Indigenous communities on several levels. Philosophically, it honours the cultural value of relationship, it emphasizes people's ability to shape and change their own destiny, and it is respectful. By relationship, I mean a sincere, authentic investment in the community; the ability to take time to visit with people from the community (whether or not they are research participants); the ability to be humble about the goals; and conversations at the start about who owns the research, its use and purpose (particularly if it is academic research). Relationship-based research can irritate the individualistic, clinical, outcome-oriented research process. However, in Indigenous communities (both urban and rural), a relationship-based approach is a practical necessity because access to the community is unlikely unless time is invested in relationship building. While the emphasis on relationship can frustrate timelines and well-charted research designs, the journey is truly amazing. As Eber Hampton says, "I had found that the cut-and-dried, rigid, cold, hard, precise facts are dead. What is alive is messy, and growing, and flexible, and soft, and warm, and often fuzzy" (1995, p. 49). Research, like life, is about relationships.

The Collective: Woven with the philosophical premise of relationship is the collective underpinning of Indigenous research. The collective nature of Indigenous culture is evident in traditional economic, political, and cultural systems. It is almost instinctive — Indigenous peoples know that you take care of your sister or brother (the extended family, not just the nuclear one), and that's just the way it is. Inherent in this understanding of life is reciprocity and accountability to each other, the community, clans, and nations. It is a way of life that creates a sense of belonging, place, and home; however, it doesn't serve anonymity or rugged individualism well. Western research tends to be individualistic with the principal researcher defining the question, determining the participants, designing the methodologies, documenting the findings, and publishing the report. In the university context, researchers (who are generally faculty) are put in the situation of publish or perish. Indigenous researchers are equally subjected to this system, but we can only get so far before we see a face—our Elder cleaning fish, our sister living on the edge in East Vancouver, our brother hunting elk for the feast, our little ones in foster care—and hear a voice whispering, "Are you helping us?" This is where Indigenous methodology must meet the criteria of collective responsibility and accountability. In protocols for Indigenous research, this is a central theme. As Indigenous research enters the academy, this principle needs to stay up close and personal.

Methods

I want to briefly explore the link between methodology and methods within Indigenous research. Research methods or techniques to gather data have expanded to fit a more expansive range of methodological choices. My sense is that Indigenous research will further broaden the range of methods in research. While traditional approaches such as surveys, in-depth interviews, and focus groups will be integral to method choices, other options that capture alternate ways of knowing will emerge as legitimate. For example, dreams have long been a source of knowledge for Indigenous cultures. Solitude with nature and the gift of insight we receive from those experiences are another source of knowledge. Methods such as dream journalling capture subjective data and are destined to be a part of discourse on Indigenous research methods. It will be an exciting new dialogue about what counts as legitimate knowledge and how that knowledge is garnered. Currently many mainstream researchers still consider this in the realm of soft philosophy and soulful words, yet given time ....

Inherent in Indigenous research is a plethora of conflicts. It is a maze of ethical issues compounded by the real need to sleep at night because there is so much work to do. The issues arising from a relational research approach rooted in a collectivist epistemology brings to light distinct dilemmas for researchers. A fundamental question about epistemology is: How much do we share? We need to ask how much knowledge do we share for the common good, and what knowledge needs to be kept sacred. Questions about purpose, benefit, and protection of research subjects may arise across a range of methodologies; however, it is the answers to these questions and the standards regarding community accountability in a collectivist, relational research model that will be different. Protocols on research with Indigenous communities in the last 10 years are defining the standards. For the past 20 years, non-Indigenous research approaches like participatory research have been debating what it means to be authentically participatory, and the dialogue continues. Indigenous methodology is an argument for a different way of research based on intellectual, philosophical, ideological, and cultural premises. It is likely that our culture will be our greatest resource in clearing a path.

Because Indigenous ways of knowing are intricately connecting to Indigenous ways of doing, I propose that epistemology, theory, methods, and ethical protocols are integral to Indigenous methodology. I refrain from narrowly defining an Indigenous methodology because, as Tuhiwai Te Rina Smith suggests, it is as much a conceptual framework as a recipe (Battiste, Bell, and Findlay, 2002). It is a methodology that shape shifts in the form of theory, methods, and ethics.

Hopes, Challenges, and Concluding Remarks

That Indigenous communities have been researched to death is not new. Researchers extracting data from Indigenous communities and then publishing "their" research with little benefit to the people has been well documented in literature and has become a part of the oral history of many Indigenous groups. The purpose of this chapter was not to spend time reviewing the history of research and Indigenous peoples but to ask: Given our uneasy relationship with Western research, why do we endure? Research is a tool that has become so entangled with haughty theories of what is truth, that it's easy to forget that it is simply "about learning and so is a way of finding out things" (Hampton, 1995, p. 48). Currently within most countries of the world, Indigenous peoples continue to experience oppression and its implications for the felt experience of life. The overrepresentation of Indigenous peoples in poverty, in prison, and in child welfare persists. Those of us who have pursued academic study and dipped our toes into the murky pool of research have obligations to use our skills to improve the socio-economic conditions of Indigenous peoples. Vine Deloria, in his article "Commentary: Research, Redskins and Reality," suggests that apart from documenting narratives of traditional culture for future generations, "there is a great and pressing need for research on contemporary affairs and conditions of Indians" (1991, p. 461). We need to take back control of research so that it is relevant and useful. By defining the research inquiry based on actual, not presumed, need and by designing a research process that is most effective in responding to our inquiries, we can use research as a practical tool. In the larger struggle for self-determination, we need to engage in what Tuhiwai Smith terms "researching back." Like "talking back," it implies resistance, recovery, and renewal (Tuhiwai Smith, 2001, p. 7).

Academic settings will likely continue as centres for research activity and I have alluded to the difficulties of conducting Indigenous research in such places. The tensions range from epistemological predicaments resulting from parallel ways of knowing and methodologies that place different values on process and product. Also, tensions arise from divergent opinions on who should define, control, and own research, and the extent to which social justice is pursued as a goal of research. The greatest ally of Indigenous research will be those non-Indigenous "methodologies from the margins" that do not hide from but embrace the political nature of research. The sustained autonomy but continued alliance between such approaches is critical. Mutually beneficial and open-spirited dialogue that is critically reflective of each other's practice will be necessary for growth. As positivism holds fast to its turf inside the academy, the methodologies from the margins will need each other.

The hope of an Indigenous research paradigm developed by Indigenous scholars, researchers, and community members is that it will have an authenticity, even if carried out within the parameters of research language. Though we may have to strategically use the "10-dollar words" of the academy, there will be breaks in the conversation for humility to surface—research is, after all, just a way to find out things. As Indigenous peoples, we have lots of work ahead of us, and taking back research is one of many tasks on the list. It will be a tough process, but it will be an exciting new discourse in a world badly in need of hope.

As I conclude this writing, I reflect on all the history, negative associations, and complexities of carving space for an Indigenous point of view, and wonder how we persist. I smile and think of a quote by Eber Hampton: "A friend of mine said, 'I know a good word for Indians.' I said, 'What?' He said, 'Relentless.' We laughed, but there is a strong element of truth in this statement" (Hampton, 1995, p. 48). Hmm, yes, … relentless, strong, and still here.

Megwetch.

Notes

1. I want to acknowledge and thank the Indigenous community in the broadest sense, of which I am a part, for being an ongoing inspiration. I also want to thank three research instructors— Leslie Brown, Susan Boyd, and Budd Hall—who created emancipatory space for me to explore Indigenous methodologies resulting in this article.
2. This is a composite accounting of several personal experiences in academia and does not refer to one incident in specific.
3. Please note that this criterion of an Indigenous framework is not meant to be definitive but rather a starting point.

References

Alford, R.R. (1998). *The craft of inquiry: Theories, methods, evidence.* New York: Oxford University Press.

Battiste, M., Bell, L., and Findlay, L.M. (2002). An interview with Linda Tuhiwai Te Rina Smith. *Canadian Journal of Native Education* 26 (2), 169–186.

Battiste, M., and Henderson, Y. (2000). *Protecting Indigenous knowledge and heritage.* Saskatoon: Purich Publishing.

Cajete, G. (1999). *Native science: Natural laws of interdependence.* Santa Fe: Clear Light Publishers.

Castellano, M. (2000). Updating Aboriginal traditions of knowledge. In G. Sefa Dei and B. Rosenberg (Eds.), *Indigeneous knowledges in global contexts: Multiple reading of our world,* pp. 21–36. Toronto: University of Toronto Press.

Creswell, J.W. (2003). *Research design: Qualitative, quantitative, and mixed methods approaches* (2nd edition). Thousand Oaks: Sage.

Deloria, V.J. (1991). Commentary: Research, redskins, and reality. In R.A. Black and T.P. Wilson (Eds.), *The American Indian Quarterly* XV, 457–467. Berkeley: The Native American Studies Program, University of California at Berkeley.

Dockery, G. (2000). Participatory research: Whose roles, whose responsibilities? In C. Truman, D. Mertens, and B. Humphries (Eds.), *Research and Inequality*, 95–110. London: UCL Press.

Esterberg, K.G. (2002). *Qualitative methods in social research*. Boston: McGraw-Hill.

Hall, B. (1982). Breaking the monopoly of knowledge: Research methods, participation and development. In B. Hall, A. Gillette, and R. Tandon (Eds.), *Participatory research network series*, pp. 13–26). Toronto: International Council for Adult Education.

Hall, B. (1998). Knowledge, democracy and higher education: Contributions from adult and lifelong learning. In B. Hall (Ed.), *Lifelong learning and institutes of higher education in the 21st century*, 17–29. Mumbai: Department of Adult Education and Continuing Education and Extension, University of Mumbai.

Hampton, E. (1995). Memory comes before knowledge: Research may improve if researchers remember their motives. Paper presented at the first biannual Indigenous scholars' conference, University of Alberta.

Harding, S. (1987). Introduction: Is there a feminist method? In S. Harding (Ed.), *Feminism and methodology*, pp. 1–4. Bloomington: Indiana University Press.

Hoare, T., Levy, C., and Robinson, M. (1993). Participatory action research in Native communities: Cultural opportunities and legal implications. *Canadian Journal of Native Studies* XIII (1), 43–68.

Humphries, B., Mertens, D., and Truman, C. (2000). Arguments for an "emancipatory" research paradigm. In C. Truman, D. Mertens, and B. Humphries (Eds.), *Research and inequality*, pp. 3–23. London: UCL Press.

Jackson, T., and McKay, G. (1982). Sanitation and water supply in Big Trout Lake: Participatory research for democratic technical solutions. *The Canadian Journal of Native Studies* II (1), 129–145.

King, T. (2003). *The truth about stories: A Native narrative*. Toronto: Dead Dog Cafe Productions Inc. and CBC Corporation.

Kemmis, S. (2001). Exploring the relevance of critical theory for action research: Emancipatory action research in the footsteps of Jürgen Habermas. In P. Reason and H. Bradbury (Eds.), *Handbook of action research: Participative inquiry and practice*, pp. 91–102. London: Sage.

Little Bear, L. (2000). Jagged worldviews colliding. In M. Battiste (Ed.), *Reclaiming Indigenous voice and vision*, 77–85. Vancouver: UBC Press.

Means, R. (1989). The same old song. In W. Churchill (Ed.), *Marxism and Native Americans*, pp. 19–33. Boston: South End Press.

Meyer, A.M. (2001). A cultural assumptions of empiricism: A Native Hawaiian critique. *Canadian Journal of Native Education* 25 (2), 188–198.

Neuman, W.L. (1997). The meaning of methodology. In W.L. Neuman (Ed.), *Social research methods: Qualitative and quantitative approaches*, pp. 60–84. Boston: Allyn and Bacon.

Royal Commission on Aboriginal Peoples for Seven Generations. (1996). *Ethical guidelines for research*. Ottawa: Libraxus Inc.

Stringer, E. (1999). *Action research* (2nd edition). Thousand Oaks: Sage.

Tandon, R. (1988). Social transformation and participatory research. *Convergence* XXI (2/3), 5–18.

Tuhiwai Smith, L. (1999). *Decolonizing methodologies: Research and Indigenous peoples*. London: Zed.

University of Victoria. (2003). *Protocols and principles for conducting research in Indigenous communities* (final draft). Victoria: University of Victoria.

Van Manen, M. (2001). *Researching lived experience*. London: University of Western Ontario.

Wilson, S. (2001). What is an Indigenous research methodology? *The Canadian Journal of Native Education* 25 (2), 175–179.

CHAPTER TWO

SITUATING ANTI-OPPRESSIVE THEORIES WITHIN CRITICAL AND DIFFERENCE-CENTRED PERSPECTIVES

Mehmoona Moosa-Mitha

Introduction

Discussions regarding the nature of anti-oppressive theories are often conducted in piecemeal fashion within relevant literature where its particular features are discussed to the exclusion of an examination of the ontological and epistemological claims within which these theories are rooted. "Anti-oppressive" is a term used in literature to mean several, often conflicting, things depending on the author's assumptions. Through the course of this chapter I provide a conceptualization of anti-oppressive theories based on a discussion of their epistemological and ontological claims, as well as by situating these claims in relation to those of other social theories. I argue that what distinguishes anti-oppressive from other theories is the juxtaposition of difference-centred and critical orientations that define it, which differs from other social theories that are positioned either on the axes of difference-centredness or critical theoretical perspective, but not on both.

Specifically I argue that liberalism, Marxism, and White feminism overlook the socio-political realities and oppression that individuals and collectivities experience on the basis of their "multiple differences" from the White, male (although White feminists do undertake gendered analysis), heterosexual, able-bodied norm. Thus, while they may reflect a critical theoretical orientation, they fail to take difference seriously. On the other hand, I also argue that postmodern theories are more inclusive in their orientation, taking a difference-centred stance without necessarily taking on a critical perspective. Hence they do not necessarily position themselves within oppositional knowledge claims that attempt to dismantle and contest hegemonic representation of the "Other."

Implicit in my discussion throughout this chapter is a critique of the view that anti-oppressive theories are discrete from other social theories. I take the view that anti-oppressive theories do not signify separate and "alternative" theorizations; rather, they engage in a conversation with other social theories that is dialectical in nature, where they contest, influence, and are in turn influenced by the ontological and epistemological assumptions of a spectrum of social theories. Representations of anti-oppressive theories as discrete result in a superficial treatment of their ideas that are animated through a deep engagement, often in the form of contestation, with other social theories. The "conversations" that influence and affect social theories, including anti-oppressive theories, is reflected in a process that is both creative and unpredictable so that over time it is not always easy or possible to distinguish all the various strands that come together in any one theoretical framework.

In this chapter, I situate anti-oppressive perspectives within a spectrum of social theories through an examination of their epistemological and ontological claims along two axes on which I locate several social theories (please refer to Figure 2.1 below). The horizontal axis represents the normative/difference-centred orientation of social theory, where theories that are invested in making singular truth claims are located closer to the left end of the spectrum as they are more normative in nature. The vertical axis represents the critical/mainstream divide, and those theories that engage in oppositional knowledge claims that dismantle mainstream representation of the "Other" are located at the north end of the axis.

While a diagrammatic depiction of this spectrum of theories is a lateral one, I do not intend to suggest that anti-oppressive theories exist to the exclusion of Marxist or liberal theories. Rather, I am arguing that anti-oppressive theories, even when they situate themselves within liberal paradigms, extend and shift the fundamental epistemological and ontological assumptions of liberal theories. It is also important to note that I acknowledge that individual theorists may choose to position themselves in ways that differ from the broad contours of their theoretical orientation as depicted in the figure below; for example, individual liberal thinkers may choose to be more critical in their analysis than others. The figure, therefore, is not meant to provide a

Figure 2.1

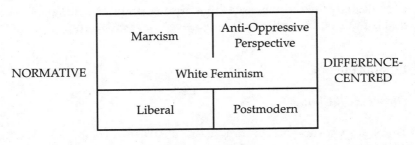

rigid classification; rather, it situates the wider parameters within which differing theories make contesting claims.

The distinctive contribution of anti-oppressive theories becomes clear when situating various social theories along these two axes. The ontological and epistemological claims of other social theories are not as inclusive in their analysis, and when they are inclusive, they are not necessarily critical in their perspective. The ontological and epistemological claims of liberalism, for example, couched as they are within a universal and transcendental language, maintain the status quo, thus positioning liberalism within a normative and mainstream orientation. White feminism, on the other hand, I position as edging more toward a difference-centred position, although this perspective is limited because it privileges gender as a difference over any other, while taking a critical perspective. Marxism, which provides the foundation for critical thought, I position at the high end of the critical edge on the vertical axis but on the normative end on the horizontal line. Postmodern perspectives, although the theorists themselves contest any form of categorization, I would argue are theoretically situated as difference-centred but not necessarily critical in their theorization. I situate anti-oppressive theories as being both critical and difference-centred.

This upper-right quadrant of the figure will provide a focus to this chapter as I discuss various social theories, namely, liberalism, Marxism,

White feminism, and postmodern and social identity theories in relation to the twin claims of critical and difference-centred perspectives that characterize anti-oppressive theories. It will also provide a focus and context to the discussions of the other chapters in the book as the book is dedicated to exploring issues that arise when undertaking research that is informed by critical, difference-centred perspectives.

Liberal Theory

Ontological Claims

There are various interpretations of liberalism that include highly individualistic (neo-liberal) interpretations at one end of the spectrum to communitarian views of liberalism on the other. Yet all of these locate themselves in the seventeenth- and eighteenth-century Enlightenment theories of Hobbes and Locke (Hobson, Lewis, and Siim, 2002; Okin, 1989). In my discussion, I will focus mostly on Rawlsian analysis due to the influential position it holds in formulating present-day liberalism. I will also be touching on the writings of communitarian liberals such as Kymlicka (1995, 2001) and Taylor (1989).

According to Rawls (1971), social reality is characterized by social relationships that are individualist and consensual by nature. His envisioning and analysis of social justice is both principled and understood in terms of a redistribution of rights and privileges. Consistent with Hobbes and Locke, Rawls argued that socially just democratic societies are governed and measure themselves against the two principles of liberty and equality. Rawls suggests that people, when asked to rationally identify principles by which a socially just society should be governed, would conclude that citizens should have the right to enjoy the greatest individual freedom possible to pursue social and economic advantage, while redistributing goods and services in a way that the least equal among them is the least worse off. Thus, concludes Rawls, people would choose to optimize their rights of freedom and equality in a socially just society.

Communitarian liberals such as Kymlicka (1995, 2001) and Taylor (1989) are less individualist in their vision of social justice. They argue that communities should live in a way that allows individuals the greatest rights of freedom or autonomy, even if they are members of minority communities in terms of numbers, while being treated with equal respect as all others in society. This "pluralist" vision of liberalism deviates from the Rawlsian view only in terms of its conception of the basic unit that makes up societies; while Rawls is more individualistic in his approach, the communitarians emphasize communal social relations. Both define their vision of social justice as being rights based, which is formal and principled in nature.

In the next section I discuss the implications of the ontological claims of liberal theory in relation to the two axes, normative/difference-centred and critical/mainstream, when undertaking research using a liberal theoretical orientation.

Liberal Approaches to Research

Ontological Claims: Universal, Individualist, Transcendental, and Singular

The ontological assumptions of liberal theories are defined in universalist terms, which assumes that all members of society, for example, are motivated by self-interest as they pursue their right of individual freedom. It also privileges one particular view of social relationships as being atomistic in nature over other views of relationships as being interconnected and interdependent (Dietz, 1987). This is equally true of liberal communitarians, where communal rather than individual forms of self-interest are emphasized.

This universalizing of particular visions of social justice and social relationships engenders normative assumptions in envisioning social justice claims that exclude the lived realities and experiences of people whose relationships and desires are characterized in ways that are different from this assumed norm. For example, feminists have contested the normative interpretation of autonomy implicit in liberal analysis by pointing out that mothers often do not necessarily wish to pursue individual freedom when looking after young children (Young, 1997). Anti-racist interpretations of autonomy, founded as they are on the basis of the experiences of anti-racist social movements, like the civil rights movement, also contest the individualist bias of White, male-stream[1] analysis of the rights of autonomy (Young, 1997).

Feminist and anti-racist theorists (Dietz, 1987; Williams, 1998; Young, 1997) have critiqued the formal and contractual assumptions that characterize liberal ontological claims, which assume that equality

41

is achieved primarily through a redistribution of rights and privileges, and minimally through that of goods and services. Male-stream liberal views of social justice are critiqued as having a limited perspective, overlooking the possibility that inequality may be experienced by people on the basis of historical oppression or as a result of being treated as inferior due to one's social identity such as race or gender (Dietz, 1987; Williams, 1998; Young, 1997).

Male-stream liberal analysis also views social justice in contractual terms in which social relationships between the state and citizens, as well as with each other, are defined in legalistic terms, usually through a charter of rights and freedoms. Contractual views of social justice, however, as anti-racist analysts have pointed out, create a binary where people are either considered to be oppressed or oppressors, overlooking the often multiple relations that people have with each other, where people can be both oppressed and oppressors (Williams, 1998). Contractual notions of social justice also assume people to be passive subjects of their rights. They do not have to do anything to merit their rights as these are considered innate and inherent to the human condition (Lister, 1997), a point that is also contested by anti-racist feminist theorists as I will discuss later in the chapter.

There are also other ways by which liberal theorists are not difference-centred; they not only universalize, but also render invisible difference through transcendental claims that overlook or ignore differences of social locations in their theorization. For example, the subjects of Rawls's theories own no social identity attributes of gender, class, or race by which to locate them (Okin, 1989; Stasiulus, 2002). It is assumed that differences can be transcended into a common language of humanity that is the "same" in its entitlement of rights and privileges. The transcendentalist claim of male-stream liberal theory is particularly clear in relation to its articulation of the rights to equality, the second foundational principle within which liberal social justice claims are envisioned. The right of equality alludes to the equal dignity that all people possess and the right to be treated with respect regardless of their race, gender, or any other differences of social identity (Dworkin, 1977). Yet the basis on which people have the right to be treated as equals is not based on an acknowledgment of their difference; rather, it is an interpretation of equality that transcends difference through an interpretation of equality that is synonymous with "same" (Phelan, 2001). People have the right to be treated as equals because underneath social difference, we are all the same in our humanity.

Communitarian liberals do acknowledge difference that is communal in nature. Their communitarian stance results in a rejection of an entirely contractual vision of social justice that can be attained through legislation of individual rights of freedom and equality. Rather, they emphasize the importance of viewing citizens, not just as rights-bearing individuals but also as members of society and participants in the culture of that society (Kymlicka, 1995, 2001; Taylor, 1989). Yet their non-structural stance, where inequality is not expressed in materialist terms, results in treating difference in non-structural terms as private. For example, communitarian liberals define racial differences in terms of difference that is "cultural." Hence the structural stratification in society, as is evidenced through socio-economic indicators, which is racialized in nature, is ignored in favour of a view that acknowledges individuals' personal choice in engaging in cultural practices (Bannerji, 2000).

Moreover, difference between communities is recognized but not difference within communities (Dietz, 1987). Multiple relationships are also difficult for pluralist liberal societies to acknowledge. As Aboriginal writers Peterson and Sanders (1998) suggest, membership is acknowledged only in one or a singular community, resulting in people having to choose between their community and the wider mainstream society. The de-politicization of difference through the use of a discourse of "individual choice" that is "private," and where difference is understood in singular terms, results in the management of difference by communitarian liberals that marginalizes difference and continues to view sameness as the norm. Thus, the ontological claims of communitarian liberals are not really difference-centred.

The contractual and normative assumptions emphasized by Rawlsian liberal theories, as well as the normative assumptions of communitarian liberals, result in a theoretical orientation that upholds the status quo within society rather than challenging these fundamentally. For example, the state is viewed as neutral in liberal theories. In the case where injustices propagated by the state in its treatment of certain citizens are acknowledged, as Kymlicka (2001) does, they are acknowledged in terms of past "mistakes" that the state needs to correct by resuming a neutral stance. Liberal theories do not fundamentally challenge normative practices and assumptions of social institutions. The legalistic view of social justice also upholds mainstream societal assumptions by viewing the law and the judicial system as independent and neutral, an assumption that is fundamentally contested by some anti-racist, feminist theorists. In that sense, liberal theory is located on normative as well as mainstream axes.

Epistemological Claims: Positivist and "Objective"

A universal vision of social justice that has its basis in formal, legalistic, and transcendental conceptions of social justice necessarily relies on rational and deductive analysis as a way of perceiving social reality and envisioning social justice. Knowledge is understood in positivist terms, which assumes that knowledge can be deduced by abstracting principles or laws that govern social relationships. Transcendental and universal notions of social justice exist independently of one's own subjective views. For example, Rawls (1971) arrives at a vision of social justice through a process of deductive thinking and by making "objective" observations about the "universal laws of nature."

Furthermore, Enlightenment thought (within which liberal visions of social justice are situated) also results in epistemological assumptions that construct dichotomies and engage in binary thinking. An example central to epistemological assumptions held by liberal theories as I have described them is the true/false dichotomy. Liberal theories assume that certain knowledge about things exists, and it is the role of theories to capture, uncover, and explain these truths (Battiste and Youngblood, 2000). In the case where liberal philosophical assumptions have been proven to be wrong, liberal philosophers usually react by adjusting these "mistakes" so as to more accurately depict the truth of the situation. For example, Kymlicka (2001) states that the liberal state's role in relation to marginalized communities in the past has proven to be biased against these communities. However, having stated this, he proceeds by discounting this fact as a mistake that can be corrected if the state were to take its proper role as the neutral arbiter of rights and privileges. Hence the epistemological assumptions of liberal theories itself never change; they are only fine-tuned.

Epistemological assumptions of liberal theories are also normative in nature. By that I mean that it is assumed that knowledge can uncover universal laws or "norms" by which nature and social relationships function. Knowledge is, therefore, used to regulate and control nature through the act of categorizing and generalizing from it (Battiste and Youngblood, 2000). These epistemological assumptions are consistent with an ontological vision that constructs its vision of social justice through a language of universality. Anti-oppressive theorists have

44

argued that normative epistemological assumptions valorize sameness and view knowledge as a way to uncover events that follow universal laws in a predictable manner. This, so they argue, is the reason why "difference" is considered a problem and a deviation within liberal theories (Yuval-Davies, 1999).

The researcher using liberal approaches to undertaking research assumes the role of the expert, who conceives of the participant as an "object" of inquiry, a receptacle of knowledge whose significance is revealed through the efforts of the researcher (Creswell, 1998; Lather, 1991). Social reality is not only knowable, but the researcher places herself in the role of a "knower" through the process of undertaking the research. This liberal approach dominates mainstream research.

Certain research methodologies and methods lend themselves to liberal epistemological and ontological assumptions. Quantitative research methodologies, for example, assume that knowledge exists as an objective truth that can be attained through deductive processes and, therefore, is particularly suitable to liberal assumptions (Creswell, 1998). Similarly, qualitative research methodologies that reflect assumptions regarding the validity and reliability of one's findings that are positivist in nature, like those found in quantitative research methodologies, also find an easy alliance with the epistemological and ontological assumptions of liberal theories. Validity is defined as the generalizability of one's findings, where one's analysis of a sample population can be seen to be equally applicable to a wider, more universal, population. Similarly, one's findings are considered reliable if one can show that they were arrived at "objectively" and are replicable through a similar process of deductive thinking. The subjective inclinations of the researcher or the participants are treated as irrelevant at best and problematic at worse, and have to be controlled so that their influence on the research process can be eradicated. Similarly, specific and context-bound findings are considered less valid unless they can be generalized on a more universal level.

Marxist/Structuralist Theory

Ontological Claims

Marxist and structuralist thought marks the beginning of theories that root themselves in critical perspectives. Mullaly (1997) defines critical theories as those that (a) provide critiques and alternatives to traditional mainstream theories and (b) are motivated by emancipatory claims informed by a critique of dominance. Leonard (1994) adds to this definition by stating that critical theories have a practical intent. Marxist/structuralist theorists undertake their analysis, including research studies, with the conscious intention of producing social change that is emancipatory in intent.

There are many variations of Marxist theories that are commonly rooted in the writings of Karl Marx, a nineteenth-century philosopher. Structuralism itself sprang out of Marxist theory, beginning with the writings of Althusser in the 1960s who attempted to modernize classical Marxist thought and make it more applicable to modern times (Lather, 1991; Mullaly, 1997). Marxism and structuralism fundamentally challenge the ontological and epistemological claims of liberal theorists. While liberal ontological claims are based on a transcendental vision of reality, Marxism and structuralist claims are based on a materialist vision of social justice. The fundamental concept integral to Marxist analysis is the concept of production and the processes by which material goods are produced for the sustenance of all members of societies. The mode of production was analyzed as being historically situated by Marx, transforming itself within different stages of history as reflected in different types of societies (Corrigan and Leonard, 1978). Marxists argue that throughout history, the mode of production is based on the oppression of the working class and for the benefit of the privileged class who own the technologies of production, such as factories. Hence the process of production is definitive in marking the social relationships in society, characterized by the proletariat (the working class) and the bourgeois (the privileged class).

Consistent with the materialist analysis of social reality, Marxists envision social justice as incorporating the overthrow of unequal class, or material relationships, in the name of the collective experience, equality, and liberty (Mullaly, 1997). Not unlike liberals, Marxists also define their vision of social justice in terms of liberty and equality. However, for Marxists, freedom can exist only if the material or social conditions within which people live allow them to be free. Social justice aims are, therefore, achieved only through liberating the oppressed class by collectively owning the technology or the means of production (Corrigan and Leonard, 1978; Lather, 1991; Mullaly, 1997).

Marx also used a stronger sense of the concept of liberty. Liberty lies in the idea that human beings are by nature productive, and that labour represents a form of self-fulfillment for people (Taylor, 1978). Labour itself is not seen as oppressive, but the social relationship within which it is situated is oppressive for the majority of the people who make up the working class. Equality is similarly translated in materialist terms where it is defined in terms of having all people's needs, however different, met equally (Lather, 1991; Mullaly, 1997).

Structural theorists have applied and translated classical Marxist theory to postindustrial societies and have defined the dominant classes to include those who have access and control of technology, media, political power, and other social structures that are integral to the functioning of society (Mullaly, 1997). As opposed to focusing on economic production solely, Althusser (1969) extends Marx's analysis by paying close attention to all concrete material practices, which produce culture, ideology, and people's sense of subjectivity. Like the cultural materialist scholar Gramsci (1971), Althusser (1971) also believed that not only the economic system but also the culture of society was political, where the institutional and structural practices that defined the culture of societies served the interests of the dominant in society over others.

Marxist Approach to Research

Ontological Claims: Materialist and Collectivist Visions of Social Justice

The ontological vision of Marxism is contradictory in relation to the manner in which it reflects the difference-centred/normative axis. On the one hand, Marxist/structuralist theories refute the atemporal claims of universalism in liberal theories. Marxist/structuralist visions of social justice are historically situated and contextualized within specific epochs and eras in time as characterized by the particular system of economic production and grounded in the specific nature of oppression that the working class experience in their lives. Yet on the other hand, Marxist analysis is predicated on claims of exposition of the fundamental laws that govern society and social relationships in society. Marxist theorization is based on abstracting the "true" nature of the laws of nature, which is used to predict social events and relationships within the lived specificities of social reality. Marx spoke very much in the language of an Enlightenment thinker, using deductive powers of

47

reasoning by which to arrive at an understanding of society through the use of the scientific discipline of economics. In fact, one of Marx's fundamental claims was that if people understood the laws of nature, they could liberate themselves from being controlled by them (Taylor, 1978). The lived realities of research participants are significant only so far as they conform and correspond to the "laws" of oppression already made explicit in the theories. Moreover, Marx is only really interested in the difference that class location makes in people's lives. Any other difference based on gender, race, and age is not discussed. For example, Marx continues to assume that all people are universally productive in the economic sense and find self-fulfillment universally by being economically productive (Lather, 1991). Similarly, Marx assumes that there is a universal expression to the oppression of the labour class (Hill Collins, 2000). Feminists have also argued that Marx does not take into account gendered differences (Pateman, 1992), and Aboriginal writers have pointed out that Marx's analysis of the economic system is entirely Eurocentric (Chrisjohn and Young, 1997).

Latter-day Marxist feminists have applied feminist analysis that incorporates gender and class analysis; however, the ontological assumption of Marxism, which is based on a universal idea of the economic laws by which society is governed as well as a universal view of "man" as productive and social reality as material in nature, results in overlooking alternative visions of society or acknowledging other differences that have also affected people's lives in fundamental ways.

Mullaly (1997, 2002), a structuralist social work theorist, claims that structuralism has the advantage over Marxism because it is more inclusive of difference in its analysis. According to Mullaly, institutional and structural practices are critiqued within structuralist analysis not only in terms of class but also other privileges such as those accrued on the basis of gender, race, and sexuality. However, an examination of structuralist theorization, including Mullaly's writings, shows that difference is treated in rigid ways in terms of fixed categories, prescribed along lines of social identity. The concept of "difference" is not complicated as it is in social identity and postmodern theories, which will be discussed later. This results in an analysis where the ontological assumptions of structuralist theories continue to be centred on material and structural inequalities.

While I think that the insistence in Marxist theory on grounding its analysis within the specificities of the socio-economic context of people's lives is an important contribution to difference-centred theorizations, it fails to live up to its own possibilities. Similarly, structuralist theories treat difference in additive terms where multiple and intersectionality of difference is not recognized as a result of fixed categorization by which difference is conceived. Hence I locate Marxist theories on the far end of the normative end of the difference/normative axis, while structuralist theories are on the normative axis but a little closer to difference-centred theorizations.

Marxism, as I suggested earlier, is steeped in critical thought. One of the significant ways by which this becomes apparent is in its insight of the close relationship between knowledge creators and the power elite in society, as I discuss in the next section. Another is its notion of praxis—that the practices of social institutions reflect the values and assumptions of society. Marxists refuse to distinguish between ontological and epistemological claims of society by refusing to distinguish knowledge claims as separate from value claims. This constitutes an important insight of critical thought as, like other critical theorists such as feminism, anti-racism, and gay lesbian movements, Marxism also grounds itself in oppositional social movements to produce alternative knowledge claims. I discuss the critical/mainstream axis within which to locate Marxist theorisations in the next section.

Epistemological Claims: Knowledge As Constructed and Ideological

The critical perspective initiated by Marxist theories and reflected in structuralist theories rests on the fundamental epistemological assumption that knowledge is socially constructed by and in the interest of the dominant in society (Lather, 1991). The assumption that knowledge is historically situated and contextualized is an important insight of Marxism and informs anti-oppressive theories that are also "social constructionist" in their epistemological assumptions (Burke and Harrison, 1998). Knowledge is understood as having an ideological function that is used to create a "hegemonic"—that is, a dominant—view of reality and social relations that is given the appearance of an authoritative version of "truth." Marx takes the example of royalty and states that royalty assume their authority over others by appealing not only to temporal power but also divinely inspired power (Corrigan and Leonard, 1978). The ideological construction of royalty as being divinely appointed provides sanction for one class of people to rule over another.

wow!

49

Hence knowledge is not assumed to be neutral as it is in classical versions of liberalism. The transference and production of knowledge signifies an important site in the fight for social justice as it does in anti-oppressive and postmodern theories. Researchers engage in the research process so as to deconstruct dominant or mainstream "constructions" of reality and expose the interests that these constructions serve both historically and contemporaneously within specific socio-cultural contexts. Paradoxically while Marxists and structuralists assume knowledge to be constructed, they seem unaware of their own complicity in using knowledge to gain a position of power through their insistence on an alternative meta-narrative (or truth claims) by which to understand how things "really" are (Lather, 1991). Thus, like all meta-narratives that preach singular visions of truth, Marxists and structuralists set up similar binaries of true/false with its attendant dichotomous lines on which knowledge claims are constructed. They also emphasize the certainty of their explanation of reality and the assumption of the importance of people to become the "knowers" of particular truths.

While knowledge is acknowledged for having an ideological function, it is also understood as being "objective," albeit used in ways that further the personal (subjective) interests of a particular class of society. Hence a fundamental epistemological assumption in Marxism/structuralism is that knowledge claims are both deductive and positivist in nature. Reality is assumed to be knowable by deducing the laws of nature through scientific observation and treated as universal through time and space. Hence Marxism/structuralism retains a critical edge on the critical/mainstream axis while continuing to maintain a normative position on the normative/difference-centred axis.

Like all critical theories, Marxism and structuralism do not see the role of their theorization to rest only in making explanatory claims, but also emancipatory claims to create social change (Habermas, 1986; Lather, 1991). This dialectical tension between theorizing and practice or acting, is what Marx termed "praxis." He asserted that in acquiring alternative and "true" knowledge of things, one eliminated false consciousness, resulting in a very different way of doing or being. Knowledge is thus directly related to practice.

Research methods using Marxist analysis are grounded in creating oppositional knowledge and critiquing the status quo, as well as in creating social change (Lather, 1991). Methods such as participatory action research have consonance with the ontological and epistemological visions of structuralism and Marxism. The outcome of the research is expected to change both the material realities of the participants and the ways by which the participants understand that reality.

Unlike liberalism, Marxism and structuralism do not view the research activity or the researcher to be neutral due to the researcher's investment in creating social change (Lather, 1991). Research that results in social change, particularly in relation to the material realities of the participants, is considered the primary criteria of validity as long as it is emancipatory in nature. At the same time the research activity is considered reliable if it is replicable by another researcher, as the "findings" of the research are based in material changes. Although there is an acknowledgment that the researcher and the participants will "shift" in their understanding or gain oppositional knowledge about social relations, this change is assumed to be material and clearly reflected in tangible ways. For example, understanding how the immigration policies of a society ensure a healthy supply of low-paid employees is valued to the degree to which this understanding results in changing the material realities of immigrant communities. In other words, reality is always knowable and the researcher works in ways that allow her to be a knower as a result of participating in the research activity.

Feminist Theories

Ontological Claims

White feminist theory, or what has come to be known as "first wave feminism" (Lather, 1991), is the particular focus of my discussion in this section. Feminism has always been engaged with centralizing difference in its theorization. As early as the eighteenth century, feminist Mary Wollstonecraft wrote a treatise entitled "Vindication of the Rights of Women" in which she argued that women should have rights equal to men because of the different but equal talents and skills they contributed to society. First wave feminism's focus of theorization was to centre gender in its analysis to correct misperceptions about women as they existed in theories about women written by men and to add women's voices and hence visibility of feminist analysis by women themselves based on their lived experiences (Reinharz, 1984;

Stanley and Wise, 1983). The singular difference that White feminism was concerned with is the difference that gender makes in the lives of women and their social relationships in society (Reinharz, 1984).

Feminist theory was therefore grounded in oppositional theorizing from its very beginning, explicitly aiming to contest hegemonic and dominant constructions of gender, particularly womanhood. The critical stance that feminism took is also reflected in its grounding within oppositional social movements, feminist movements, rather than relying on a canonical tradition, as is the case with liberalism and latter-day Marxism (Huyssen, 1990). Feminists, like Marxists and other critical theorists, clearly intend their theorizations to serve emancipatory ends, more specifically using theory as another site of struggle for the liberation of women from gendered oppression (Lather, 1991). In order to do this, feminists have not used only one theoretical lens to conduct their analysis; in fact, I would argue that one of the most significant contributions of feminism is its use of multiple theories to make its point. One can have liberal feminists, postmodern feminists, Marxist/structuralist feminists, and so on, all of whom use gender as the focus of their analysis in combination with other theoretical insights.

A common theme of White feminist thought was to theorize about injustices that occur as a result of patriarchal conventions and assumptions that exist at an ideological, institutional, and societal level (Dominelli, 2002b). Women's oppression is viewed as resulting from normative gendered assumptions. There are basically three ways in which feminist theories formulate their vision of social justice based on their theorizations about gender.

The first, as argued by "individualist feminists," emphasizes women's sameness with men (Offen, 1992). These feminists, such as Pateman (1989), MacKinnon (1990), and to some extent Okin (1989), find that normative theories and visions of social justice are inherently patriarchal. All of these theorists give examples of how "maleness" is constructed as rational, individuated, and capable of making decisions for the common good, while "feminine" is constructed as being emotional, interdependent or even dependent, and incapable of forming judgments that are disinterested and applicable to defining the common good of the public. Individualist feminists argue against the privileging of a male norm and the gendered construction of "male" as opposed to "female" where women are constructed as being inferior. Central to their analysis is the contestation of binaries that are constructed as a result of societal gendered norms. One of the more important binaries is the notion of public versus private, where women are supposed to subsist in a private realm without the rights and privileges that exist in the public realm, which is properly considered the domain of men. These feminists argue that both men and women should participate equally in the public realm as well as contest the construction of a private/public divide, stating that the "private realm," such as home and the family, are in fact public institutions that reflect societal norms and values. The focus of their theorization is on dismantling any notions of difference that may exist between men and women (Offen, 1992).

On the other hand, relational feminists emphasize differences between women and men, seeking to valorize "feminine" virtues of women and contest the patriarchal construction of women as inferior. Feminists writing in this vein, such as Carol Gilligan (1982), argue that women as mothers and caretakers live more interconnected lives than men do and are better at maintaining social relationships. This they consider to be an important contribution of women to society and one that complements men's role in society. Rather than viewing women as deficient, relational feminists insist on valorizing women's difference from men.

Central to feminist theorization is a vision of social justice that opposes patriarchy and gendered social relations wherever they are found to be unjust. Liberal feminists such as Okin (1989) argue against the patriarchal assumptions embedded in liberal visions of social justice, forming an alternative analysis that is more inclusive of women within male-oriented liberal analysis. Marxist feminists focus on the labour laws and the production of labour, including women's reproductive "labour," and argue for a more inclusive analysis of reproduction (Weedon, 1997).

More recently feminist writing has moved to theorizing about gender roles in ways that move beyond the binary of "same" versus "different." As a result of challenges that have been posed by theorists who are lesbians, women of colour, postcolonial theorists, women with disabilities, as well as those who position themselves as queer, some feminist theorizing has become more difference-centred. Women of colour, writing from both the postcolonial as well as colonized world, contest the universality with which White feminists analyzed gendered oppression. Hill Collins (1998), for example, points out that while White feminists were engaged in debating whether women's role in the home was "natural" or "constructed," they overlooked the plight of Black women in Western societies, who did not have the relative privilege of having the choice to stay at home. Similarly, women writing from postcolonial societies such as India rejected the universality with which White feminists assumed that their own experiences of oppression were the same for women everywhere (Mohanty, 1991). Other women, such as lesbian writers, contested the heterosexist assumptions in the writings of first wave feminists, as did queer theorists who extended feminist analysis of the construction of gender by questioning if "gender" was even a useful or necessary concept to have (Jagose, 1997). I will explore difference-centred feminism later in my discussion of social identity theory.

Feminist Approaches to Research

Ontological Claims: Collectivist, Women-Centred, Grounded in Lived Experience

Feminism, like Marxism, privileges the specific and the contextual over the transcendental and the universal in its theorizations. However, a fundamental break between feminist and Marxist, as well as liberal theories, is its contestation of the notion of one truth or one true reality. Truth claims are contextualized within subjective and specific lived experiences of gendered oppression. They are seen as multiple and outside of the dichotomous oppositions of truth/false statements by which ontological assumptions of meta-theories, such as Marxism and liberalism, are defined. Hence feminist theorizations are oriented toward difference-centred analysis, where normative assumptions on the basis of universal claims are eschewed for multiple ones.

Yet first wave feminism theorization, which is what I am discussing in this section, did not confront the possibilities of its own theoretical assumptions. While theorizing about the multiplicity of truth claims and allying themselves with various and multiple theoretical frameworks when undertaking their analysis, White feminism continues to privilege and single out gender as its focus of analysis. White women's experiences of injustice are privileged over those of women of colour. As Hill Collins (1998), a Black feminist, has argued, White feminists fought for women's rights to become members of the workforce outside the home, yet Black women had always worked outside their homes as enslaved or indentured labour. The universalizing of White women's experiences of oppression in early feminist theory was, and continues to be, hotly contested by women of colour (Mohanty, 1991).

The main charge against White feminist thought then is the difficulty in being inclusive of difference, whether that is race, sexuality, or any other basis of difference, in its analysis. Hence by privileging White women's experiences of oppression over multiple and intersecting oppressions that women who occupy multiple social identities experience, first wave feminists continue to envision social justice in singular and universal terms. Therefore, although I position White feminism as on more of a difference-centred rather than normative edge of the difference/normative axis, I find that the focus of their theorization is not difference and the many ways by which it is interwoven in the lives of women; rather, their focus is on gender and the many ways that gender interweaves with other factors in women's lives to produce the oppression that women experience in their lives.

In terms of their orientation toward critical analysis, feminists, like other critical theorists, also base their theorization within lived experiences and oppositional social movements (Weedon, 1997). Feminist theorization, as in the case of all critical theories, is emancipatory in intent and is seen by feminists as a contiguous site for the struggle for social justice. Feminism therefore occupies a position at the critical end of the critical/mainstream axis, although the ambit of its critique does not result in the examination of White privilege within White feminist writings. In the next section I discuss the critical orientation of feminist writing through a discussion of feminist epistemological assumptions.

Epistemological Claims: Knowledge as Subjective and Inductive

Feminist theories challenge the assumptions of enlightenment thought as articulated in meta-theories (Stanley and Wise, 1987). Therefore, they contest the assumptions of knowledge as being positivist and deductive, emphasizing instead inductive thinking that has its basis in the subjective and lived experiences of women (Reinharz, 1984). The specific rather than the general provide the definitive background within which feminist theorizing takes place.

Feminists, like Marxists, are social constructionists who regard mainstream knowledge as the purview of privileged men who construct particular views about women that are then accepted by society to be "natural" (Lather, 1991). Therefore, like other critical theories, feminism assumes knowledge production to be an important site in the struggle for social justice. There is also an acknowledgment within feminist theory of multiple ways of knowing. Rather than validating literate, "academic," and positivist ways of knowing only, feminists accept the knowledge that is derived from everyday experience as it is reflected in song, art, personal narratives, etc. (Trinder, 2000).

Hence feminist researchers consider knowledge to be value laden and partial in nature, situated within the assumptions of the privileged and in the interest of maintaining patriarchy. When conducting research, feminists do not define the reliability of their analysis to consist of statements that are measured by the degree to which they are seen to be objective or neutral. Rather, they seek to make their own biases and values transparent, consistent with their epistemological assumptions (Lather, 1991).

Research participants are considered to be subjects at the heart of the research project, which is itself viewed as emancipatory in nature (Smith, 1990). The participant is not viewed as a repository of knowledge, an object of the research intervention used to "collect data" (Lather, 1991). The researcher and the participant are engaged in self-reflexive activities where their collaborative efforts at making meaning reveals to both the different possibilities of ways of understanding social realities (Stanley and Wise, 1983). Like most research projects that are undertaken using critical theory, feminists are also concerned about linking their research to social justice claims and not to "merely justify and rationalise the power relationships, which oppress women. They also provide the concepts, models and methods by which experience can be translated and transformed" (Stanley and Wise, 1987, p. 163).

Feminist research, due to its epistemological and ontological assumptions, is largely undertaken using qualitative research methodologies that include focus group discussions, narrative research methodologies, semi-directed interviews, etc. These approaches to research use inductive reasoning and are more conducive to feminists' attempts at undertaking theory in order to understand rather than predict the multiple meanings and patterns that emerge from the narrative of people's lives (Lather, 1991).

Postmodern Theories

Postmodernism, a term that was first used in architectural criticism, has become a philosophical movement that is embraced by a growing number of social scientists (Lather, 1991). The fundamental theoretical contestation and claim of postmodern theories is that social reality cannot be described or explained with certainty or in authoritarian terms (Huyssen, 1990). Reality, according to postmodern theorists, is too complex, multiple, and fluid to be captured by singular, universal explanations found in enlightenment based theories, with their attendant false/true dualisms (Huyssen, 1990).

Knowledge about reality is not only constructed, but reality itself is understood to exist solely on representational terms (Weedon, 1997). In other words, to the question of what constitutes social reality and the social relations that characterize it, postmodern theorists would respond by saying that one cannot answer this question in generalities or universal terms. Reality is both multiple and fluid as well as historically specific in character, hence one cannot say anything for certain about social reality; one can only interpret it based on one's own culture, values, biases, etc. (Lather, 1991). Postmodern theories, therefore, do not make normative statements when analyzing social reality or envisioning social justice claims.

Historically, postmodern theorists, or theorists with whom postmodern writers ally themselves, have always been engaged in difference-centred theorizing. For example, Edward Said (1986; Said and Hitchens, 1988) in his works deconstructed the images and representations that were used by White or European scholars to depict the Other, in this case Muslim societies, as inferior. Said, who did not label himself a postmodernist, was co-opted as a forerunner of postmodernism due to the attention he paid to deconstructing representations of the Other. Postmodern theorists understand truth as being representational, fluid, evolving, and thus refusing categorization. Similarly, Michel Foucault (1979, 1980), who is influential in postmodern analysis, undertook genealogical analysis to examine the language by which the Other, such as gay men or those who were treated as criminals in society across various historical epochs, were represented within mainstream society. Foucault analyzed the use of religious, medical, or scientific discourse in making particular constructions of the Other in society. The use of medical discourse, for example, to construct homosexuality as a "disease" was used to make truth claims that were, in fact, grounded in the desire to control or regulate same-sex behaviour. For postmodern thinkers, therefore, there are no truths; however, there are "regimes of truth that occupy a dominant space in representing and creating certain "truths" about the Other on the basis of their "difference" (Foucault, 1980).

Knowledge is, therefore, clearly linked to relations of power, but unlike Marxism where power is understood in binary terms with the oppressed having no power as victims of "false consciousness," power is analyzed as existing in multiple relationships in postmodern theories (Lather, 1991). Taking their cue from Foucault, postmodern theorists consider everyone to be a participant in maintaining particular representations or discourses of themselves and others in society. Hence postmodern thinkers are concerned with analyzing how "we are constituted as subjects of our own knowledge" (Lather, 1991). For example, hierarchical relationships in society are viewed as being maintained by all those who participate in the system and not just those who dominate it. Hence postmodernists would argue that people who occupy the lower echelons of power internalize the need for hierarchy in societies and their place within it, if not for always, then at least for the present. Thus, the subject within postmodern theories is treated as an active subject and is centralized in postmodern analysis, very much like it is in feminist and anti-oppressive analyses.

Postmodern theorists contest the role played by traditional theories in explaining the "true" nature of social reality and envision social justice claims that are consistent with these explanations. According to postmodern theorists, there is no "true" or "singular" reality that can be explained with certainty (Rorty, 1998). What exists are representations and interpretations of reality, which need to be deconstructed so as to better understand the processes and interests that such interpretations of reality serve (Weedon, 1997). Therefore, social justice claims that are singular in nature cannot be made, and deconstructing mainstream representations is seen as participating in acts of justice.

Postmodern Approaches to Research

Ontological Assumptions: Multiple, Representational, Individuated, and Fluid

Postmodern theorizing does not necessarily aim to explain, predict, or emancipate but simply to deconstruct. As postmodern theorizing does not make any normative assumptions, there is no other imperative to postmodern theorizing but to deconstruct through a historical process that is genealogical in nature, the manner by which certain phenomena came to take on the meanings they do (Spivak, 1987). Fishkin (2004) has argued that postmodern theorizing in fact makes another ontological assumption—that of assuming that differences of voices and diversity of multiple meanings are an important facet of social reality and have to be acknowledged. There is some validity to this argument, although one could argue that as postmodern theories do not commit themselves to certain notions of "good," then it is difficult to assert that postmodern theorizations affirm anything fundamentally. Postmodern theorists have been critiqued for not making a distinction between difference-centred analysis that perpetuates dominance and theorizations that contest oppression (Spivak, 1987).

On the difference-centred/normative axis, postmodern theories very much position themselves on the lines of difference-centred analysis. Their stance against normative assumptions clearly marks them as theories that are governed by the very specific context within which their work is situated. I would argue that this results in an analysis that is individualist in orientation. In their emphasis on the particular and the specific, postmodern theories lack the language by which to speak in terms of solidarity and collectivities (Dominelli, 1997). To generalize about the experiences of collectivities or to speak in terms of group solidarity can result in a level of universalizing with which postmodern theorists are not necessarily comfortable. On the axis of critical/mainstream, postmodern theorists pose a quandary as they are not clearly positioned within critical analysis, yet their analysis, which is often used to deconstruct mainstream assumptions, can result in upholding mainstream assumptions because of their lack of a political agenda, specifically in the fact that they treat all claims to difference equally, ignoring the majority/minority positions of the people making those claims.

There is an abiding assumption within postmodern theories that "in the knowing is the doing," suggesting that ontological and epistemological separation does not exist in reality (Lather, 1991). This is consistent with the postmodern notion that one's subjectivity, including one's participation in various social systems, remains a reflection and extension of one's knowledge.

Epistemological Assumptions: Fluid, Subjective and Subject Making, Representational

Knowledge is understood as being fluid, impossible to cast into rigid categories, as reality is multiple and always changing. Hence postmodern theorists align themselves to varying and multiple theoretical frameworks by which to analyze situations. For example, there can be postmodern, feminist critical theorists or postmodern, Marxist feminist theorists, etc. (Weedon, 1997). Like feminist theory, one cannot speak of postmodern theory in singular terms.

Knowledge is assumed to exist not only in the formal structures and institutions of society, but also as it constitutes the subjectivity of individuals. Foucault (1980) defines this theorizing as "thinking more about how we think." Postmodern theorists presume self-reflexivity on the part of individuals and researchers. They consider it possible and necessary for individuals to be the subjects of their own knowledge and to be able to examine their own knowledge base, how it came to be that they acquired the knowledge they did, and what their assumptions are (Lather, 1991).

The multiple nature of social reality and the fact that postmodern theorists consider reality to be unknowable and largely interpretative results in postmodern theorists' fundamental assumption that all individuals possess only partial knowledge and are never in a position to know anything completely (Lather, 1991). Anti-oppressive theorists also emphasize the not-knowing stance over that of the "expert." However, for postmodern theorists it is the universal, meta-narratives and the authoritative voice that they position themselves against. The researcher, therefore, is always positioned as the "learner" when undertaking research using postmodern theories (Lather, 1991). Fundamentally postmodern theorists move away from theorizing through the research process to constructing a narrative about their observations and endeavours at deconstructing social reality (Rorty, 1998).

Depending on the researcher's interpretation of postmodern theories, research undertaken using this stance is likely to be qualitative in nature. It is also likely to include narrative methodology, using genealogical research by deconstructing mainstream narratives that are either textual or verbal as revealed by the participants. Generally, postmodern thinkers prefer research methodologies that use interpretative methods, such as hermeneutics, of undertaking research where there are no certain truths, only interpretations of truths (Creswell, 1998). Attention is likely to be paid to the participants' experiences and the meanings that they make of their experiences so as to deconstruct dominant representations of participants' realities as well as to understand participants' subjectivity through their meaning-making processes.

The researcher is self-reflexive when undertaking research, being open and ready to shift from her own assumptions upon understanding the meanings and definitions that others place on their own understandings (Lather, 1991). One of the hallmarks of postmodern approaches to research is that it is participant-centred, ensuring that the participant's voice is central to the analysis and/or deconstruction effort of the research project.

Social Identity Theories

I use the term "social identity theories" to refer to those theories that are grounded within oppositional social movements organized around social identity locations such as race, ability/disability, queer, gay, lesbian, bisexual, transgendered, and so on. Anti-oppressive theories developed historically from theorizations by "social identity theorists" who sought to go beyond the confines of analyzing the nature and experiences of oppression on the basis of singular social identity to an analysis of multiple and intersectionality of identity locations. As with feminist theories, no one ontological or canonical tradition defines social identity theories. The commonality that has historically bound social identity theorists is the adoption of a critical stance, contesting mainstream theories that characterize "difference" as problematic or inferior (Dominelli, 2002a). Social identity theories are clearly situated within oppositional social movements such as the anti-racist, queer, disability, Aboriginal, and other social identity-based movements, all of which have the elimination of oppression, as experienced by their collectivity, as its central focus.

Like other theories discussed in this chapter, anti-oppressive theories offer an analysis of social reality and a vision of social justice. While there are a diversity of views by which social reality is analyzed by theorists who write in this vein, a commonality is the acknowledgment of subordinate/dominant power relations that characterize social relationships in society. The basis on which people experience differential and subordinate power lies in the ownership of their social identity, where "difference" from an assumed White, heterosexual, able-bodied norm results in various forms of oppression that are structural, relational, and cultural in nature. Injustice, unlike Marxism, is defined not only in materialistic terms, but also in relational and cultural terms that define the normative values, assumptions, and beliefs of society. While Marx defined injustice as occurring in material and cultural terms, Marxist analysis regards culture as "false," forming a part of the superstructure of a society whose "real" nature was economic or material. Social identity theorists, like postmodern theorists, take seriously the cultural representations of society, particularly representations of the Other in society without excluding analysis of the material conditions of society. However, unlike postmodern theories, "oppression" both in its collective as well as in its intersectionality, a term I explain in the next paragraph, is the focus of its analysis.

The first wave of anti-oppressive theories, which began to be more explicitly articulated as such by the mid-1990s, was characterized in two ways; it was grounded in the lived experiences, both collective and individual, of intersecting and multiple oppressions. Intersectionality, as a concept, was foundational to the inception of anti-oppressive theories, and provided a more complex analysis of the processes by which "Othering" took place for marginalized communities. This can be seen in the works of Crenshaw (1991), Razack (1998), Fine (1997), Hill Collins (1998), and Phoenix (2004), among many other writers. Intersectionality was defined as the interweaving of oppressions on the basis of multiple social identities as well as marginalization that was both relational and structural (Phoenix, 2004). The focus of anti-oppressive analysis, therefore, is apparent in the stand that theorists take against all forms of oppression in their analysis, a development from analyzing oppression on the basis of singular social identities such as gender or race.

Secondly, it was characterized by analysis that spoke in terms of resistance to and a contestation of mainstream theorizations of a transparent and universal truth that excluded differences of social identities, and an attempt at self-definition, of giving voice to one's own experiences and knowledge derived from the experiences of marginalization. One can clearly see examples of this "theorizing as a matter of survival," as hooks has termed it, in the writings of anti-racist, queer, and disability theorists (Hill Collins, 1998, 2000; hooks,

1990; Jagose, 1997; Wendell, 1996). This theorization is situated in the particular and specific nature of oppressions that are historically situated and contextualized (Burke and Harrison, 1998). Hence, as in the case of all critical theories, theorization becomes yet another site of struggling against oppression. As Hill Collins (2000) states: "social injustice is the maintenance of intersectionality of oppression that has to be eliminated both in practice and ideas."

A particular contribution of anti-oppressive theorists is their analysis and conceptualization of oppression. Binary thinking about oppression that assumes the existence of an oppressed and oppressor is deconstructed to include a more complex notion of oppression that acknowledged multiple relationships in which one could be the oppressed and the oppressor at the same time (Razack, 1998). Concepts that treat the margin as being in a dichotomous relationship with the centre are also disrupted; the "margin" is also recognized for being a space of power (hooks, 1989, 1990). "Essentializing" people on the basis of their social identity that has its basis on singular social locations such as race is also challenged by complicating the multiple identity locations of people (Hill Collins, 1998) and by decentring notions of a "norm," such as is assumed within White or male-stream analysis.

More recently, anti-oppressive theorization has developed a sharper focus on the concepts of intersectionality and multiplicity by complicating and theorizing about the concept of "difference." Difference has always been implicit in anti-oppressive theories, but it has come into the foreground as theorists attempt to move beyond theorization of representations and resistance to "Othering" to an analysis that envisions the possibilities, both practical and theoretical, of what it means to have a society that is difference-centred. In so doing, difference-centred (anti-oppressive) theorists interrogate "normative" assumptions and practices that exist both in marginalized as well as privileged spaces, resulting in the social exclusion of people on the basis of their difference from an assumed norm (Dietz, 1987; Yuval-Davis, 1999; Yuval-Davis and Werbner, 1999). They also envision the transformations that would occur when difference is treated as the basis, rather than the site of exclusion, for membership in society. Yuval-Davis (1999), for example, discusses an inversion of the liberal visions of social justice in which citizens have the right to be equally different to one in which citizens were "differently equal." Similarly other writers (Hall and Held, 1989) discuss what it would mean if rights

63

of autonomy were to be recast from their liberal, individualist definition to a participatory and relational one.

Difference is complicated within this analysis as being multiple, challenging earlier theorization within critical theories that assumed what Mouffe (1992) has called "false universals," such as that all women or people of colour are universally the same or different (Mouffe, 1992; Pateman, 1992). Moreover, difference, which is seen to have its basis in the social identities of people, is viewed as fluid and changing rather than fixed and reduced to a single position (Yuval-Davies, 1999). Not all claims based on difference are considered equally legitimate. As Mouffe (1992) suggests, only those claims of difference that are liberatory and address themselves to emancipating people's lives from oppression are acknowledged.

While postmodern theories are difference-centred, they are not necessarily critical or emancipatory in their claims. On the other hand, critical theorists such as Marxists are critical in their theoretical orientation but not difference-centred. Anti-oppressive theories reflect both a normative stance against oppression, and are difference-centred by seeking to interrogate normative assumptions, acknowledge multiplicity of social positions, and disrupting essentialist thinking. The juxtaposition of these two axes — critical thought and difference-centerd analysis — characterizes and distinguishes anti-oppressive theories from other theories discussed in this chapter.

I find the increasingly explicit difference-centred stance of anti-oppressive theories to provide very interesting theoretical possibilities. Their theoretical contributions provide a language that acknowledges and roots experiences of oppression in the particular experiences of people while working in solidarity against common injustices (Yuval-Davis, 1999). They are also more easily able to critique the limitations of normative theories precisely on the basis of their "normative" character. Finally, they acknowledge complicity of all communities in perpetuating injustices on the basis of an inability to accept difference.

Difference-Centred Approaches to Research

Ontological Assumptions of Anti-oppressive Theories: Specific, Dialogical, Fluid, and Anti-oppressive

Anti-oppressive theorists contest the ontological assumptions of Enlightenment-based theories that are rooted in universal, transcendental, and singular truth claims. The ontological assumptions of anti-oppressive theories are rooted in the subjective and specific as well as particular socio-historical experiences of people that are simultaneously multiply positioned. Yet unlike postmodern theories, there is an acknowledgment of tensions or contradictions that result from such theorizing between the universality of social justice claims and the specificities of acts of oppression (Crenshaw, 1991). The specific and differential nature of oppression is acknowledged, but without losing the sense of collective experiences of oppression. For example, Hill Collins (1998, 2000) acknowledges differences in individual people's experiences of racism while also hearkening to the collective Black communities' experiences of oppression. Similarly within queer theory, there is an acknowledgment of differential experiences of oppression that are gendered and intersect in particular ways with other forms of oppression while grounding this analysis in the experiences of oppression that the queer community faces as a result of transgressing gender lines (Vaid, 1995).

The ontological vision of anti-oppressive or difference-centred theorists is also multidisciplinary in nature, using various rather than one framework of theorization. Anti-oppressive theorists consider it important to form a strategy of resistance that is multidisciplinary, using multiple positions—such as, formal, structural, and cultural analysis—in resisting oppression and moving toward a vision of a difference-centred society.

Dichotomous and binary constructions of reality are also contested within the ontological assumptions of anti-oppressive theories that emphasizes the multiple, fluid, and interweaving or intersectionality of social phenomena (Brah, 1996). As I discussed in the earlier section, the concepts of race, gender, sexuality, ability, oppression, and social identity that form the theoretical foundations of anti-oppressive, difference-centred analysis are defined in ways that emphasize their fluid and multiple nature, albeit within very stable and systemic social conditions of injustice.

The ontological assumptions of anti-oppressive theories also treat the subject of its theorization or, in the case of research, the research participant as active and as owning agency (Dominelli, 2002a). Hence analyses of injustice are not predicated on one or more rigid forms of categorization, nor are they normative, allowing for differences in self-identity and responses to oppression to be free from prescribed expectations. The self is also deeply dialogical or relational where it affects and is also affected by the multitude of relationships and experiences of oppression that it faces in society.

Epistemological Assumptions: Knowledge as Partial, Multiple, Situated, and Subjugated

Positivist epistemological assumptions are contested and multiple ways of knowing and knowledges are acknowledged within anti-oppressive theories. Knowledge is not only understood as subjective, grounded as it is in one's lived experiences, it is also conceived of as situated and subjugated. Situated knowledge contests the notion of an omniscient or omnipotent viewpoint from which anything is knowable (Haraway, 1988; Harding, 1987; Hill Collins, 2000). Knowledge is understood as situated by one's social location as a result of privileges and oppression that one has experienced. Hence it is not possible for someone to know what it feels like to be racialized unless one has had the experience of being racialized and even then, there are differences within the experiences.

Knowledge is also subaltern when people who have lived in subjugation own knowledge that is the result of their lived circumstances and/or is the experience of living in a world where, due to their oppressed status, they are always translating from one sort of knowledge to another. Hence knowledge is not only subjective, it is also many times a form of translation (hooks, 1992; Spivak, 1987). There are many examples of "translated" knowledge, such as in the case of immigrant communities who are aware of both their own traditions and value systems as well as those of the country in which they have settled. This is even more true in the case of Aboriginal communities who interact with White settler societies through an intimate knowledge of those cultures, through a prism of their own knowledge, and understandings about the world they live in (Battiste and Youngblood, 2000). Transgendered writings also speak to the translation that transgendered communities are faced with as they combat a culture of gender dichotomy with their own more fluid understanding of gender.

An important insight of difference-centred or anti-oppressive theorists rests on the assumption, which follows from what I have just stated earlier, that not everything is knowable; for example, subaltern knowledge is owned by and belongs to particular marginalized communities (Burke and Harrison, 1998; Dominelli, 2002a). The researcher holds the attitude of a learner, of one who is a "not-knower," but, through the act of empathetic imagination and by possessing critical self-consciousness, comes to gain a sense of what the Other knows. The researcher is reflexive in her practice, whereby the knowledge of the subaltern or subjugated is used to reflect dominant practices and assumptions in which the researcher herself is complicit (Lather, 1991).

As with all critical theories such as Marxism, anti-oppressive theorists also make a connection between knowing and doing, and research as "praxis" (hooks, 1996). Knowledge, therefore, is not conceived of as neutral, nor is it abstract in nature. For this reason, knowledge holds the potential for "liberatory" practice because "knowing" things differently results in acting differently (Freire, 1967).

Epistemological assumptions within difference-centred theories also refute the stance that knowledge is objective as is defined within positivist theories. At the same time, difference-centred theorists, aware that difference is a fluid concept, consider knowledge to be intersubjective and dialogical. Knowledge about something is gained by the interaction of the subject and the observer, where both are understood as having agency and are involved in defining "difference" (Hall, 1996).

Difference-centred theorists, writing on race, gender, ability, class, or sexual orientation, employ a variety of research methods to undertake research. Qualitative, inductive methods of research are most suited to the ontological and epistemological assumptions of these researchers. Research methods such as narrative, some forms of ethnography, and phenomenological methods of research can be used in a way that facilitates the centring of the participants' voice that critique and contest mainstream or dominant perceived truths and representations of the Other and have been used by difference-centred theorists.

Conclusion

The purpose of this chapter was to define and clarify the theoretical assumptions of anti-oppressive theories, a task that has been overlooked within the relevant literature, so as to provide an overview of the theoretical orientation that provides the background to the various chapters of this book. I have undertaken to do so by situating anti-oppressive analysis in relation to a spectrum of other theories by examining their ontological and epistemological assumptions with reference to their orientation on two axes: a critical/mainstream as well as a difference-centred/normative one.

I characterize those theories that view knowledge in positivist terms as neutral and objective as having a mainstream orientation. Similarly, I characterize those theories that use universalist and transcendentalist language to characterize their ontological visions as mainstream in orientation. On the other hand, theories that view knowledge in social constructionist terms as rooted in subjective experiences and power relations I characterize as critical. I define those theories that situate their ontological visions in the particular and in ways that are rooted in the specificities of experiences that are differential on the basis of "difference" as difference-centred.

I have argued that anti-oppressive theories, which have their basis in social identity theories, are distinguishable from other theories by being both difference-centred as well as critical in orientation. I situate liberal theories as normative and mainstream, Marxism as critical but normative, White feminism as critical but gender normative, and postmodernism as difference-centred but not necessarily critical.

In an attempt to retain a sense of the fluidity of theoretical analysis, and in keeping with the philosophical stance of difference-centred theories, I have cast my analysis in the form of a "conversation" between theories that allows for a continual reshifting of the boundary lines that characterize the envisioning of particular theories. I have also allowed for the possibility of individual reinterpretation and repositioning of one's own ontological views that challenge the broader theoretical orientation within which one may choose to locate oneself. For example, I think it is possible for individual theorists or researchers to consider themselves liberal but in ways that expand and extend liberal ontological assumptions through a more critical edge of the individual's analysis, or indeed by the individual researcher's ability to combine several theoretical views as his or her own. It might be interesting for readers to consider their own location within the spectrum of these theories along the axes I have proposed as a way to clarify their own ontological and epistemological assumptions.

Note

1. By male-stream I mean the dominant or mainstream point of view that is gendered and patriarchal.

References

Althusser, L. (1969). *For Marx.* London: Allen Lane.

Althusser, L. (1971). *Lenin and philosophy and other essays.* London: New Left Books.

Bannerji, H. (2000). *Essays on multiculturalism, nationalism and gender.* Toronto: Canadian Scholars' Press.

Battiste, M., and Youngblood, H. (2000). *Protecting Indigenous knowledge and heritage: A global challenge.* Saskatoon: Purich Publishing.

Brah, A. (1996). *Cartographies of diaspora: Contesting identities.* New York: Routledge.

Burke, J., and Harrison, V. (1998). Anti-oppressive social work practice. In R. Adams, L. Dominelli, and M. Payne. (Eds.) *Social work: Themes, issues and critical debates,* pp. 157–182. Basingstroke: Macmillan.

Chrisjohn, R.D., and Young, S.L. (1997). *The circle game: Shadows and substance in the Indian residential school experience in Canada.* Penticton: Theytus Books.

Corrigan, P., and Leonard, P. (1978). *Social work practice under capitalism: A Marxist approach.* London: Macmillan.

Crenshaw, K. (1991). Demarginalizing the intersection of race and sex: A Black feminist critique of antidiscrimination doctrine, feminist theory, an antiracist politics. In K.T. Bartlett and R. Kennedy (Eds.), *Feminist legal theory,* pp. 57–80. Boulder: Westview Press.

Creswall, J. (1998). *Qualitative inquiry and research design: Choosing among the five traditions.* London: Sage.

Dietz, M. (1987). Context is all: Feminism and theories of citizenship. *Daedalus* 116 (4), 1–24.

Dominelli, L. (1997). *Anti-racist social work: A challenge for White practitioners and educators.* Basingstoke: Macmillan.

Dominelli, L. (2002a). *Anti-oppressive social work theory and practice.* New York: Palgrave.

Dominelli, L. (2002b). *Feminist social work theory and practice.* Basingstoke: Palgrave.

Dworkin, R. (1977). *Taking rights seriously.* Cambridge: Harvard University Press.

Fine, M., Weiss, L., Powell, L., and Mun Wong, L. (Eds.) (1997). *Off white: Readings on race, power, and society.* New York: Routledge.

Fishkin, J. (2004). Who speaks for the people? Paper presented at the Colloquim on Social, Political and Legal Theory. April 2, 2004. University of Victoria, Victoria, British Columbia.

Foucault, M. (1979). *Discipline and punish: The birth of the prison.* New York: Vintage Books.

Foucault, M. (1980). *The history of sexuality: Volume 2, The use of pleasure.* New York: Vintage Books.

Freire, P. (1993) *Pedagogy of the oppressed (20th anniversary edition).* New York: Continuum.

Gilligan, C. (1982). *In a different voice.* Cambridge: Harvard University Press.

Gramsci, A. (1971). *Selections from the prison notebooks.* Edited and translated by Q. Hoare and G. N. Smith. London: Lawrence and Wishart.

Habermas, J. (1986). *Autonomy and solidarity: Interviews.* London: Verso.

Hall, S. (1996). *Questions of cultural identity.* London: Sage.

Hall, S., and Held, D. (1989). Citizens and citizenship. In S. Hall and M. Jacques (Eds.), *New times: The changing face of politics in the 1990's,* pp.173–188. New York: Verso.

Haraway, D. (1988). Situated knowledges: The science question in feminism and the privilege of partial perspective. *Feminist Studies* 14 (3), 575–599.

Harding, S. (Ed.). (1987). *Feminism and methodology: Social science issues.* Bloomington: Indiana University Press.

Hill Collins, P. (1998). *Fighting words: Black women and the search for justice.* Minneapolis: University of Minnesota Press.

Hill Collins, P. (2000). *Black feminist thought: Knowledge, consciousness and the politics of empowerment* (2nd edition). New York: Routledge.

Hobson, B., Lewis, J., and Siim, B. (Eds.). (2002). *Contested concepts in gender and social politics.* Cheltenham: Edward Elgar Publishing.

hooks, b. (1989). *Talking back: Thinking feminist, thinking Black.* Boston: South End.

hooks, b. (1990). *Yearning: Race, gender & cultural politics.* Boston: South End.

hooks, b. (1992). *Black looks: Race and representation.* Boston: South End.

hooks, b. (1996). *Boneblack: Memories of girlhood.* New York: Henry Holt.

Huyssen, A. (1990). Mapping the postmodern. In L. Nicholson (Ed.), *Feminism/ Postmodernism.* New York: Routledge.

Jagose, A. (1997). *Queer theory.* New York: Routledge.

Kymlicka, W. (1995). *Multicultural citzenship: A liberal theory of minority rights.* Oxford: Clarendon Press.

Kymlicka, W. (2001). *Politics in the vernacular: Nationalism, multiculturalism, and citizenship.* Oxford: Oxford University Press.

Lather, P. (1991). *Getting smart: Feminist research and pedagogy with/in the postmodern.* New York: Routledge.

Leonard, P. (1994). Knowledge/power and post-modernism: Implications for the practice of critical social work education. *Canadian Social Work Review* 11(1), 27–54.

Lister, R. (1997). *Citizenship: Feminist perspectives.* New York: Macmillan.

MacKinnon, C. (1990). *Toward a feminist theory of the state.* Cambridge: Harvard University Press.

Mohanty, C. (1991). *Under western eyes: Feminist scholarship and colonial discourse.* Bloomington: Indiana University Press.

Mouffe, C. (Ed.). (1992). *Dimensions of democracy.* London: Verso.

Mullaly, R. (1997). *Structural social work: Ideology, theory, and practice.* Toronto: Oxford University Press.

Mullaly, R. (2002). *Challenging oppression: A critical social work approach.*Toronto: Oxford University Press.

Offen, K. (1992). Defining feminism: A comparative historical approach. In G. Bock and S. James (Eds.), *Beyond equality and difference: Citizenship, feminist politics and female subjectivity,* pp. 69–88. London: Routledge.

Okin, S. (1989). *Justice, gender and the family.* New York: Basic Books.

Pateman, C. (1989). *The disorder of women.* Cambridge: Polity Press.

Pateman, C. (1992). Equality, difference, subordination: The politics of motherhood and women's citizenship. In G. Bock and S. James (Eds.), *Beyond equality and difference: Citizenship, feminist politics and female subjectivity,* pp. 17–31. London: Routledge.

Peterson, N., and Sanders, W. (Eds.). (1998). *Citizenship and indigenous Australians: Changing conceptions and possibilities.* Cambridge: Cambridge University Press.

Phelan, S. (2001). *Sexual strangers: Gays, lesbians and dilemmas of citizenship.* Philadelphia: Temple University Press.

Phoenix, A. (2004). Centering marginality? Otherness, difference and the psychology of women. Paper presented at Psychology of Women Conference, Brighton, U.K., July 7–9, 2004.

Rawls, J. (1971). *A theory of justice.* Cambridge: Harvard University Press.

Razack, S. (1998). *Looking White people in the eye.* Toronto: University of Toronto Press.

Reinharz, S. (1984). *On becoming a social scientist.* Brunswick: Transaction.

Rorty, R. (1998). *Truth and progress.* Cambridge: Cambridge University Press.

Said, E. (1986). *After the last sky: Palestinian lives.* New York: Pantheon Books.

Said, E., and Hitchens, C. (1988). *Blaming the victims: Spurious scholarship and the Palestinian question.* New York: Verso.

Smith, D. (1990). *The conceptual practices of power: A feminist sociology of knowledge.* Boston: Northeastern University Press.

Spivak, G. (1987). *In other worlds: Essays in cultural politics.* New York: Methuen.

Stasiulis, D. (2002). The active child citizen: Lessons from Canadian policy and the children's movement. *Citizenship Studies* 6 (4), 507–538.

Stanley, L., and Wise, S. (1987). *Breaking out: Feminist consciousness and feminist research*. London: Routledge & Kegan Paul.

Taylor, C. (1989). *Sources of the self: The making of the modern identity*. Cambridge: Harvard University Press.

Taylor, C. (1978). Marxist philosophy. In B. Magee (Ed.), *Men of ideas*, pp. 28–42. Oxford: Oxford University Press.

Trinder, L. (2002). Reading the texts: Postmodern feminism and the "doing" of research. In B. Fawcett, B. Featherstone, J. Fook, and A. Rossiter (Eds.), *Practice and research in social work: Postmodern feminist perspectives*, pp. 39–61. New York: Routledge.

Vaid, U. (1995). *Virtual equality: The mainstreaming of gay and lesbian liberation*. New York: Anchor Books.

Weedon, C. (1997). *Feminist practice and post-structuralist theory*. Cambridge: Blackwell Publishers.

Wendell, S. (1996). *The rejected body: Feminist philosophical reflections on disability*. London: Routledge.

Williams, P. (1998). *The alchemy of race and rights: Diary of a law professor*. Cambridge: Harvard University Press.

Young, I.M. (1997). *Intersecting voices, dilemmas of gender, political philosophy, and policy*. Princeton: Princeton University Press.

Yuval-Davis, N. (1999). Ethnicity, gender relations and multiculturalism. In R.D. Torres, J.X. Inda, and L.F. Miron. *Race, identity and citizenship: A reader*, pp. 112–125. Oxford: Blackwell.

Yuval-Davis, N., and Werbner, P. (1999). *Women, citizenship and difference*. London: Zed.

CHAPTER THREE

STEPPING OFF THE ROAD:
A NARRATIVE (OF) INQUIRY

Sally A. Kimpson

Elsewhere I have written about how narratives grounded in my everyday experience as a disabled woman reveal the potential for constructing a transgressive self in an academic setting (Kimpson, 2000). This chapter focuses on research that similarly uses an autobiographical narrative approach to inquire about my experience of being a beginning researcher struggling with issues of power and representation at work in the research I was doing as part of a graduate degree. Used primarily by feminist researchers, these kinds of critical autobiographical narratives themselves transgress academic and disciplinary expectations about "acceptable" research topics, and violate norms about how research is "supposed" to be conducted. In undertaking this kind of anti-oppressive research methodology, I have felt the power of these disciplinary norms and their role in suppressing the experiences of women (Richardson, 1992), in this case myself as a disabled woman.

Autobiographical narratives also create an opportunity for us to construct ourselves and our research in ways that may be of methodological and political interest to others struggling with alternate forms of representation of the lives of marginalized people. This text, then, is intended for those embarking on graduate school research for the first time, or who are otherwise new to research, and for those researchers seeking to understand what anti-oppressive research is. More personally, this chapter is intended to be a text that would have been helpful for me to read as I struggled with/in the research, something I might recommend to those who are also struggling. Or perhaps it is something I might suggest to established researchers who want to understand alternative research methodologies and how marginality connects to research.

Feminist Research Using Autobiographical Narrative

There has been debate in both academic and grassroots women's communities as to a clear definition of "feminist research." Some claim that it is always research by and for women; others insist that the value of subjectivity and personal experience are central principles of feminist research; still others assert the importance of using methods that are not oppressive (Acker, Barry, and Esseveld, 1991; Black, 1989; Stanley, 1983). What is clear is that women's lives and experiences are the subjects of research and that making these visible and developing knowledge about them constitutes a political act. A specific challenge for feminist scholars is to find suitable methods within their disciplinary traditions while working toward an intellectual revolution aimed at transforming those traditions (Acker, Barry, and Esseveld, 1991; DeVault, 1990).

The use of personal narratives in feminist research initially began as a challenge to the androcentric bias in most research and brought forward women's voices that formerly had been silenced. Feminist researchers also began to attend to and write about the ways their own biographies intersected with those of their research participants (Jackson, 1998). Many, but not all, feminist researchers are aware that reflexivity—the reflection upon and critical examination of the nature of the research process and their role in it—is key to the generation of insight (Fonow and Cook, 1991). This feminist "self-reflexivity" about the research process constitutes a significant challenge to traditional understandings of the researcher as male, neutral, disinterested, objective, and disembodied. Indeed, most traditional academic writing is textually disembodied, systematically effacing "[t]he producer of knowledge and the means by which it is produced" (Gill, 1998, p. 24). Researchers writing in the social sciences using the third person attempt to suppress their humanity, disguising it in the omniscient voice of science, but "no writing is untainted by human hands, pure, objective, 'innocent'" (Richardson, 2001, p. 34). In contrast to traditional scholars, those using narrative approaches that are explicitly self-reflexive acknowledge that (research) writing is a practice that is inevitably informed by who we are and how we live our lives.

74

Research using self-reflexive personal narratives provides researchers with a method that illuminates the partial and perspectival nature of knowledges and the texts that we as researchers create (Lincoln, 1997). When knowledge is considered this way, other, different perspectives become possible, opening us to "a multiplicity of positions in fields that up to now have been governed by a singular, exclusive, and privileged access to true representations and valid methods of knowing reality" (Grosz, 1993, p. 194). Further, by including the body, especially my disabled body, in the text as a source of knowledge, I underscore the ways "bodies ... are essential to accounts of power and critiques of knowledge" (Grosz, 1993, p. 196). Collectively, these research practices substantially contribute to the feminist critique of the politics of knowledge construction and the marginalizing effects of traditional methods in the social sciences.

Critical self-reflexive autobiographical narrative, such as described here, is an innovative feminist strategy challenging the dictates of scientific objectivity, which conceals the social and institutional locations from which research is conducted (Jackson, 1998). More specifically, I demonstrate its usefulness not just for addressing the experiences of those who are marginalized in society and the marginalization of feminist researchers in academic settings, but also for foregrounding the experiences of those researchers whose marginality is linked to race, sexuality, class, gender, age, and, in this case, ability.

The narrative research presented here is an account of the disruption of a standard ethnographic methodology by insight generated through self-reflective writing. The move to foreground the ethical, personal, and political problems that confronted me as a researcher reveals an explicit consciousness about how we shape our texts. In particular, it illuminates how doing so is "a political issue ... not just the way the world is written" (Jones, 1992, p. 25), thus rendering problematic our assumptions about the social while acting in (and upon) it and taking a stand (Lather, 1991).

Autobiography is a powerful tool for making visible the everyday and embodied world of women's lives. Feminists and postmodernists recognize the distant voice of the objective observer/writer to be "a fiction ... a mechanism of power which ensures the domination of certain accounts" (Jones, 1992, p. 18). What becomes central in autobiographical narratives is "I," our accounts of the world, which are constructions made up of language and meanings, and our own histories of thinking about the topics that interest us. Learning to critique our experience by reflection and analysis is one way we as researchers can explore and make visible the biases and assumptions organizing our particular ways of working (Brookes, 1992).

Telling Stories: Using the First Person[1]

So what is this particular narrative inquiry about, and why might it be significant to other marginalized researchers? The simple answer lies in the study's abstract: "This account of my struggles to understand the experience of being a (disabled) woman returning to study in a university setting, first from the stories of others, then shifting to my own, renders visibility to the process of meaning making .... Changing direction by altering the method reveals the joining of two landscapes: a landscape of consciousness, and a landscape of action" (Greene, as cited in Kimpson, 1995, p. ii).

I had entered graduate school directly from a nursing degree program in which I had learned about and adopted the academy's ideas about what "legitimate" research methodologies were. In part, these were believable to me because I lived with acquired disability and, as a nurse, had adopted the medical view of disability—the "personal tragedy" model. Like many disabled people, I had subscribed to traditional societal attitudes toward people with disabilities as individuals who had experienced the tragic misfortune of becoming disabled. Along with this was the belief that disability was entirely connected to my physical impairment, something to be treated, fixed, or cured.

What might have prompted me to think differently? There was little in my life or the social context of the academy that countered this view, and authoritative voices on disability, like those of the medical community, dominated. The treatments and curative practices that physicians and allied health professionals use had been developed by scientists and researchers with well-established careers and the authority to define how people with disabilities are treated, using "rigorous"—objective, neutral, valid—research methodologies. These researchers were also predominantly able-bodied, economically secure White men, likely well established in their careers—everything I was not. Indeed, my nursing career—and economic security—had been significantly interrupted because of disability.

The story at the heart of the narrative, from which I draw excerpts for this chapter, recounts how I came to be included in the research I had undertaken as a graduate student, and how I came to see the necessity of challenging the canon. In the narrative constructed as part of the research, I characterized myself as a beginning or "neophyte" researcher who struggled with important research issues in a self-reflective way. Early in the research text I articulated four narrative threads woven together so that they recreated the fabric of my experience and my knowing. The threads comprised the following interwoven stories:

1. doing research as a graduate student, but more importantly how I came to be included in that research
2. coming to recognize my own authority and voice, and myself as a credible knower and creator of knowledge
3. learning how I learn and create knowledge, which is different from when I thought learning was a result of certain structured activities prescribed and practised in schools and other educational settings
4. living in a body with an unpredictable and disabling chronic illness, and how this influences what I know and how I experience the world, especially while conducting research in an academic setting

I do not pretend to have the answers or the truth. Adrienne Rich's (1979) words ring in my ears: "There is no 'the truth,' 'a truth' — truth is not one thing, or even a system. It is an increasing complexity" (p. 187). Indeed, the truth of any situation is to be found through the interweaving of many voices and perspectives, and is socially constructed. I arrive here not just through critical reflection on (the practice of) my research, but through reflection on situations as they have arisen and presented themselves to me in the course of my research/writing. By focusing in a self-reflective way on what and how I have learned, I can identify what is transformative for me in this process, and some possible implications for other researchers. In writing this chapter, reconstructed from my master's thesis (Kimpson, 1995), I am once again attempting to join landscapes of consciousness and action to demonstrate how a critically self-reflexive autobiography might function as a research text.

An Ingot of Time and Space[2]

It is difficult for me to remember when I decided to approach doing research/being in academia differently. In trying to recall how this unfolded, I am reminded of Novak's (1971) words about discerning our own standpoint: ascending the mountain—those deliberate, effortful steps forward, a different and more expansive perspective with each new rise, and, yes, the flight of the dove, serendipity—unexpected events, occurring seemingly unconnected to the whole, but which produce flashes of insight and knowing, moving us to new standpoints.

Having to bow to the limitations on my energy as a result of living with a disabling chronic illness seems central to this decision, but I sense there was more. Initially, like my peers, I had also chosen not to "have a life" and to pursue my academic work relentlessly, using up most of my energy on my studies. Institutional imperatives bore down on me, a transport truck of rules, regulations, and codes of conduct, leaving me whirling, like so many fallen leaves, in deadlines, meetings, assignments, and presentations. Also, the silence surrounding the sexual harassment of two women students by a tenured professor[3] in our small department, which erupted in my first term, left me confused and angry.

Responding proactively, I added political action to my heavy academic load, and became part of a small group of women students who decided to meet regularly for dialogue, support, and response to ongoing issues of concern. I would often reflect on how amazing it was that I had been blessed with such unusual energy, given the day-to-day limitations I was living (and still live) with.

In retrospect, I see how I had been trying to construct a decontextualized life in an attempt to put aside the challenges of living with disability in order to meet the demands of my academic life. In an effort to mirror the lives of those who are dominant in the academic setting, upon which the messiness of daily living as a woman with a disability is not to intrude, I chose to push myself physically beyond the limits of my energy.

The imperatives that demanded this pace from me became disabling. I had no choice about having emergency abdominal surgery near the end of my first year as a graduate student; my life was threatened. Yet this frightening event represents a divergence that was important because it forced me to reflect on my life once again in an altogether different way, to formulate not just new meanings, but a new self. I could no longer allow myself the questionable luxury of putting most of my life on hold in order to undertake graduate-level research. Surgery and recuperation forced me to slow down enough that I could carefully consider my previous experiences as a disabled BSN student, and current ones as a graduate student. From this reflection emerged my proposed thesis research, which I undertook in a self-reflexive way, creating not just different understandings about research and methodology, and the contexts within which these are located, but something new and often tenuous—a different way of doing research.

Writing was central to everything I did. Independently, I elected to begin a research journal in the first week of my M.A. program to provide a place to chronicle my experience, to store information and insights, to work through questions and concerns, thoughts and feelings, and to struggle. And as I repeatedly revisited my ongoing experiences of doing research and the entries in the research journal I was creating about these experiences, these recursive moves revealed important elements of my experience of learning to do research. As such, the journal became fertile ground from which pieces of my thesis began to grow.

What I brought forward was a story about doing research in a way in which I came to honour my unfolding (and unlearning and relearning) as a disabled woman, a student, a researcher, and a knowledgeable person with growing personal authority. It was also a story about (researching) women's lives, but more than that it was a story about conducting research—context, method, and self-reflexivity.

Ethnographic Intentions: Choosing a Topic and Method for Study

My original intention upon embarking on research for the graduate degree was to use phenomenology to study nurses returning to school to obtain BSN degrees. My exposure to feminist women (and theory) in the context of our women's group led me to consider that the stress BSN students experience and exhibit might be linked in some way to the fact that they are predominantly women studying in a male-dominated institution. To illuminate the contours of my biases and assumptions, I wrote in my research journal of my own stressful experience as a BSN student, including social and economic disadvantages I had experienced as a disabled woman. This was a first step in bringing these to light. The qualitative research literature had recommended that illuminating my biases and assumptions was important so I could "bracket" them during the research, even though later I asked critical questions about the extent to which bracketing[4] was/is possible.

These questions arose from my developing sense that I couldn't completely eradicate my preconceptions—was this not the same move to become a disinterested observer that I was becoming increasingly uncomfortable with? Wouldn't these preconceptions either bear out or not, i.e., be "critically tested" (Gitlin, Siegel, and Boru, 1989) in the research dialogues with BSN students I was planning? So why would I want to set them aside? And how on earth might I actually do this?

One of my assumptions about the method was that phenomenology would uncover the meaning of the experience for these women, but the interruption of my graduate research program because of surgery created space for questioning, and ultimately reconsideration of this method. I questioned whether it would actually uncover BSN students' implicit understandings about power. From my own BSN experience, I assumed that these women students would not be aware of the influence of their gender socialization on their experience of returning to school. It had never occurred to me to examine these influences while I was a BSN student, and nothing in my BSN program was designed to heighten awareness of this reality.

Being a beginning researcher, it was not apparent to me how this so-called "false (or submerged) consciousness" could be revealed using phenomenology. At the time I was engaged in this research, nurses and nursing educators had not actively investigated or subscribed to feminist critiques of women's gendered roles in society, and especially nurses' roles in male-dominated health care settings and universities. Thus, a general lack of awareness of the critical importance of gender persisted in nursing and nursing education, with androcentric ways of knowing predominating. Freire (1990) is credited with articulating this kind of false or submerged consciousness, wherein dominant groups—in this case men—prescribe or impose their version of reality/ views of the world on the others such that the consciousness of the subordinate group—women—is transformed into one that conforms with that of the dominant group. I was not convinced phenomenology had the critical capacity to bring this to the surface because it lacked a theory of power adequate to the critical task in which I was engaged. Thus, I became increasingly disenchanted with the idea of conducting phenomenological research.

I realized that I needed a method that revealed tacit understandings about power, and how these elements informed the BSN students' experience. A colleague had used Spradley's (1979) ethnographic interview method to study women's lives, revealing important issues of gender and power submerged in their consciousness. Building on my existing understandings of qualitative method, I was able to readily grasp the usefulness of ethnographic design for my proposed study. In essence, I chose Spradley's method for both personal and political reasons. I thought that it would simplify the research process for me, a neophyte researcher for whom disability-related time and energy considerations were paramount, and that it would reveal implicit understandings of different aspects of power embedded in the experience of women returning to school.

To a certain degree, expedience seemed important at the time; I had been cautioned to "keep it simple," and figured that Spradley would help me do this. I was seduced by the apparent simplicity of the method, and how detailed and well mapped out it was. My hope was that by following the 12 steps outlined by Spradley,[5] the complexity I understood to be inherent in qualitative methods would be reduced, and that perhaps it would make my work easier and proceed faster. This was important to me because I felt institutional pressure to finish within allotted time frames in the face of a variety of ongoing disability-related interruptions.

It is clear now that choosing ethnography marked my developing awareness of the importance of fit between method and topic, or research question. Reflective writings mapped out the concrete beginnings of my struggle with the issue of researcher bias, particularly my own biases, and questions about their place in the research I had undertaken. These doubts were articulated in my journal as assumptions that my understandings of the BSN experience would likely differ from the informants' because I now had a well-developed feminist analysis, and I was worried that I might somehow impose this on the women I intended to interview. At the time, because I did not completely understand what "interpreting the data" meant, my concerns were primarily focused on the effect that my bias might have on the women themselves and what they might tell me during interviews. Again, naively, I thought Spradley's method would "control" for this effect. I was unconcerned about the equally problematic effect my biases might have on the analysis of the data. Thus, any problems with a priori theorizing and its imposition on the data were at this time either absent or beyond my awareness.

Likewise, I naively understood reciprocity to be the mutual effect of researcher and researched on each other, not the more sophisticated and "emancipatory" view subscribed to by many feminist researchers, i.e., the involvement of research participants in the construction and validation of knowledge (Lather, 1991). Also, my belief in the power of Spradley's method to provide validity reveals that I was still willing to trust an "authority" (male) when uncertain. Choosing ethnography also gave me confidence, and I thought that doing this research was possible; it was not just something I read or dreamed about, or struggled with. I was also pleased that I had found a method that I thought would reflect my beliefs about power and that would easily incorporate my feminist perspective.

My first reading of Spradley's book found me confused by unfamiliarity with the ethnographic method and the strange terminology I was encountering. I reassured myself that this confusion was because I did not know the method, and clarity would emerge as I immersed myself in the research. What I did not share with others were my ongoing doubts about my own ability as a researcher, in part because of my biases, but also due to my inexperience. As my journey unfolded, even Spradley's "simple" 12-step sequence was not able to ease these doubts and, in fact, created new ones.

Time and "Place"

Missing from this account was my desire to situate myself in the research endeavour, a constant wrestling with the ambiguity of being positioned as a female graduate student with a physical disability in a place of privilege in Western society, the halls of academe. Of no less importance was the way in which I had been working, my relationship with myself as a writer, and the tensions generated between equally compelling prescriptions to be creative and scholarly. Clearly, prescriptions about who is the idealized graduate student—male, able-bodied, White, heterosexual, middle class—were constructing my experience in problematic ways.

Some professors in the department who thought I was taking too long to finish my degree levelled derogatory (and discriminatory) comments at me. I always felt ridiculed when this happened and spent considerable time feeling inadequate or berating myself for not being able to finish on time, even though I knew at an intellectual level that these comments told me more about the people who uttered them and their particular view of the world than about me. In vulnerable moments, the weight of my socialization—like that of a well-used bowling ball—knocked over any notions I had about honouring my own voice or my rights as a woman with a disability. My deeply ingrained belief that people in authority knew better and that there was something wrong with me if I was not able to finish on time seemed like blemishes on my skin, masking any clear, strong, authoritative self lying below the surface.

Not surprisingly, the women I interviewed also felt considerable time constraints with respect to completing their BSN degrees. But taking longer to complete the degree allowed for deeper reflection and learning, and in my case provided me with the time needed to reconsider my methodology. It also meant that I could spend time in the company of other women struggling to complete graduate degrees, sharing experiences with each other and mutually supporting each other's learning. In fact, I believe I learned more in the company of other women students and through my own ability to pursue in a systematic, in-depth, and reflective way what interested me than I did from many of the professors (all male in our department). I shared with these women the common experience of doing research qualitatively, a way that is not generally valued in the academy, intensifying my experience of feeling like an outsider and acting as a stimulus to personally challenge what I thought was unfair in the culture of the university. As Anyon (1983) points out, this challenge can be seen as part of my active "response to social contradictions" (p. 19), an attempt to cope with and resolve discrepant social messages about how I was supposed to be as a graduate student/beginning researcher and a woman in this context. University is the site of higher learning, yet only certain forms of learning are valued and rewarded.

Power, Representation, and Research

The interviews I conducted with four BSN student "informants" revealed much about their experience and, unexpectedly, about my own experience as a researcher and graduate student. Some of my questions had been directed at finding out how they lived with the cultural contradictions embedded in the experience, many of which were mirrored in my own experience as a disabled woman doing a graduate degree. These parallel worlds intrigued me, further prompting me to pose questions about the ambiguities they had revealed to me.

What I was not prepared for were the kinds of questions our dialogues raised for me in terms of power in the research process. I was not prepared for the difficulty and perhaps lack of fit I had with Spradley's ethnographic interview method past the initial interviews, during which I had asked primarily descriptive and clarifying questions. I had felt awkward using "structural" and "contrast" questions (Spradley, 1979)—the next two levels of ethnographic questioning—which went against my natural style of interviewing using open-ended descriptive questions and clarifying and summarizing as I proceeded.

I was not prepared for the immense struggle trying to discover "cultural themes"—themes I knew implicitly, buried just beyond my awareness, borne of my own experience of being situated in the same "culture" of women returning to school. I was not prepared to deal with my personal "battle with bias," trying to bracket my own assumptions, all the while questioning whether or not bracketing was possible, and to what ends. I was unable to see how this aspect of qualitative research, whose literature instructs researchers to bracket biases, mirrored quantitative research—"doing the police in different voices" (Con Davis, 1990, p. 109)—and did not in fact resist, critique, or discard the traditional research canon.

Of course I had biases—knowledge about being a woman living with disability while pursuing a university degree—but was unaware of "valid" ways to incorporate them into the research. Yet I was coming to question whether my "epistemic privilege" (Bar-On, 1993), grounded in the identity and practices of being a socially marginalized person, was something to be "controlled for" or treated as suspect in the research. And because I was not prepared for any of these questions I did not initially recognize their importance as they arose, tending to view them as researcher errors or something I should have been able to see and understand in a certain way, a way predetermined and "authorized" by the method I had chosen. I forged on with the interviews, transcriptions, and each of the four levels of analysis.

As I began to experiment with writing the "ethnographic text," I considered more deeply some of the problems I was having being situated (more or less) in the culture I was studying. Reflections brought more questions and I asked myself, "In what ways might I be unconsciously exercising my power as a researcher?" What emerged was the "authorship" of the ethnography and related issues with respect to writing about the BSN students' experiences (e.g., how to foreground each person's experience in the text with verbatim quotes, and how to relate his or her experiences to the existing literature). I became aware that I was the one who was creating the end product of our labours and was stunned to read Stacey's (1988) words: "In the last instance an ethnography is a written document structured primarily by a researcher's purposes, offering a researcher's interpretations, registered in a researcher's voice" (p. 23). My feminist understandings were being challenged. What about their purposes, their interpretations, their voices?

Wolf (1992), echoing Stacey, called the creation of text an "exercise of power" (p. 11), but she also spoke of the dilemma of trying to represent the differing experiences and interpretations of each of the informants, and I began to feel even more burdened by my "ethnographic responsibility." Both Stacey and Wolf invite exploration into the postmodern and feminist issue of whether or not it is possible to share voice/authority/authorship with informants. This was something about which I had also wondered, but was not willing to consider seriously at that point because, again, I feared the extra work entailed in altering my method. I imagined a huge drain on my limited energy having to renegotiate the research relationship with all four informants, and the different responsibilities each of us would assume. Since the surgery I had paced my studies in ways that respected my limited physical abilities and energy, and was not willing to compromise my health by increasing my workload. At this point, I had already asked for and had been granted an extension from the Faculty of Graduate Studies based on disability, but was uncertain whether a further extension would be granted if I requested it.

Questions about whether or even how the method I was using might not be "liberating" or anti-oppressive for the informants had also been subsumed by my firm conviction that it would reveal aspects of their experience that were oppressive, thus opening the possibility of freeing them from submerged consciousness. I was asking them to talk about their lives using a method that I had difficulty with. Although they were "teaching" me about their experience, I was also teaching them that, as a researcher, I was in control. For instance, I had been using specific kinds of structured questions to elicit more detailed and meaningful information. Although useful for eliciting "folk terms," for discovering the relationships between these terms and thus how meaning is constructed in the culture I was studying, having to ask these types of questions left me with serious doubts. I wondered whether the questioning process (and ethnographic methodology) truly represented the interests of those whose experience it was designed to uncover and explicate. Simply put, it seemed like too much structure for me and I began to wonder if I was imposing structure on the women's experience in an effort to make sense of it, especially with the analysis, and in doing so exercising power as a researcher in oppressive ways.

I began to realize that I could not ignore or minimize these doubts about the methodology and its lack of fit with my self-understandings as a disabled woman, along with my feminist values and beliefs about power. Spradley's method implied that life was ordered, observable, and congruent, but living every day with disability had taught me that is was messy, disordered, and incongruent. The method called for me to make interpretations, judgments, and evaluations and I began to see that my original intention of doing "member checks"[6] (Lincoln and Guba, 1985) of the text with each informant would not eliminate the problem of unequal power and authority. These were not just my concerns; the literature I was reading assured me that there was a history in ethnography of grappling with these issues (see Clifford, 1986). I took this to be intellectual support for what I was thinking, at the very least validating my questioning and doubts.

Stepping Off the Road

> I looked up the road I was going and back the way I come, and since I wasn't satisfied, I decided to step off the road and cut me a new path.
>
> —Maya Angelou

Wouldn't Take Nothing for My Journey Now

Reflecting on my own experience, cultural themes about power had been constantly repeated in my everyday life as a disabled woman returning to school, and seemed to confound my understandings of the informants' experience, but really our lives were like mirrors for each other. Just as all of the BSN students had talked to me about the different ways they had to "jump through hoops" and "play the game," I knew that I had been doing some of the same things as part of my graduate education, and using some of the same folk terms. Perhaps I was having trouble seeing the emerging cultural themes of power because they were so familiar to me. Every time I would try and articulate them, I judged myself to be imposing my own biased understandings on the data.

When I asked myself, "How does doing this research mirror what the BSN students are telling me about their experience?" I began very slowly to see how I had "jumped through the hoops" set out by Spradley's method, in part because I was a beginning researcher and also because I had not yet learned to trust my own authority and ways of knowing as a disabled woman. So assiduously had I been following the rules, trying to bracket my assumptions and biases as I had been instructed that I had negated my own parallel experience and knowing, obscuring the cultural themes. The contradictions with which I had been living were in my face. Not only had I been exercising authority vis-à-vis the informants and the research, I was appropriating power that was not really mine to use, authority that was external to me and that also held power in my life. I was caught in the unavoidable ambivalence germane to the relationship between feminism and ethnography.

The critical self-reflexivity I had been engaging in and the sense that my situation as a student (inside the academy) might allow me to cross over into my own research prompted me to think that these might be possible ways of reducing some of the power-based limitations of creating the ethnographic text. The autobiographical narratives of Anne-Louise Brookes (1992) and Carol Schick (1992) about their experiences as doctoral students (at OISE) inspired me to consider the possibility of including a personal narrative and I then turned again to my research journal. Reading and writing reflectively in response to entries in the journal revealed to me that my own experience, especially with chronic illness and disability, but also as a woman student, gave me authority to speak:

> Schick's (1992) words strongly influenced my decision to write autobiographically: After much deliberation, she decided to include her own responses and become another research subject, rather than pretend that she had remained unaffected by the research process. The woman's inclusion of her own responses could be interpreted by some as having transgressed the mythical bounds of objectivity; but

it is also an example of scrupulous honesty in the process of doing feminist research. (Kimpson, 1995, p. 29)

What is the significance of the move to tell the story of my struggles as a disabled woman doing research for the first time? It represents a new respect and honouring of not just what I knew, but the myriad ways of knowing that lay close to the heart of my personal authority. It was a difficult decision, one that played on my insecurities but that ultimately felt right. I was finally listening and attending to my own intuition, voice, and embodied knowing after deferring for so long to the disembodied "experts." While learning to value my own knowing, I was unlearning values I had learned about the knowledge of these experts and the methods they espoused.

With respect to the research I had undertaken, I was moving myself from the margin to the centre, while paradoxically moving from the centre of a dominant discourse within the qualitative/ interpretive paradigm (ethnography) to the relative margins (narrative/autobiographical inquiry). In the midst of shifting from the margins closer to the centre, or at least centring myself as a disabled woman undertaking graduate level research, I remained a woman with a disability removed from the dominant centre of the culture in which I was living. Marginality is thus not a unitary but a multiple experience.

I had often felt like I had been groping in the dark, looking for light somewhere between the lines on Spradley's page when in fact there was light within me. In some ways, I merely had to turn inward. This was a move that was ever more difficult because of my marginalized identity as a woman living with disability for whom so many aspects of life are authorized by those who construct me as devalued and worthless. Giving myself the authority to value my own insights and to focus undeterred on my knowing was a transgressive move, a stepping off the road.

I had sensed that the ethnographic method of interviewing did not quite fit with who I was, yet I had doggedly continued to fit myself into it rather than attend to what my body was telling me I knew. At the outset, with a nascent critical consciousness similar to my informants' as they learned about nurses and oppression theory, I did not have the research experience or skills to critically understand or analyze the method I had chosen or to change it. Indeed, the marginalization I had experienced as a disabled woman—and the method itself—constrained me from asking such critical questions as, "Where is Spradley's method situated?" "Who does this method serve?" and, perhaps most importantly, "How does it construct both me as a researcher and my informants?" Like the informants' preoccupation with survival as BSN students, I had been caught in my own survival as a woman and a disabled graduate student, which interfered with my understanding of how the power enacted through the method was affecting my life as a researcher. When I was unable to see what the method promised it would reveal to me, I mostly blamed myself.

Seduced by ethnography, I had believed it to be well suited to several important elements of doing this research: my purpose of revealing women's tacit knowledge during their experience in the male-dominated academy; my beliefs about the importance of myself as the primary instrument in the research; and my ability to draw on my resources of empathy, connection, and concern for women and nurses. I assumed that the caring relationships I had developed with my informants and the quality of understanding emerging from those relationships would erase any potential for exploitation inherent in the method. But mostly I had worried about my biases, my radical views of nursing education, and my need to redeem myself within academic nursing, having been for so long at the margins of this profession because of disability.

I now see how my biases were inevitable and valid, borne of being located as a disabled woman in a male-dominated setting structured to privilege non-disabled, White, heterosexual, middle-class men, rather than subscribe to the academic pretense that biases can and should be eliminated because of their potential invalidating effect on the research. Reflecting on my attempts to deal with my own biases and assumptions brought me face to face with the reality that I had obscured the cultural themes emerging in the research despite their insistence. I discovered that I had been doing the same thing the informants had reported doing during their BSN education—not honouring my own voice and authority. I would minimize or devalue my interpretations of the data, or get caught in a judgment of myself as being incredibly biased, which affected my ability to do the interpretive part of the study. In this silencing of self, my creative, embodied, knowing self was not free to emerge and play with the data in ways that made sense to me as a disabled woman studying in the same social context as the informants. I had focused instead on being as "true" to the data as I could while trying to erase myself and any influence I might exercise. But as I began to trust my own authority based on the knowledge I was generating from my own experience of being a disabled student, I recognized my ability to interpret the data in an insightful and critical way and to write about the experience with some authority.

The move to pursue what had become both fascinating and compelling for me—the questions I had been asking in my journal—was supported by my advisers and peers, though not those in the broader academy. Their support awakened in me the possibility of my own support in the form of listening to the voice that speaks from my own experience and knowing about learning and research.

Clearly, I was developing a critical consciousness of research, my university education and that of my informants, learning to perceive social contradictions and taking action to change oppressive elements of this particular reality, similar to a process suggested by Freire (1990). Having become aware of the "inevitably political nature of knowledge production" (Gill, 1998, p. 39) and the power imbalances extant in all research, I was seeking to alter these by making myself and my experiences more transparent, rather than hiding myself as a researcher in the text through careful use of language and the exclusion of personal information. To a degree, I was on the elusive quest to get it right, even while learning from Margery Wolf's experience in *A Thrice-Told Tale* (1992) that there is no right way.

In fact the right way for me was, ultimately, to realize the importance of the questions I was posing, and to pursue them while writing self-reflectively. Creating an inquiry of the research experience as it continued to unfold seemed like a direct move toward the kind of authenticity that rang true for me. Ostensibly, I was unlearning some of what I had learned over my life in formal educational settings. How was I doing this? By beginning with myself. Like many academic feminists I had unconsciously subscribed to traditional scholarship, needing to do so to generate a level of knowledge sanctioned by disciplinary authorities that could "free" me to validate what I knew, or have known, or was coming to know, like the idea that stepping off the road—moving from ethnography to autobiographical narrative inquiry—would present me with new and strangely familiar challenges. But that is another story.

Conclusion

In returning to the original text of the thesis to decide what to include in this chapter, I remain, as all writers do, exquisitely conscious of my potential audience. I am cautious about summarizing or drawing out themes from this story for your benefit and wonder about the wisdom of distilling the text in such a way. Like myself, I know that you will also make your own meanings from the text and I encourage you to do so.

Clearly, returning to seek higher education and the attempt to excel, which in the university context requires aggressiveness, perseverance, and independence, places women, especially those at the margins, in resistance to societally prescribed behaviours. How much difference do acts of resistance make in terms of reorganizing or transforming institutions of higher education or the relations of power that govern them? Although I did not elaborate on the collective action of our women's group, I believe some of our work did benefit the department and to some degree the wider university at the time, but no significant structural changes resulted.

Unfortunately, all of us had busy and exhausting personal and academic schedules—some were working, others were single parents or both—mitigating against our ability to keep a solid, constant challenge to professorial and institutional authority. We would reflect upon how the pressure on graduate students to get through quickly acted as one barrier to organizing and gaining some momentum in terms of resistance and change. I often felt powerless during these discussions, realizing that organizing and engaging in this type of resistance would likely be a full-time job, not something any of us were prepared to do. This was particularly true in terms of what was required for me to live with a physically impaired body in the context of limited financial resources and other disabling social practices. Almost insurmountable academic demands in terms of time and energy, combined with busy and complex lives, constituted another barrier to substantive change.

Feminist and critical social theory were notably absent from my formal graduate education. What I learned about these perspectives I taught myself and this learning clearly had a transformative effect on me and the research I undertook. These two perspectives are important to understanding the lives of women and other marginalized groups and individuals with whom we do research, and ought to be incorporated into our graduate education. Gender issues of power and equity exist on personal, social, and political levels. Notwithstanding our own marginalization, graduate student researchers have influence and power in our relationships with research participants, as supervisors do with graduate students. Neither research nor the education of researchers is a neutral process; each is inherently political.

A call to incorporate critical perspectives into the education of researchers in ways that make visible researcher biases is one that recognizes the political reality of our intellectual endeavours. As a feminist, using my own experience as the ground for my research practice is a deeply subversive and political move that is enacted by naming "that location from which I come to voice—that [embodied] space of my own theorizing" (hooks, 1990, p. 146)—autobiographical writing. As my story illustrates, there are different realities and other paths to follow as we learn to conduct research as part of our graduate education. This narrative then "takes place," marking the territory that is the ground for meaningful action (Grumet, 1987). Reflecting on the tensions and contradictions experienced while doing qualitative research with other women, leaving the ethnography behind, and subsequently writing a critically self-reflexive autobiographical narrative about these transgressive moves are meaningful actions, at once both personal and political. In doing so, I reconstruct myself in ways that call into question dominant understandings of what constitutes research, who the subjects of research might be, who does research (and for whom), and how it gets done in the context of living on the margins.

Notes

1. Readers will notice that I am using the first person singular. This is appropriate to highlight salient aspects of the narrative inquiry conducted as part of my master's degree and to further reflect on the implications of this work for marginalized researchers. It also makes visible a conscious challenge to academic canons that privilege the objective, authoritative voice in research texts.

2. Following Connelly and Clandinin's (1990) recommendation, I have created in this section a "narrative sketch," which they suggest might be called "an ingot of time and space" (p. 11), an overview of the inquiry.

3. A university committee found this particular professor guilty of the offences, and sanctions were placed against him. In an effort to defend

himself publicly, he went to the local newspaper with his version of the story. Interestingly, if he had not done this, the university policy of keeping the identities of the women private, which also functions to keep perpetrators' identities private (and perhaps out of the legal system) would mean officially, at least, the public would not have known that he had harassed two students. I would have been prevented by university policy from including this episode, however generally depicted, in my research narrative or even this article.

4. The phenomenologist Max van Manen (1990) defines bracketing as "the act of suspending one's various beliefs in the reality of the natural world in order to study the essential structures of the world. The term 'bracketing' was borrowed from mathematics by Husserl (1911/80), the father of phenomenology, who himself was a mathematician" (pp. 175–176).

5. Spradley (1979) describes in detail the following steps in what he calls the Developmental Research Sequence: (1) locating an informant; (2) interviewing an informant; (3) making an ethnographic record; (4) asking descriptive questions; (5) analyzing ethnographic interviews; (6) making a domain analysis; (7) asking structural questions; (8) making a taxonomic analysis; (9) asking contrast questions; (10) making a componential analysis; (11) discovering cultural themes; and (12) writing an ethnography.

6. The member check is a technique used in many qualitative research methods for establishing the trustworthiness of the findings. In a member check, "data, analytic categories, interpretations, and conclusions are tested with those members of stakeholding groups from whom the data were originally collected, and is the most crucial technique for establishing credibility" (Lincoln and Guba, 1985, p. 314). Member checking is carried out throughout a study in both formal and informal ways.

References

Acker, J., Barry, K., and Esseveld, J. (1991). Objectivity and truth: Problems in doing feminist research. In M.M. Fonow and J.A. Cook (Eds.), *Beyond methodology: Feminist scholarship as lived research*, pp. 133–153. Bloomington: Indiana University Press.

Angelou, M. (1993). *Wouldn't take nothing for my journey now*. New York: Bantam Books.

Anyon, J. (1983). Intersections of gender and class: Accommodation and resistance by working-class and affluent females to contradictory sex-role ideologies. In S. Walker and L. Barton (Eds.), *Gender, class and education*, pp. 19–37. Sussex: Falmer.

Bar On, B. (1993). Marginality and epistemic privilege. In L. Alcoff and E. Potter (Eds.), *Feminist epistemologies,* pp. 83–100. New York: Routledge.

Black, N. (1989). *Social feminism.* Ithaca: Cornell University Press.

Brookes, A. (1992). *Feminist pedagogy: An autobiographical approach.* Halifax: Fernwood Publishing.

Clifford, J. (1986). Introduction: Partial truths. In J. Clifford and G. Marcus (Eds.), *Writing culture: The poetics and politics of ethnography,* pp. 1–26. Berkeley: University of California Press.

Con Davis, R. (1990). Woman as oppositional reader: Cixous on discourse. In S.L. Gabriel and I. Smithson (Eds.), *Gender in the classroom: Power and pedagogy,* pp. 96–111. Urbana: University of Illinois Press.

Connelly, F.M., and Clandinin, D.J. (1990). Stories of experience and narrative inquiry. *Educational Researcher* 19 (5), 2–14.

DeVault, M.L. (1990). Talking and listening from women's standpoint: Feminist strategies for interviewing and analysis. *Social Problems* 37 (1), 701–721.

Fonow, M.M., and Cook, J.A. (1991). Back to the future: A look at the second wave of feminist epistemology and methodology. In M.M. Fonow and J.A. Cook (Eds.), *Beyond methodology: Feminist scholarship as lived research,* pp. 1–15. Bloomington: Indiana University Press.

Freire, P. (1990). *Pedagogy of the oppressed.* Translated by M.B. Ramos. New York: Continuum.

Gitlin, A., Siegel, M., and Born, K. (1989). The politics of method: From leftist ethnography to educative research. *Qualitative Studies in Education,* 2(3), 237–253.

Gill, R. (1998). Dialogues and differences: Writing, reflexivity and the crisis of representation. In K. Henwood, C. Griffin, and A. Phoenix (Eds.), *Standpoints and differences: Essays in the practice of feminist psychology,* pp. 18–44. London: Sage.

Greene, M. (1987). Sense-making through story: An autobiographical inquiry. *Teaching Education* 1 (2), 9–14.

Grosz, E. (1993). Bodies and knowledges: Feminism and the crisis of reason. In L. Alcoff and E. Potter (Eds.), *Feminist epistemologies,* pp. 187–215. New York: Routledge.

Grumet, M. (1987). The politics of personal knowledge. *Curriculum Inquiry* 17 (3), 319–329.

hooks, b. (1989). *Talking back: Thinking feminist, thinking Black.* Boston: South End.

hooks, b. (1990). Choosing the margin as a space of radical openness. In b. hooks, *Yearning: race, gender, and cultural politics,* pp. 145–153. Toronto: Between the Lines Press.

Jackson, S. (1998). Telling stories: Memory, narrative and experience in feminist research and theory. In K. Henwood, C. Griffin, and A. Phoenix (Eds.), *Standpoints and differences: Essays in the practice of feminist psychology*, pp. 45–64. London: Sage.

Jones, A. (1992). Writing feminist educational research: Am I in the text? In S. Middleton and A. Jones (Eds.), *Women and education in Aotearoa*, 2, pp. 18–32. Wellington: Bridget Williams Books.

Kimpson, S.A. (1995). Stepping off the road: A narrative (of) inquiry. Unpublished M.A. thesis, University of Victoria, Victoria, B.C.

Kimpson, S.A. (2000). Embodied activism: Constructing a transgressive self. *Disability Studies Quarterly* 20 (3), 319–325.

Lather, P. (1991). *Getting smart: Feminist research and pedagogy with/in the postmodern*. New York: Routledge.

Le Guin, U.K. (1989). Bryn Mawr commencement address (1986). In U.K. Le Guin, *Dancing at the edge of the world: Thoughts on words, women, places*, pp. 147–160. New York: Harper & Row.

Lenzo, K. (1995). Validity and self-reflexivity meet poststructuralism: Scientific ethos and the transgressive self. *Educational Researcher* 24 (40), 17–23.

Lincoln, Y.S. (1997). Self, subject, audience, text: Living at the edge, writing in the margins. In W.G. Tierney and Y.S. Lincoln (Eds.), *Representation and the text: Reframing the narrative voice*, pp. 37–55. New York: SUNY Press.

Lincoln, Y., and Guba, E. (1985). *Naturalistic inquiry*. Beverly Hills: Sage.

Novak, M. (1971). *Ascent of the mountain, flight of the dove: An invitation to religious studies*. New York: Harper & Row.

Rich, A. (1979). *On lies, secrets, and silence*. New York: Norton.

Richardson, L. (1992). The consequences of poetic representation: Writing the other, rewriting the self. In C. Ellis and M.G. Flaherty (Eds.), *Investigating subjectivity: Research on lived experience*, pp. 125–137. Newbury Park: Sage.

Richardson, L. (2001). Getting personal: Writing stories. *International Journal of Qualitative Studies in Education* 14 (1), 33–38.

Roberts, S.J. (1983). Oppressed group behavior: Implications for nursing. *Advances in Nursing Science* 5 (4), 21–30.

Schick, C. (1994). *The university as text: Women and the university context*. Halifax: Fernwood Publishing.

Spradley, J.P. (1979). *The ethnographic interview*. New York: Holt, Rinehart & Winston.

Stacey, J. (1988). Can there be a feminist ethnography? *Women's Studies International Forum* 11 (1), 21–27.

Stanley, L. (1983). *Breaking out: Feminist consciousness and feminist research*. London: Routledge & Kegan Paul.

Van Manen, M. (1990). *Researching lived experience: Human science for an action sensitive pedagogy.* London: The Althouse Press.

Wolf, M. (1992). *A thrice-told tale: Feminism, postmodernism and ethnographic responsibility.* Stanford: Stanford University Press.

CHAPTER FOUR

PUTTING OURSELVES FORWARD:
LOCATION IN ABORIGINAL RESEARCH

Kathy Absolon and Cam Willett

Locating Ourselves

It is our opinion that one of the most fundamental principles of Aboriginal research methodology is the necessity for the researcher to locate himself or herself. Identifying, at the outset, the location from which the voice of the researcher emanates is an Aboriginal way of ensuring that those who study, write, and participate in knowledge creation are accountable for their own positionality (Owens, 2002; Said, 1994; Tierney, 2002). We are of the opinion that neutrality and objectivity do not exist in research, since all research is conducted and observed through human epistemological lenses. Therefore, in this chapter we advocate that location is essential to Indigenous methodologies and Aboriginal research/world view/epistemologies. As Aboriginal researchers, we write about ourselves and position ourselves at the outset of our work because the only thing we can write about with authority is ourselves (Allen, 1998; Monture-Angus, 1995). When it comes to research by/about Aboriginal peoples, location is an essential part of the research process. The actual research cannot take place without the trust of the community, and one way to gain trust is to locate yourself.

This chapter is written to validate Indigenous world views and knowledge, and those seeking validation of self within the research process will benefit from it. Although this chapter speaks clearly from an Indigenous voice to Indigenous researchers/students, researchers who sees their position, history, and/or experiences as pivotal to their research process may benefit from it.

In our experience as Indigenous peoples, the process of telling a story is as much the point as the story itself. We resist colonial models of writing by talking about ourselves first and then relating pieces of our stories and ideas to the research topic. Rather than revealing the lesson or central point in an epiphany within a key statement, we hope that we have woven our ideas in this chapter within and beyond our dialogue and discourse. We rely on the intelligence and imagination of readers to draw their own interpretations and conclusions about the role and purpose of putting ourselves forward in research. As our chapter illustrates, location is more than simply saying you are of Cree or Anishinabe or British ancestry; from Toronto or Alberta or Canada; location is about relationships to land, language, spiritual, cosmological, political, economical, environmental, and social elements in one's life. We begin by putting ourselves forward, then proceed with a discourse on the purpose of location in Aboriginal research. Our conclusion connects location with contextual validation.

Putting Ourselves Forward

Kathy: As an Anishinabe woman I assert a specific set of experiences based on my cultural, racial, geographical, and political location. My name is Minogiizhgo kwe (Shining Day woman) and I am Anishinabe kwe (Ojibway woman) from Flying Post First Nation. I am born of an Ojibway mother and a British father and grew up in the bush. My mother was "dis-membered" from her Nation because of the patriarchal Indian Act legislation. She has since been re-membered as a result of Bill C-31. I too have been re-membered. Becoming re-membered is also about being re-membered in terms of who I am. Searching and re-searching has been central to my journey of recovery and discovery of my history, culture, and community. Society's acknowledgment of my existence as an Anishinabe kwe (Ojibway woman) did not come naturally or easily. If Indian policy had fulfilled its goals, my ancestors and I would have been extinguished. The fact that I can say this sets forth the complexities of my political, racial, or cultural location as an Aboriginal woman in Canada. The memories of who I am accompany a position that asserts the survival of my cultural identity and location. My memories are the antithesis of contemporary attitudes toward Aboriginal peoples that permeate popular media in which we are portrayed as a vanishing race and are relegated to museums and history books. I am remembered and I re-member and this makes my existence visible.

Searching was also central to my experience in the bush. I spent most of my childhood to young adulthood in the bush. The absence of fences, neighbours, and physical boundaries led way for the natural curiosities of a child to grow and be nurtured. My curious nature led me to find my way in the bush. Exploring the woods was my favourite pastime. The wonders that awaited and the possibilities of discoveries made my journeys into uncharted territories even more exciting. I learned to search for food, wood, plants, medicines, and animals. Trees provided markers; streams, rivers, and lakes marked boundaries; plants indicated location, and all this knowledge I developed out of just being in the bush. I believe that growing up in the bush equipped me with an extraordinary set of research skills. My bush socialization has taught me to be conscious of my surroundings, to be observant, to listen and discern my actions from what I see and hear. Elements of the earth, air, water, and sun have taught me to be aware and move through the bush accordingly. My experiences both of being lost in the bush and of knowing the bush really well and learning about its markings have become the roots of my skills as researcher. From these experiences I have also come to understand that, traditionally, Anishinabe people were well-practised researchers whose methodologies were rooted in Aboriginal epistemologies.

Today I am an educator, researcher, coordinator, facilitator, designer, developer, and helper. Because of who I am, I have accepted that my location at times can be isolating as I strive to introduce ideas, methods, and practices of different ways of knowing, thinking, being, and doing. In my work I often find myself trail-blazing, cutting through ideologies, attitudes, and structures ingrained in Euro-Western thought that can make the path for Aboriginal self-determination difficult, even impassable. I expose people to new ideas and different ways of thinking, being, and doing. I am a visionary with thoughts and dreams about life as an Anishinabe person. In this chapter I am again challenged to embark on a study, a journey of self-determination in Aboriginal education and Anishinabe pedagogy. Yet, I know that I speak and write truly from my own position, experiences, and perspectives and do not represent the Aboriginal peoples' voice. The only voice I can represent is my own and this is where I place myself.

Cam: I am a Bill C-31 status Indian from Little Pine First Nation in Saskatchewan. My mother is Cree and my father is of Scottish/British ancestry. My mother was "dis-membered" when she married my father, who is White. The government of Canada no longer considered her an Indian and, under the rules of the Indian Act, her treaty status and band membership were taken away. Although, as her son, I too was dis-membered, my generation has begun the process of re-membering, of reclaiming, and of re-searching our Aboriginal heritage. The following is my process of re-membering.

After spending half of her life in residential school, my mother returned home to her reserve and travelled every day to and from the nearest town north of her home to attend high school. It was at Paynton High School that she met my father, a third-generation farm boy whose grandfather had homesteaded about 10 kilometres north of town. After graduation, my parents both moved to Saskatoon where my mother attended a business college and my father attended a program in commercial construction. They soon married, had two boys, and moved around wherever my father could find work. After working in the construction trade for a few years, my father bought a half share of the family farm and moved us back to the homestead. It was there that my earliest memories were formed: the smell of freshly mown grass, clear days with piercing blue skies, and the sound of caragana pods popping in the hot sun. As a child, I remember trying to avoid the bare white-hot light bulb that hung down from a bent nail above the sink where my mother bathed us, getting dressed in the morning beside the diesel-burning furnace in the middle of our tiny house, and eating canned nuts while listening to the Beatles "Let It Be" album on our eight-track stereo.

I have happy memories of growing up on the farm: doing farm work with my family, playing with the neighbour's kids, and going to town to pick up the mail. My memories of school are equally happy: making friends, participating in class, and riding the bus. Yet in retrospect, as I remember and discuss my childhood with my colleagues in graduate school, I have realized that what is missing from my memories is as revealing as the memories themselves. Since my brothers and I were the only Aboriginal students in the entire school, I have always wondered why I could recall so few experiences of racism during those early years. As I remember the context of my experience, the answer to my question is unveiled. My family did not live on the reserve and we associated mostly with our White relatives in and around Paynton. We participated in community associations and events in Paynton: 4-H, softball, curling, library, sports days, auctions, dances, and church. We conducted all of our business in White communities. For all intents and purposes, we lived like White people and because of our connections at many levels (family, business, friends), we were accepted as White.

To be sure, my family suffered many experiences of racism. I remember the way that many of my father's relatives shunned my mother and spoke of her in a patronizing or demeaning manner. I remember my mother crying when the captain of the Paynton ladies' softball team pushed her and said, "Go home! We don't want to play with you!" I remember my brother (whose complexion was visibly darker than my own) being teased and getting his ears pulled until they bled by an older boy on the bus. Yet I retain a certain nostalgia for my early childhood, when I did not yet understand what was going on around me. It wasn't until I left the comfortable confines of our rural community for the city that I began to experience racism in a more direct way, which had a dramatic effect on me.

For me then, my life experience had left many questions unanswered. Remembering and reflecting on my experiences as an Aboriginal person is Aboriginal re-search. Through the telling and retelling of my story, I am able to reclaim, revise, and rename it so that I come to a new understanding about it.

Kathy: What we've experienced and seen people do in our communities is that we always introduce ourselves. We say who we are and where we come from. People will ask us who our family is. "Oh, so you're so and so's daughter or you're so and so's girl." Sometimes you tell people what your territory is: "This is where I come from," and you locate that geographically. Sometimes people will ask what it's like there.

Cam: When you're walking around the First Nations University and you meet someone you don't know or you've never met before, the first question is always "Where are you from?" and you don't mean "Are you from Saskatoon or Vancouver or Ottawa," but "Where geographically is your Aboriginal community?" There's an assumption that we have that community. Some Aboriginal peoples don't have that land base.

Kathy: Yeah, but I don't think community is reserve. I think that's kind of a boxed-in definition. I think a reserve is a fabricated and constructed mythology and so when I say, "Where are you from?" I don't mean,

"What reserve are you from?" I mean in a broader sense, "Where do you come from?"

Cam: So you're talking physical, spiritual ....

Kathy: Yeah, and geographically too because we're not all from a reserve and to just make that assumption, I think, is almost to ethnically cleanse ourselves when we think that. Who you are is related to where you are from in terms of place, family, clan, and nation. Yesterday I met another Aboriginal woman and I told her that I was Anishnabe. If somebody doesn't ask right away when I meet them, then I'll tell them who I am and where I come from; that I'm not from here, I'm from Ontario. And I think that's important because then they have a bit more of an idea of the reference point that I have, but also the reference point that I don't have. In terms of having knowledge of Saskatchewan, right away if they know that I've just moved here, they know that I don't necessarily know some things yet. I think that when we say who we are, it's almost like knowing who we are is connected to our healing as Indigenous peoples. It's connected to what we stand for individually and collectively. Who you are speaks to your ancestors. When you say who you are, it acknowledges them. It acknowledges them if you have a name that is your spirit name or saying your name in your language also acknowledges who you are in relation to the creator and the spirit because that's your spirit name.

Cam: It's kind of like ... because we don't all look brown and you might not know someone is Aboriginal. I mean you look at someone and you make assumptions based on how they look. When I meet someone who is working in an Aboriginal community, I ask myself, "What stake does this person have in this community?" So when you locate at the outset, I think I can make assumptions about people based on that. I assume that a person has more of a stake in a community because of their connections or ties or family that might be in that community. The things I might say depend on whether I believe I am talking to an insider or an outsider. I will express views that I think might be shared and see whether they are reflected in the person that I'm talking to. It's a way of connecting. If you locate and that's reflected back to you, then you have something in common and there's a connection and you've moved beyond a certain boundary, landmark, or hurdle and you're into the next stage in a relationship where you ask, "What are some other connections we could make? Are there other people that we know that are in common? Is this someone that should be closer to my circle?"

Kathy: How does that benefit us as researchers?

Cam: We never make the assumption that our positionality is neutral. We never think to ourselves that we can treat each other the same, that there is some sort of generic Canadian person and that we can all be friends because we are *not* the same. Other people don't have an Indian Act. White people are not subject to funny looks or funny things that people say. We are not treated the same way.

Kathy: I think that as researchers when we put ourselves forward, when I say who I am and where I'm from, we have those exchanges where we identify ourselves. As a researcher in a community, when I've done community-based research and I've talked to elders or people in the community about seeking answers or searching for something, I let them know who I am and what my intent is because they are suspicious of people extracting knowledge. We are suspicious of people misrepresenting us. We are suspicious of people who take knowledge and use it and we are suspicious of being exploited and used. That knowledge that we give sometimes gets turned around and used against us. So, say, when Statistics Canada comes into the community and they want to enumerate, a lot of communities don't let that happen because, number one, that's our knowledge. Also, at times information is used against the community and not for the benefit of the community, but to create policy or create funding guidelines that really marginalize communities. I think when I've gone into communities and I locate, there's an openness from people in the community. I think they're more willing to talk with me and there's a bit more of a trust that's already there.

Cam: People make assumptions about who you are about, what your intentions might be, because you are an insider, not an outsider.

Kathy: The other thing is that when you locate, they know that the reason you're collecting information is to make things better, that hopefully there will be an outcome that will be useful to the community in some way.

Cam: Well, I think they make that assumption because they know that you have a personal stake in it, so you're not likely to use or misuse information for your own personal benefit if there is another personal cost to your family.

Kathy: And I think that saying who we are and where we come from is just something that's always been done. It's putting ourselves forward. It is part of your honour and your respect not only for yourself, but for your family, your nation, your clan, your genealogy. It's respect for who you're addressing, or who you're talking to, or who you're representing. It lets people know your relatedness. It's like when we were in our research class (in our doctoral program) and people did their presentations, we would often ask them, "So what does this have to do with you? Why are you doing this?" It's almost connected to your motive. "How are you invested in this research?" and if people have an investment, then they're going to do the best that they can do, be responsible and accountable.

Cam: This reminds me of a quantitative research course in which my professor taught us never to pick a topic that's too close to your heart, the logic being that you'll be so caught up in it that you'd never finish your thesis. I never took his advice, but the assumption there is that it is possible for a person to conduct research that is completely unrelated to you personally, that you're not interested in, that you have no experience or connection with whatsoever. That you could come in as an objective scientist, take a topic, study it, and make a valid representation or some valid generalizations about the subject based on the data that you collect. I think that's not possible because if you have no stake in a subject, I don't see how you can do an adequate job of researching that topic.

Kathy: We're saying that if you want to do ethical research that accurately represents who it is for and who it represents, then you have to be positioned in it and connected to it.

Cam: I believe that it is unethical to do research in which you have no stake whatsoever—no interest, no personal connection with, no reason other than your training as a scientist. You need to have some reason for doing it. When you explain your methodology, you need to be able to answer the question "Why are you doing research?" and you don't have to be able to say that you're carrying on your father's research as you promised him on his deathbed, but you have to at least have an interest in the topic.

Kathy: Well, what happens if you have no connection? Some of the anthropological accounts of Aboriginal ceremony or society or culture that we read in articles or books are inaccurate representations and racially biased.

Cam: Why are they inaccurate?

Kathy: I think it's because they don't have a cultural lens upon which to base their research, or the kind of authority of knowledge to study Aboriginal peoples.

Cam: I think that if a researcher studies any question in which they have no stake, then they really don't care what the answer to the question is. They collect the data without any understanding of its context and without any personal connection or stake in the data. They make no attempt to guess what the stories collected in a study might mean to the people who tell them. For example, the creation stories are often dismissed as some sort of superstitious myth. Both the research and the researcher lose respect and validity. There are lurking variables that are not accounted for. The data are skewed.

Kathy: Part of the point of Indigenous research methodology is to take ownership of our own language, so taking language from mainstream research and plopping it in here is not what we should be doing. We need to speak from our own position and in our own voice. Sometimes we recreate language.

Cam: When we locate, we are saying, "This is just my view." It's not the view of the Anishnabe nation because I'm not Anishnabe. It's not the view of the Coastal nations. It's not the view of a 100 percent, full-blooded Cree. It's not the view of women. It's just my view and this is who I am. This is my mother. This is my father. These are my ancestors. This is where I grew up geographically. This was my experience as I grew up. And based on all of those things, this is what I think. You might say that any part of my experience accounts for my opinion and that is the whole point—that who I am mitigates what I say. I might make any number of seemingly radical statements and the reason I might say any one of those things is based in part on my personal experience. We locate because what you remember about what anyone says depends in large part on who is doing the talking.

Kathy and Cam: Our dialogue voiced our expressions about location as a research methodology. Through our dialogue we hoped to model and convey some initial ideas upon which to base further discussions. We both spoke about remembering, community, ownership, representation, and connection.

   The section that follows expands on the ideas we discussed and challenges us to unlearn colonial research agendas and processes. Today we must be creative in revising research methodologies to make our research more Indigenous and counter-colonial. Through their work, authors such as Tuhiwai Smith (1999); Nabigon, Hagey, Webster, and MacKay (1998); Deloria (1998); and Monture-Angus (1995) have encouraged us to turn around, to look back, and to rethink the language, terms, and methods we employ in research. In our discourse on the significance of location in research we found a recurrent use of the prefix *re-*. Accordingly, we have employed the prefix *re-* to divide issues into different sections as we examine the purpose of location in Indigenous research, thus serving the larger purpose of rehumanizing research, which is to foster a knowledge creation process that takes into account the underlying and often hidden factors of the researcher and producer of knowledge.

The Purpose of Location in Aboriginal Research

   It means revealing our identity to others; who we are, where we come from, our experiences that have shaped those things, and our intentions for the work we plan to do. Hence, "location" in Indigenous research, as in life, is a critical starting point. (Sinclair, 2003, p. 122)

There are a number of reasons why location is essential to Aboriginal research methodology. First, researching Aboriginal knowledge and Aboriginal peoples without the consent of the Aboriginal community is unethical. Aboriginal peoples have been misrepresented and exploited for countless generations as the subjects of academic, "scientific" studies conducted by non-Aboriginals. As a result, Aboriginal communities today are no longer content to be passive objects of "scientific" study, but demand to know who is doing the research and for what purposes. Many Aboriginal communities have appointed research units to govern research inquiries and projects related to their community. In doing community-based research, for example, the Aboriginal community and cultural protocols demand to know three basic things: (1) Who is doing the research?; (2) How is the research being done?; and (3) What purpose does the research serve to the community? When it comes to Aboriginal peoples and Aboriginal knowledge, researchers today must be prepared to explain who they are and what interest they have in the proposed research before they are allowed to proceed.

Second, location helps to offset existing unbalanced scholarship about Aboriginal peoples. Aboriginal scholars echo that it is no longer acceptable to have non-Aboriginal researchers publishing voyeuristic accounts of Aboriginal peoples in the absence of community sanctioning (Gilchrist, 1997; Tuhiwai Smith, 1999). If location were a more widely used component of Aboriginal research methodology, readers would be more easily able to distinguish between authors who have a vested interest in the research and those who do not.

Third, Fixico (1998) asserts that one of the roles of ethical Aboriginal research is to eradicate ethnocentrism in the writing of Aboriginal history and representation. We believe that research conducted from a "neutral" or "objective" location is Eurocentric and is, therefore, unethical. Ethnocentric writing can be avoided, however, if the writer reveals his or her epistemological location at the outset through a brief introductory autobiography.

Finally, when we talk about research in Aboriginal circles we are not just talking about the goal and the finish; we are talking about everything that happens in between. Between the beginning and the end of any given research project is process. Aboriginal research methodologies are as much about process as they are about product. It is in the process of conducting research that the researcher engages the community to share knowledge, recreation, and work. As Tuhiwai Smith (1999) says, "Indigenous methodologies tend to approach cultural protocols, values and behaviors as an integral part of methodology" (p. 15). The final product is always secondary to the community benefiting from the process, and in order for this process to happen, the researchers must locate themselves. The actual research is in the research process, which cannot take place without the trust of the community, and one way to gain trust is to locate yourself.

If research about Aboriginal peoples and Aboriginal knowledge is to be useful to Aboriginal communities, location is critical for a multitude of reasons, which we discuss here under headings that we call the "Re's." "Re" means to redo; to look twice, and is the teaching of respect in the West direction of the Medicine Wheel. In our dialogue and through our process of considering knowledge creation and research, we found ourselves inadvertently returning to the notions of respectful representations, revising, reclaiming, renaming, remembering, reconnecting, recovering, and researching. All of these ideas are associated with looking again to uncover, unlearn, recover, and relearn how and why location is a fundamental principle of Indigenous research. Since much of our knowledge, experiences, stories, histories, and lives have been disrespected and misrepresented, it seems only natural to begin our "Re's" with respectful representations.

Respectful Representations

> Representation is important as a concept because it gives the impression of "the truth." When I read texts, for example, I frequently orientate myself to a text world in which the center of academic knowledge is either in Britain, the United States or Western Europe; in which words such as "we," "us," "our," "I" actually exclude me … they still do not entirely account for the experiences of indigenous peoples. (Tuhiwai Smith, 1999, p. 35)

To look twice is to practise respect. Respect calls upon us to consider how we are represented by others, the expectations that others have of us, and how we represent ourselves. As Aboriginal scholars, we have both been highly dismayed by the realization that our experience as Aboriginal peoples is poorly represented in the academy. There are few places that accurately reflect Aboriginal reality, where we can see and say, "This represents who I am." Thus far, Aboriginal peoples have been represented in curricula, research, and scholarship (if at all) as a savage, noble, stoic, and, most disturbingly, a dying race. Images and representations of Aboriginal peoples that predominate in media, popular culture, and research studies portray us not as we are, but as non-Aboriginals think we are. To various degrees, we all struggle to free ourselves from the colonial beliefs and values that have been ingrained in us. Throughout the world such "neutral" and "objective" research has been used to justify the oppression and genocide of the Other for the good of humankind. Gilchrist (1997) explains that:

> [t]he fact that much research does not confront ideologies of oppression prevents the application to research of critical knowledge regarding traditional culture, colonial history and racist structure. This results in research which does not use appropriate concepts as variables and defines one's culture using the cultural beliefs of another. (Gilchrist, 1997, p. 76)

This lack of accurate representations of Aboriginal peoples in almost every facet of popular culture leads us (Aboriginal peoples) to seek validation in one another. This is a two-edged sword; while Aboriginal peoples are extremely proud of Aboriginal individuals who become famous in sports, politics, or the media, generalized representations of Aboriginal role models can negate the reality of oppression. A minority of Aboriginal peoples who have successfully negotiated Western culture are too often held up as proof that the problems of oppression, racism, and inequity can be easily overcome or, worse, that the roots of these problems lie not within institutions or systems of governance but within Aboriginal peoples themselves.

There are inappropriate expectations placed upon us from both inside and outside of the Aboriginal community. We ourselves perpetuate the notion that one person can be a positive role model for the whole Aboriginal race. At times we replicate, reinforce, and support misrepresentations of Aboriginal peoples through the use of stereotypical images. As we mirror and model ourselves after one another in search of our true identity, we form a framework for how we think we should be.

Further, unlike White researchers, we are conscious that putting our individual representations into "writing can be dangerous because sometimes we reveal ourselves in ways which get misappropriated and used against us" (Tuhiwai Smith, 1999, p. 36). We are asked about our opinions as if they represent the opinions of all Aboriginal peoples in Canada. As students, as staff, and simply as individuals we are always expected to be the Aboriginal voice and the Aboriginal expert. We are expected to carry the flag of diversity, of tolerance, and of Aboriginal achievement.

When we self-locate, we represent our own truths. We represent our own reality. In Indigenous circles one rarely sees an Indigenous person speaking on behalf of another nation or another person. Instead, we generally hear people stating up front that they are expressing only their own experiences and opinions. They represent only themselves because, as the old cliché goes, you do not know another person's journey unless you have travelled in his or her moccasins. You cannot speak about or represent something that is not yours. To do so would be perceived in Indigenous communities as arrogant, audacious, and disrespectful. Stating at the outset that you speak only for yourself also means who you do *not* represent or speak for. In terms of representation, location as a research methodology is ethical. As an anti-oppressive methodology, location brings ownership and responsibility to the forefront. When researchers own who or what they represent, they also reveal what they do not represent.

The concept of representation is significant because it leaves an imprint of what is true. Location brings to the forefront both our commonalities and our distinctiveness, distinguishing us from one another and avoiding the "pan-Indian myth" that Aboriginal peoples are all the same, one race, and one people. We are *not* all the same. We say Aboriginal peoples as a plural in order to denote our diversity. There are many facets that make us who we are. To be accurate, our representations must take into account cultural and colonial histories and contexts. We must consider who we are relationally, interracially, intergenerationally, geographically, physically, spiritually, politically, socially, and economically. Being an Aboriginal person today is not easy, and it is no simple task to represent ourselves respectfully. We need a hologram to illustrate the multiplexity, multidimensionality, and interconnection of all aspects of our Aboriginal realities.

Locating oneself is as lively and active as Aboriginal reality today. Each time we locate ourselves, our representations change and, depending on the context in which we locate, we may or may not emphasize certain aspects of our realities. Yet, as we locate, we must still account for the relative aspects of who we are and thus represent ourselves accordingly and distinctly. Location will not simply be about your name or where you are from, but will reflect more of a dynamic and transformative representation. For example, Kathy has received two Anishinabe names and walked with two different clans thus far in her life. At one point in her life she located using her first name and clan and now locates using the second name and clan. Life changes transform our locations and thus our locations become dynamic. An Indigenous scholar, knowing that location is transformative, is challenged in academia and in written research because academia is dominantly based in written text and print. Indigenous knowledge and culture is dynamic—ever flowing, adaptable, and fluid. In a truly transformative research process, opinions, thoughts, ideas, and theories are in a constant flux. Yet writing on paper is one-dimensional, permanent, and fixed, a snapshot of a single moment in time. Thus, to Indigenous scholars, location becomes a crucial means of contextualizing their lens and reference points in a given time. Location is transformed as our lenses, perceptions, understandings, and knowledge are transformed.

Representations are either broadened or limited by world view, socialization, internalization, and perceptual lenses. It is impossible to represent all Aboriginal peoples in research, and respectful researchers should not try to do so. It is better to locate relevant and distinct aspects of oneself rather than to make broad general statements. Location forms the basis of representation and is integral to writing and representing oneself with respect. When we look twice, we create our own checks and balances regarding respectful representation.

Re-Vising

> You must understand that for people like us, there are no such things as models. We are called upon to constantly create our models .... Colonialism means that we must always rethink everything. (Sembene, as cited in hooks, 1992, p. 2)

Any illumination of past, present, and future First Nations conditions demands a complete deconstruction of the history and application of colonial and racist ideology and, most importantly, of the impact (personal and political) of racism. That is, we need to know how we got into the mess we're in. Historical written texts about Aboriginal peoples reveal more about the ideological perspective and position of the authors (patriarchy, paternalism, racism, White supremacy, fear, ignorance, and ethnocentrism) than they do about their subjects (Voyageur, 2000). We need to have an analysis of colonization (Tuhiwai Smith, 1999) and our cultural past to decolonize our mind, heart, body, and spirit. Without this critical knowledge, we are operating in a vacuum. Thus, recontextualizing and revising Aboriginal experiences, events, and history can help us make sense of our reality (Henderson,

2000). Location in research has a role as we revise and recontextualize our past, present, and future.

Aboriginal knowledge and Aboriginal peoples are wonderfully dynamic and diverse. As we recover from colonization, racism, residential schooling, and genocidal policies, we are retrieving and locating bits and pieces of who we are. Essentially, we are in the process of pulling ourselves together. Location means that we begin by stating who we are and we revise this statement over and over again. We each locate ourselves differently at various points in our lives. As our recovery from colonialism progresses, we speak about our past and present experiences with more awareness, understanding, and knowledge, and we revise the stories of our lives. Revision through location is essential and integral to our recovery process. We will tell our stories one way today, then revise and retell them tomorrow. The means by which we locate may also be revised. Sometimes we locate with song, dance, or story or we locate using ceremony, language, or tradition. For example, when we open a class with a smudge, we locate our cultural identity through a traditional ceremony. When we open a meeting with a prayer, we locate ourselves through our spirituality. We can also locate in more contemporary avenues through our dress, hair, jewellery, or general presentation. When we walk into a room wearing clothing with Indigenous motifs and symbols, we are locating our cultural identity or alliances. Some people wear feathers in their hair; others wear beautiful earrings of silver, turquoise, feathers, carvings, Medicine Wheels, or beading. Location as a cultural protocol provides us with an important opportunity to revise our self-concept and the way in which we present ourselves.

Re-Claiming: Avoiding the Extraction of Knowledge

> Native scholars and writers are demonstrating that "voice" can be, must be, used within academic studies not only as an expression of cultural integrity but also as an attempt to begin to balance the legacy of dehumanization and bias entrenched in Canadian studies about Native peoples. (LaRocque, 1996, p. 13)

To locate is to make a claim about who you are and where you come from, your investment and your intent. To put yourself forward means to say who you are, give yourself voice, and claim your position.

Reclaiming creates space for Aboriginal authors to name who they are and to claim their location in relation to their research topic. At the onset of this chapter, we (the writers) each claimed a specific location based on our individual experiences. Aboriginal peoples must now say who we are directly and proudly, in the glory of our traditional regalia, songs, ceremonies, and languages and in the reality of contemporary issues. In reclaiming our location we assert our presence and power to define ourselves. By asserting our presence we refuse to be relics of the past. In defining ourselves we establish authority over our own knowledge. Thus, we begin to counter knowledge extraction and define our location in our own reality. Taking a position and owning your location is a reclaiming of your personal space and territory in the context of research and writing. Claiming your personal space within your research and writing counters objectivity and neutrality with subjectivity, credibility, accountability, and humanity. We will no longer be the subjects of objective study; we are the subjects of our own knowledge creation. When we claim our location, we become congruent with Indigenous world views and knowledge, thus transforming our place within research.

The writing of Indigenous knowledge is a delicate topic. First, there is the issue of which Indigenous knowledge should be put into text and which should not. Non-Indigenous writers have historically extracted Indigenous knowledge for their own interests, with Indigenous peoples receiving little acknowledgment and practically no benefit. Further, while there have been innumerable misrepresentations and wild inaccuracies, Indigenous peoples "have never been able to stop the traffic in distorted and sensationalized imagery" (Miller, 1998, p. 106). Indigenous authors, producers, actors, researchers, artists, songwriters, and others have invested incredible time and energy to counter racist images as they tell, sing, write, act, and paint from an Indigenous perspective. Many of the references for this chapter evidence Indigenous voice and representation. While there has been some movement toward more accurate representations of Indigenous peoples, the onslaught of distorted images continues through such media as television, movies, literature, school curricula, and popular culture. As Aboriginal writers perform the critical role of countering and critiquing these misrepresentations, we must be considerate about what knowledge we put into text. Considerations such as cultural protocol, sacredness, oral traditions, copyright, and ownership all must be factored into deciding what Indigenous knowledge goes into text. However, as we record our own Indigenous histories, stories, and experiences via location, we reclaim ourselves.

Re-Naming Research in Our Own Language

There are at least two issues around what we call "renaming." The first centres on the word "research." In many Aboriginal communities the very word "research" makes our skin crawl as we remember the way our knowledge has been misrepresented and extracted. The word "research" evokes images of ethnographers, missionaries, explorers, and social scientists voyeuristically noting their observations and labelling Indigenous peoples as hedonistic, barbaric, and savage. We are reminded of White archaeologists who have extracted the bones of our ancestors and displayed them ceremoniously like flags in museums around the world. The word "research" has too much racist and colonial baggage attached to it to be used in an Indigenous context. If we are to gather and share knowledge in an Indigenous way, we must find new words to liberate and decolonize our processes for doing so. We call on Indigenous peoples to rename our process of gathering and sharing knowledge (aka: research) to distinguish it from the exploitation, sterility, and individualism inherent to Western positivist research. It is necessary to rename "research" in order to exemplify that the Indigenous process for gathering and sharing knowledge is of a completely unique paradigm.

The second issue around renaming is related to language usage. Learning the English language from mothers whose first language is not English has given us unique epistemological lenses. Cultural world views are embedded in language. Therefore, as native Ojibway and Cree speakers, our mothers held world views that were distinctly Indigenous. As we grew up, these world views were transmitted to us linguistically in English, but also physically and psychologically in Cree and Ojibway. Although English is our first language, we learned to speak it and write it through lenses (our mothers') that were distinctly Indigenous. Therefore, the rules and structure of the English language make it inadequate to express what we truly mean. In order to express ourselves, we have no choice but to break these rules to make the words work for us, or to create new words. We must use the English language in a way that is congruent with Indigenous experiences and cultures. For example, a friend of ours, Professor Gale Cyr of Timiskaming First

Nation, created the term "matrifocalist Indigenist" in locating herself at a public lecture. Her term represents a perspective that is unknown to Western ways of knowing and for which there was, until now, no English term. As another example, Indigenous peoples often say that we "Indigenize" ideas, concepts, and processes by bringing an Indigenous world view to them. Although we Indigenize things every day, the word "Indigenize" is not in the English dictionary.

We need to transcend the rules and limitations of the English language to make it work for us as Indigenous peoples. Cole's (2002) research and poetry is an example of such transcendence. In poetic form, Cole demonstrates First Nations' knowings as a legitimate discourse in education and research through the analogy of a canoe journey. His poetry integrates Aboriginal epistemology and validates frameworks derived from Indigenous knowledge. Cole (2002) contends that paragraphs and chapters are meaningless, and that academically correct punctuation distances Aboriginal research methods from Indigenous concepts of space, time, and speech patterns. Cole writes for meaning rather than grammatical correctness and offers his experiences/location as a reference point rather than as expert testimony.

Ultimately, we know that the meaning of our words will often be overlooked or misunderstood not only because there is no adequate way to express our meaning in English, but also because many people lack the epistemological framework to understand it. Yet it is a burden we must accept as we forge the sword of research into an implement that works for Indigenous peoples.

Re-Membering

> Through the re-membering process, individuals are absolved of blame and the community is brought into re-connecting. (Nabigon, Hagey, Webster, and MacKay, 1998, p. 114)

Locating ourselves is a remembering process. The word "remember" can have two different meanings: (1) to recall from memory or (2) to reconnect. Location establishes connection through memory. When we locate, we search through our memory banks and retrieve information about who we are, where we come from, and our roots. Everyone has the capacity for this kind of memory. For Aboriginal Canadian peoples, locating re-members us with our ancestors and with our Nations. We were externally dis-membered as Indian or non-Indian, status and non-status according to the Indian Act and the government of Canada, which has only attempted to dis-member us from our cultural origins. Despite the intrusions into our membership, we can re-member ourselves through our DNA, through our spirituality, and through our blood memory of cultural origin.

As Nabigon, Hagey, Webster, and MacKay (1998) explain, "research is understood in Native terms to be a quest for the roots of problems, and a convening of the voices needed to re-member the history and assess the future" (p. 114). Research as a "learning circle" (Nabigon et al., 1998) is a process that generates information sharing, connections, builds capacity, and seeks balance and healing. A learning circle also facilitates the remembering process and re-membering of individual experiences into a collective knowing and consciousness. The idea of re-membering as a research method and process facilitates a full reconnection, which is also healing to our recovery process. Re-membering facilitates recovering stories, experiences, teachings, tradition, and connections.

The general discourse that is propagated in the academy is that we as Aboriginal peoples are losing our culture, languages, and traditions. The truth is that we have been subjected to centuries of programs and policies deliberately calculated to strip us of our language and culture. We have not "misplaced" anything. We have survived and continue to survive countless political, educational, legal, and military mechanisms that are meant to eradicate our ethnicity from the face of the earth, yet we are still here. We are proud to stand beside McGuire (1997) in pointing out that Aboriginal peoples, "of course, never vanished, nor did they forget their own histories and heritages. They have always taught their children this culture" (p. 77).

Fortunately for us, human beings have an amazing capacity for memory both on individual and collective levels. Elders have evidenced their memory capacity through oral tradition as histories, events, songs, dances, ceremonies, and traditions have been retold and passed from one generation to the next. Memory is more than a mental process of recalling facts, experiences, and information. Human beings also have a capacity for sensory, physical, spiritual, and emotional memory. Physical or body memory refers to the body's capacity to remember how to skin a moose, snare a rabbit, or where to pick medicines. Sensory memory is the kind of memory where smells, sounds, or tastes evoke vivid memories of other times, people, and places. These memories, for example, come alive when we smell a burning fire and remember the cabin our grandparents lived in. Spiritual memory is the extrasensory perception or connection we have with the spiritual world. Some say that *déjà vu* is a form of spiritual memory and that at a spiritual level we are remembering the earth journey our spirit was shown prior to our birth. Emotional memory rests in our hearts and in our capacity to remember emotional connections with other people. We associate feelings from the past with feelings in the present and we make assumptions about feelings in the future. Holistically, our memories are activated when we locate, and through location we re-member, reconnect, and recover our very identity. We are proud that after so many generations of oppression and genocide (attempts to make us disappear, be forgotten, and forget), we are able to "re-search" and "re-member" ourselves with the mental, physical, spiritual, and emotional aspects of our beautiful heritage. Location within the research process is essentially both remembering who we are and "re-membering" within our Nations. Indigenous researchers, we believe, research to remember and re-member.

Re-Connecting

> Indigenous researchers are expected, by their communities and by the institutions which employ them, to have some form of historical and critical analysis of the role of research in the indigenous world. (Tuhiwai Smith, 1999, p. 5)

Colonization and genocide have disconnected Aboriginal peoples from our natural contexts. Henderson (2000) states that if the context does not allow people to move in their world to discover as much about themselves as they can, then such a context is artificial. As Aboriginal researchers locate themselves, the context from which they come becomes validated. Contextual validation makes our reality, experiences, and existence as Aboriginal peoples visible. Aboriginal researchers are then challenged with making transformative changes in research processes and practices. A revolution or transformation is a shift in context. "We do, however, have a common struggle—that is to decolonize ourselves and our knowledge production. We need to change research methods to end the objectification of Aboriginal communities, and to encourage action based knowledge that is useful on the road to self-determination" (Gilchrist, 1997, p. 80). Subjectivity via location is one way to counter dehumanizing objectification in research.

As we (Aboriginal peoples) put our knowledge, experiences, and world views into written text, we must do so in connection to our communities (whoever, whatever, or wherever they may be). Location in research authenticates relations within community. To write in the absence of connection to community or tribal group could be perceived and interpreted as second-hand writing or as writing in a vacuum. Library research and writing is not enough. We need to talk to other Aboriginal peoples and to go beyond the library (Mihesuah, 1998). We need to be coming from a context that is based on a current reality and that reflects representations of that reality.

Location exposes the researchers' current context as details about the researchers such as where they are from, their race and gender, who they are connected to, and what their research intentions are become revealed. We take the position here that it is impossible to conduct valid and ethical research about Aboriginal peoples without locating because location asserts the identity of the writer and the importance of the research. For example, a quick scanning of the "Aboriginal" section of any bookstore will reveal countless books written about Aboriginal peoples by non-Aboriginal authors passing themselves off as "Indian experts." Very few books about Aboriginal peoples reveal anything substantial about the identity and location of the author. It is as if these authors have no connection or affiliation with any community whatsoever, Aboriginal or non-Aboriginal. Yet all researchers must certainly have connections either with an Aboriginal or non-Aboriginal community or with both. Unfortunately, with no knowledge of these connections, we are unable to assess the lens through which the researcher views the data and there are no mechanisms to flag Aboriginal community participants of biased research results (Gilchrist, 1997). While such studies collect, interpret, and present data as scientific truth, it is often not useful to Indigenous peoples.

Location as an Aboriginal research methodology is one way to ensure that researchers of Aboriginal peoples and Aboriginal knowledge are connected with and accountable to the Aboriginal community. As Kathy stated in the initial dialogue, ethical research on Aboriginal peoples and Aboriginal knowledge is conducted with the goal of enhancing life for Aboriginal peoples and communities. Location makes the researcher accountable to both Aboriginal and non-Aboriginal communities. Putting yourself forward as a researcher tells the community whether or not you are connected and committed to those you are researching. Further, our sections on respectful representation, remembering, reconnection, and recovery all clearly identify how location makes the research ethical and accountable. When the community knows who you are and what you are doing, the nebulous, neutral, objective voice is overcome. Through location the researcher reconnects the research to self and to the Aboriginal and non-Aboriginal community.

Re-Covering

In recovering our truths, we have a responsibility to uncover and realize our historicity. That is, we have to know our historical truth. Recovery of truth is evident in how, what, when, and where a person locates himself or herself. For example, we (the writers) can both locate residential school experiences in our families, which is essential to recovering elements of our historicity. In the beginning of the chapter, we also located our racial ethnicity, geographic upbringing, and absences of cultural teachings. Seeking our truth in our location aids us in recovering ourselves and our strengths, and in uncovering historical oppressions. Our perceptions of who we are and how we locate ourselves are a result of our own personal and political consciousness. Nonetheless, recovering truth inherently implies taking off the blinders to become conscious. Another example is Cam's earlier references to how he didn't experience racism in his youth. But as he grew and learned more about his own history, he began to see that he had not escaped experiences of racism or oppression. The very fact that his ethnic heritage was not acknowledged or celebrated, as if it were something to be ashamed of, was racism. By this same principle, we (Kathy and Cam) cannot just say that we are Cree or Anishinabe, but we must also acknowledge our European heritage. The search for our truth is often marred with inaccurate images and representations that diminish or ignore our cultural identity. Many Aboriginal peoples experience internal chaos, conflict, and confusion about who they really are. It is as if they are being torn in two. A critical turning point in healing and recovering our truth is the moment you recognize that today there are many truths and that within the collective Indigenous experience there are many individual diversities. Recovering, accepting, and becoming proud of who we are as we tell and retell our individual stories is a difficult challenge. Yet location is essential to the recovery of our individual and collective experiences and identities as Indigenous peoples because it honours individual diversity and recovery of self from internalized colonialism, racism, and oppression.

Aboriginal and non-Aboriginal researchers today who tackle any facet of Indigenous study must have a critical analysis of colonialism and an understanding of Western scientific research as a mechanism of colonization. For location to be insightful and conscious, a critical analysis is required among all researchers. Recovering truth in history implies the necessary element of uncovering history. That is, we need to be able to re-examine, question, contemplate, and comprehend how research has been used to reinforce racist notions of evolutionary thought and how research has therefore justified and legitimized genocide in policy and action. Only when we have decolonized ourselves can we recover, contemplate, and envision ways in which research can be used to eradicate racism and lift the oppression. The answers, our Elders tell us, are in our own Indigenous knowledges, cultures, and ways. In recovering Indigenous paradigms and methods, the knowledge set that is expected of an Aboriginal researcher far exceeds what has been expected of non-Aboriginal researchers. As Aboriginal researchers, we must be masters of both our own world views and Euro-Western world views. We must have the ability to critically examine Western research methods and to develop methods that will work within Indigenous paradigms. Also, we must have knowledge of the cultural context, protocols, and issues within which we are researching. Gilchrist (1997) further explains:

> We cannot blame the individual for underlying racist assumptions acquired through socialization and education. However, it is not unreasonable to expect researchers, non-Aboriginal and Aboriginal alike (McNab, 1986), to bring with them a thorough background on the history of colonialism and a broad based knowledge of Aboriginal cultures when engaging in research with our communities. Researchers must have a critical interpretation of colonialism and western domination embedded in research methodology. They must be prepared to engage with community representatives so that their research methodology more accurately reflects an Aboriginal point of view. (Gilchrist, 1997, p. 80)

We must also know our own Indigenous epistemologies, genealogies, traditions, and cultures. The origins of our roots are there for us to learn. Our ancestors call to be remembered and recovered into our present. Cultural traditions, ceremonies, stories, songs, dances, and rituals are our responsibility to learn. Because colonization has attempted to erase our roots, ancestors, and traditions, we must work hard to recover all that we can. Recovering museum artifacts, the bones of our ancestors, and remnants of our cultural identity are the responsibility of Indigenous peoples today. We cannot trust non-Aboriginal researchers to record the stories of our creation and our survival. Indigenous researchers today are hard at work recovering stories, songs, histories, experiences, ancestors, traditions, and cultural identities. And location is a critical part of our recovering process. When it comes to the research of Indigenous peoples and Indigenous knowledge, to be ethical and diligent researchers, we must reveal the lenses that each of us, as human beings, look through.

Re-Search Methods: Affirming Indigenous Paths

Free Your Minds, Aboriginal Brothers and Sisters
Free your minds, Aboriginal brothers and sisters
Brothers and sisters of turtle island
Now is the time to wake up
Get up!
Rub the sleep from your eyes and wake up!
Let go of your colonial dreams and wake up!
Splash cold water on your face, take a drink, and look in the mirror!
Your cheeks are the gentle curves of grandmother moon
Your hair is the breeze of mother earth
There is ice in your breath
and fire in your eyes
You are beautiful!
Aboriginal
Proud

—Cam Willett, 2004

Aboriginal realities are unique and diverse, and expressing these realities demands creativity and innovation. We encourage Indigenous writers to develop and utilize styles of writing such as narrative, self-location, subjective text, poetry, and storytelling that better reflect Aboriginal realities than do academic prose. Tuhiwai Smith's (1999)

121

decolonizing methodologies, Monture-Angus's (1995) anger, and Cole's (2002) poetry are only a few examples of literature that exemplify and validate Indigenous world views. LaRocque describes Indigenous voice and location as "Native resistance scholarship" (1996, p. 13). Sinclair (2003) examines how Indigenous scholars operationalize Indigenous world views in their research. Interestingly, she finds that many Indigenous scholars have inherently and creatively integrated their world views into their research in resistance to the restrictive methods of Western positivist research.

Resistance to colonizing research methods involves envisioning and utilizing research methods that better reflect Indigenous world views. In doing so, we help build a foundation for the ongoing development of Indigenous cultural knowledge production in a pattern that is congruent with Indigenous ways of knowing. When Aboriginal scholars in Canada bring our voices to our research, we bring "the other half of Canada into light ... we offer new ways of seeing and saying things ... and provide new directions and fresh methodologies to cross-cultural research" (LaRocque, 1996, p. 12). The distinction and innovation of Indigenous philosophy, Indigenous thought, and Indigenous methodology is, by definition, contrary to Western epistemology and positivist research methodology. There is no dignity for Aboriginal peoples in a philosophy that attempts to destroy, distort, and/or reject oneself. Aboriginal researching calls upon us to examine research motives, values, beliefs, and methods by questioning, reflecting, and acknowledging our locations (Archibald, 1993). Movers and shakers trail-blazing in the terrain of Aboriginal research methodology must, therefore, have tenacity, courage, and faith. Research of Indigenous peoples by Indigenous researchers remains an emerging, yet powerful, body of literature. We can only reassure Indigenous scholars that you are not alone; it is there if you seek it out.

Location Equals Contextual Validation

When we have overcome the myths of value neutrality and objectivity; when we insist on historical contextualization and cultural acknowledgement, and when we have complete access to technical knowledge and ownership of our research; we will improve the quality and value of research concerning Aboriginal people. Only then will we fully realize the rights of Aboriginal people and construct our own reality. (Gilchrist, 1997, p. 80)

It is time that academics recognize the validity of research processes that account for the influence of the researcher's reality and experience. Locating self in research brings forward this reality. Critical authors advocate doing so as a response to the crisis in representation where the objective neutrality of writing is no longer considered real (hooks, 1992, 1993; Mihesuah, 1998; Monture-Angus, 1995; Monture-Okanee, 1995; Owens, 2002; Said, 1994; Tuhiwai Smith, 1999; Tierney, 2002). Many authors encourage writers to "get real" and to see ourselves as an important element in the work of social science research, writing, and representation (Tierney, 2002).

When researching Aboriginal knowledge and Aboriginal peoples, Aboriginal Elders and communities expect researchers to foster a knowledge creation process that accounts for many variables, including epistemological, cultural, colonial, historical, and contemporary contexts of both the researched and the researcher. It is *putting ourselves forward* that establishes these contexts, guides the research process, and determines research outcomes. Research outcomes, in turn, affect policy, programming, practice, and societal perceptions.

In short, location is good protocol for research methodology because it accounts for the context of the researcher. Further, research becomes transformative both for researched and researcher as individual stories are told and retold. Location ensures that individual realities are not misrepresented as generalizable collectives. Our ancestors gave us membership into nations and traditions; location both remembers and "re-members" us to those things. The recovery processes of location facilitate healing by restoring pride in ourselves.

Gathering and sharing Indigenous knowledge requires pride in self, family, community, culture, nation, identity, economy, and governance; it requires courage to resist the rules and rigours of the dominant culture; and it requires faith that change can be made for the betterment of society as a whole, qualities that ought to be reflected in the location of the researcher. Following the example of a genre of writers who choose to represent themselves via storytelling, poems, or personal narrative (Cole, 2002; hooks, 1992) we end this chapter with a poem. Its meaning and impact depend on you, the reader.

The Story of Me
I saw a picture of myself and said "Hey? That's not me!"
"Yes I am!" said the picture
"No I'm not!" I said

"In all of the pictures I have ever seen
and all the stories I have ever read, I could not see myself"
So I made up a story about me
And whispered it softly to myself at night as I went to sleep
The next day I wrote it down and read it slowly over and over again
It wasn't right so I crumpled it up, threw it away, and made a new one
Which I hid beneath my pillow and pulled out to look at from time to time
I would have conversations with myself
As I looked in the mirror
And soon
My reflection changed
I began to argue with myself
And very nearly had a falling out with me
Before I forgave myself and made up
And now I've gotten used to living with me
I find out something new about myself every day
And sometimes we fight, but usually we get along just fine and
I know the story of me by heart
And sometimes I share it with people around me
Like when I'm meeting a group of people for the very first time
Or when I get close to someone and I want them to know who I really am
Or when I write about things other than myself
So that people don't get me confused with anyone else

—Cam Willett, 2004

References

Allen, P.G. (1998). Special problems in teaching Leslie Marmon Silko's "Ceremony." In D.A. Mihesuah (Ed.), *Natives and academics: Researching and writing about American Indians*, pp. 55–64. Lincoln: University of Nebraska Press.

Archibald, J.-A. (1993). Researching with mutual respect. *Canadian Journal of Native Education* 20 (2), 189–192.

Cole, P. (2002). Aboriginalizing methodology: Considering the canoe. *International Journal of Qualitative Studies in Education* 15 (4), 447–460.

Deloria, V.J. (1998). Comfortable fictions and the struggle for turf: An essay review of The invented Indian: Cultural fictions and government policies. In D.A. Mihesuah (Ed.), *Natives and academics: Researching and writing about American Indians*, pp. 65–83. Lincoln: University of Nebraska Press.

Fixico, D.L. (1998). Ethics and responsibilities in writing American Indian history. In D.A. Mihesuah (Ed.), *Natives and academics: Researching and writing about American Indians*, pp. 84–99. Lincoln: University of Nebraska Press.

Gilchrist, L. (1997). Aboriginal communities and social science research: Voyeurism in transition. *Native Social Work Journal* 1 (1), 69–85.

Henderson, J.Y. (2000). The context of the state of nature. In M. Battiste (Ed.), *Reclaiming Indigenous voice and vision*, pp. 11–38. Vancouver: UBC Press.

hooks, b. (1992). *Black looks: Race and representation*. Toronto: Between the Lines.

hooks, b. (1993). *Sisters of the yam: Black women and self-recovery*. Toronto: Between the Lines.

LaRocque, E. (1996). The colonization of a Native woman scholar. In C. Miller and P. Chuchryk (Eds.), *Women of the First Nations: Power, wisdom, strength*, pp. 11–18. Winnipeg: University of Manitoba Press.

McGuire, R.H. (1997). Why have archaeologists thought the real Indians were dead and what can we do about it? In T. Biolsi and L.J. Zimmerman (Eds.), *Indians and anthropologists: Vine Deloria Jr. and the critique of anthropology*. Tucson: University of Arizona Press.

Mihesuah, D.A. (Ed.). (1998). *Natives and academics: Researching and writing about American Indians*. Lincoln: University of Nebraska Press.

Miller, S.A. (1998). Licensed trafficking and ethnogenetic engineering. In D.A. Mihesuah (Ed.), *Natives and academics: Researching and writing about American Indians*, pp. 100–110. Lincoln: University of Nebraska Press.

Monture-Angus, P.A. (1995). *Thunder in my soul: A Mohawk woman speaks*. Halifax: Fernwood Publishing.

Monture-Okanee, P.A. (1995). Self-portrait: Flint woman. In L. Jaine and D.H. Taylor (Eds.), *Voices: Being Native in Canada* (2nd edition), pp. 109–117. Saskatoon: University Extension Press.

Nabigon, H., Hagey, R., Webster, S., and MacKay, R. (1998). The learning circle as a research method: The trickster and windigo in research. *Native Social Work Journal* 2 (1), 113–137.

Owens, L. (2002). As if an Indian were really an Indian: Native voices and postcolonial theory. In G.M. Bataille (Ed.), *Native American representations: First encounters, distorted images, and literary appropriations*, pp. 11–24. Lincoln: University of Nebraska Press.

Said, E.W. (1994). *Culture and imperialism*. New York: Vintage Books.

Sinclair, R. (2003). Indigenous research in social work: The challenge of operationalizing worldview. *Native Social Work Journal* 5, 117–139.

Stalker, J., and Prentice, S. (Eds.). (1998). *The illusion of inclusion: Women in post-secondary education*. Halifax: Fernwood Publishing.

Tierney, W.G. (2002). Get real: Representing reality. *International Journal of Qualitative Studies in Education* 15 (4), 385–398.

Tuhiwai Smith, L.T. (1999). *Decolonizing methodologies: Research and Indigenous peoples*. London: Zed.

Voyageur, C.J. (2000). Contemporary Aboriginal women in Canada. In D. Long and O.P. Dickasone (Eds.), *Visions of the heart: Canadian Aboriginal issues*, pp. 81–106. Toronto: Harcourt.

CHAPTER FIVE

INTERRUPTING POSITIONS:
Critical Thresholds and Queer Pro/Positions

Fairn herising[1]

Thresh-old: *n.* the plank or stone at the bottom of a doorway // a beginning, the threshold of a career // the point at which a stimulus of increasing strength is first perceived or produces its specific response, auditory threshold.
— *Webster's New Lexicon Dictionary* (1988, p. 1030)

Like clockwork I awake to the sun diffracting through slits on my blinds. My right thigh feels slightly cool, and there seems to be an ache between my shoulder blades. There's a bird, no two, maybe more talking from the few precious trees in our urban backyard. The lines of light from my blinds seem longer and brighter. I move my shoulders up and down in hopes of shifting what was once a barely perceptible ache. The light has turned to heat and I realize it is going to be another hot day. I remember I forgot to wash out a T-shirt. I wonder about what I will now wear under my shirt. I remember how strange you think it is of me to wear so many layers. I wonder if today is a good day to bind my chest. Maybe today I could pass through the men's washroom. Maybe today is too hot, maybe I should buy more T-shirts.

Thresholds—like my awakening, like my bed, like my T-shirt, and like the bathroom—are places and locations. Thresholds as place and location provoke questions of where: where an object is located, where a practice is done, and where a person is situated. These questions of where can allow us to articulate and analyze the specificity of locations. Also, questions of where are never disconnected from other where locations. For example, the place of waking is connected to the place of sleep, which is also connected to the place of light, to the place of birds, to the place of trees, to the place of urban living. By paying attention to the relations between locations, and the ways in which various locations intersect (or collide) with each other, we[2] can develop a fuller and more complex understanding of locations. As a result we can move our analysis of where through questions of who and why certain relations interact and intersect in particular ways. For example, another hot summer morning connects across to a shortage of T-shirts intersecting with public curiosities of why I wear what I wear and intersecting with questions of who can enter gendered spaces. When we engage the multiplicities of where locations can connect and move questions of where through relations of who and why, we can give shape, reshape, and move toward engaging the many shapes of location. We might then be in a position to see how specific relations influence and intersect with the thresholds of where we are located and the ways in which our location intersect with people, places, and how we shape and are shaped by our locations.

Thresholds are also about passageways between and through locations. We enter thresholds, cross thresholds, traverse thresholds, and exit thresholds. As such, thresholds as passageways are about entries and exits between, among, and through locations. Thresholds are, in other words, transitions "to other realities, archetypal, primal symbols of shifting consciousness" (Anzaldúa, 2002, p. 1). Thresholds as passageways are not about ensuring arrivals to any fixed ground but rather ways of being and living " ... amidst, among, atwixt" dwelling only within "the realm of questioning, experiment, and adventure ... " (Heilbrun, 1999, p. 98). Thresholds are always shifting, and our relationship to and with particular thresholds vary, where some invoke momentary familiarity and comfort, others may be fraught with ambiguity, discomfort, and danger. What is most exciting and creative about thresholds as passageways are the possibilities that are produced by letting go of destinies and expectations, by learning to live with and through uncertainties.

This chapter presents some ways to critically explore the stances of researchers who work with/in marginal communities. More precisely, I am concerned with exploring and rethinking the politics of location between the researcher and the communities that we propose to enter, or the relational locations that I call "the thresholds of passages." These "thresholds of passages" contain continuities and discontinuities between the researcher and the entryways to the communities we desire to work with and for under the rubric of research. Focusing

128

attention on thresholds of passages, I examine researchers' socio-political locations (politics of location) and their relationships to and tensions within research. I propose and explore queer flexibilities and the ex-centric researcher as counter-hegemonic positions and stances that researchers can employ in forging politically ethical relations with marginal communities. Before situating and re-examining the politics of location and queer flexibilities, I want to explore some of the potential contexts and contours of thresholds and passageways and raise some critical questions that inform the project of this chapter.

Before continuing, I wish to elaborate on the use of the term "research" in the context of this chapter. First, I do not separate the discipline of social work research from the discipline and practices of social work for "despite our desperate, eternal layers to separate, contain, and mend, categories always leak" (Minh-ha, 1989, p. 94). Formulating research as distinct from practice can become a strategy for ignoring the inherent flaws of social work practice—flaws that comprise many of the skills and techniques of our pedagogical imperatives. The separation of practice and research as two spaces is troubling given the failure to catch the many pitfalls and "moments" of research in practice. In our everyday practice, various "how-to practice social work" tools provide the necessary skills and means to research the margins. These skills tend to neglect the processes of how social work develops, analyzes, and replenishes itself in the everyday. Whether research practices are engaged in the seemingly benign techniques of building trusting relationships with its skills of empathy and active listening, or assessing the feasibility of a client's access to services, research is constantly engaged but rarely articulated to make these processes visible. Consequently, I want to challenge the notion that there is a fixed point or moment when one is a researcher or when one does research. I want to envision each and every process of researching as thresholds, where we critically attend to the complexities, tensions, and possibilities of arrivals and exits, and where we are accountable to our different research relationships within various passageways. In deploying the term "research," I insert a critical position where historical conditions and relations are centralized within the need and desire to change contemporary social and political conditions. This position does not deflect or undermine differences, or deflect from contextualizing and shifting the multiple relational sites of privilege that researchers may/do occupy. In other words, I understand research to mean re/search/in-g: that is, the ongoing social, historical, and political dialectical processes whereby subjects, disciplines, and practices are engaged in renewal, critical interruptions, and critical praxis.

Que(e)rying the Thresholds

Talking about thresholds of passageways is to centre on the physical and psychological places of entry into communities and in forging relationships. The threshold is both the entryway and the marker for the spaces that demarcate the boundaries of inside and outside, of belonging and un-belonging. By attending to thresholds of passageways, the borders that exist between the researcher and the research participants are contested; it is essential to continually turn to negotiate these borders given the cultures and knowings that exist and are produced in relationship to each other. I envision the "threshold of passages" to be what Toni Morrison (1992) describes in the following quote: "I want to draw a map, so to speak, of a critical geography and use that map to open as much space for discovery, intellectual adventure, and close exploration ... without the mandate of conquest" (p. 3). Dionne Brand (2001) offers another important reading that points to the complexity of passageways: "The door is a place, real, imaginary and imagined .... It is a door many of us wish never existed. It is a door which makes the word door impossible and dangerous, cunning and disagreeable" (p. 19). By paying attention to space and spaces, my intent is to move away from notions of origin and fixed identities to specific subjectivities and subject positions, highlighting the relational nature of spaces and concepts of spaciousness. My hope is that the experimental (ad)venture of this chapter has connected with Soja's call for "the creation of a politicised spatial consciousness and a radical spatial praxis" (as quoted in Kaplan, 1996, p. 152).

In order to engage critical research that attends to thresholds of passageways, there are substantive questions that researchers must consider. Some of these questions include: how do we negotiate the chasm between ourselves and the communities we propose to research? How are the places between these relational sites envisioned? What is the significance of negotiating the spaces between researchers, the communities in which we reside (including the marginal communities we are a part of), and the communities we are researching? What are the frictions and dissonances within and between these spaces? What aspects of our beliefs, values, identities, and knowledges do we need to disinherit, disavow, decentre, disrupt, claim, reinsert, or centre in order to work with various communities? What are the necessary politically ethical grounds that need to be cultivated and sustained to engage and recognize various thresholds in and through multiple research passageways? In what ways do we attend to our knowledges, and ethically and politically align ourselves to the vision and struggles of marginal peoples and politics in research?

It is essential that we critically question and consider the value of finding passages to and through research thresholds. Thus, it is important to ask in what ways is the act of "finding" these passages different from any imperialist/colonizing project? In recent years, there has been attention paid to emancipatory and participatory forms of research practices with marginalized communities. A significant and problematic discussion occurs within these frameworks. Often emancipatory and participatory forms of research seek to understand the ways in which researchers can allow for greater accountability and transparency of the researcher and research processes. Discussions often centre on ways to make visible our ideological and political biases. This process is often referred to as "understanding [or unpacking] our conceptual baggage," and more recently, "reflexivity." These vital discussions are related to, and a response to, critiques of researcher objectivity, and the colonial and colonizing project of research. My concern is twofold: first, this discussion resituates objectivity by proposing that we can fully know ourselves, and that the Self is now transparent to others and Others. However, the notion of transparency, of making visible our biases, may become an excuse for not fully attending to the complex interrelationships and socio-political conditions of and in research. Second, these discussions can collapse into regulatory prescriptive methods of "working with marginalized communities," thus neutralizing and masking the political foundations and emancipatory possibilities of such forms of research. This form of premeditative prescriptive rapport requires researchers to explore such questions as: Who is the Other? What can and/or does the Other know? How do we work with the Other? What are the social conditions of the Other's life? This practice shifts potential critical terrains to liberal discourses where the position of researcher is the standpoint and norm that defines "Others." Unquestioned is the taken-for-granted inherent right of entry; that one has the ability or right to travel to/through/via or enter into another's community.

These latter questions and former discussions neglect to "interrogate" and discern the contexts and tensions of entering communities, notably the ways in which the context of history, colonizations, discipline, and institutions shape research priorities and formulations. How might we decentralize the focus on research that these questions engender, and instead shift to centralizing communities and forging collectivity and solidarity of visions? What questions enable me/us to attend to the various passageways that we travel and negotiate as we come to and through various thresholds? There needs to be a challenge, interrogation, and clarification of the desires and needs for "entering the passages that lead to Others." Questions that might engage a queering of thresholds and passageways could include: How and why are the borders of Otherness created? How and why might research and researching reconstitute the borders of Otherness? What are the imperatives that guide the "need to know" that inform and shape the ways in which we enter communities? Why, and in whose interests, are differences enacted that highlight research participants as Othered?

Guided by these questions while probing for new ones, I want to further politicize the threshold of passages by critically examining the stances, attitudes, and encumbrances of researchers, in particular, the role that the researcher occupies in researching marginal communities. In undertaking research with marginal communities, researchers have been (and continue to be) accused of participating in research that is asymmetrical and lacking in reciprocity in their excavation or retrieval of information (Abu-lughod, 1993; Bishop, 1998; Minh-ha, 1991). Some forms of such researchers include "the expert," "the appropriator," "the discoverer," "the explorer," and "the traveler," who extract and exploit knowledges, or construct a partial knowledge that serves within institutional containment of valued narratives without much, if any, critical interventions or transformative shifts with marginal communities. A premise of critical theories is that our research must have socio-political value; that our work must be guided by principles of social justice (Dominelli, 2002). I base my assumptions about research within a social justice framework grounded in emancipation of social oppression. In attempting to answer some of the questions raised earlier, I will argue that critical researchers need to substantially rethink what it is we are doing when we conceive research as we do by unravelling places of privilege within research relations.

Critical Thresholds: Thinking through the Politics of Location

In speaking to marginality, my focus is on the positionality of the researcher. Regardless of our relative distance and location between "insider" and "outsider," the position of researcher has its vestments in power. A central component of critical research practice within marginal communities is to interrogate and challenge the various fields of power, authority, and privilege that are embodied and practised by researchers. In order to engage our research with politicized ethic and integrity and to attend to the nuances and specificities of our work, it is necessary to attend to the varying plexus and intersecting trajectories of power, authority, identity, difference, subjectivity, agency, dissent, resistance, and suspicion. Accordingly, we trace the nuances of the politics of location as a means of dislocating the researcher from the threshold.

The term "politics of location" was first coined by Adrienne Rich in *Blood, Bread, and Poetry*, a collection of essays written between 1979 and 1985. In these essays, Rich examined the borders and limits of Western feminism, specifically, the racist and homophobic assumptions of U.S. feminism in its unitary and hegemonic categorical analysis of "woman." This term has since been picked up and expanded in multiple writings, and has been employed to create alternative discourses on the "politics of location." These discourses are contingent upon the term's varied utility, the discipline in which it is situated, and the contexts of how "politics of location" is formulated, employed, and interpreted.

In order to consider the linkages and ways in which "politics of location" can be employed and interpreted within critical research discourse, I wish to read this term as a means of interrupting and accounting for the formulations and constructions of one's social-political locations. To do so requires the researcher not simply turn hir[3] gaze critically and reflectively inward but rather to engage in critically reflective processes that speak to multiple power relations. As Rosi Braidotti (2002) asserts, "Self-reflexivity is, moreover, not an individual activity, but an interactive process which relies upon a social network of exchanges" (p. 11). This continuous and embodied process of internal contraction and external expansion of the researcher's gaze must move beyond mere considerations and individualized reflection and reflexivity. The imperative for researchers, then, is to take a critically active stance that takes into account (and accounts for) multiple histories and traces diverse trajectories that give shape to various meanings, authorities, power, and ways of knowing.

An imperative of the politics of location was a critique of dominant articulations of White, Western feminists, particularly those in the academy. Thus, the politics of location was a call for feminists to interrogate the linkages between feminist theory and feminist practices and to examine whose theories/practices were being privileged. In its broadest usage, the term is used as a means of acknowledging differentially situated subjects (difference), and to interrogate the positions of privileged identities and histories. Adrienne Rich wrote that in order to shift unequal dynamics, those of us in relative sites of privilege needed to account for our marginalizing practices, and to uncover the ways in which such privileging allows for participation in or complicitness with maintaining hegemonic relations. She argues for this because she believes "the movement for change is a changing movement, changing itself, demasculinizing itself, de-Westernizing itself, becoming a critical mass that is saying no in so many different voices, languages, gestures, actions: it must change; we ourselves can change it" (1986, p. 225).

In challenging privileged stances, Rich vocalizes the need to decentre the very spaces that locate our identities and subjectivities. Decentring and dislocating our assumptions, values, and knowledges are critical practices for establishing the groundwork for articulating the processes and relationships of our research and research subjects. In order to ensure that research does not occur in a social and political vacuum, and that researchers are constituted in relation to and with (O)thers,[4] engaging in a process of disinheriting our assumed narratives is essential. Further, it is a means of clarifying our interests in (O)thers, our desire to uncover (a) truth(s) of various communities. Consequently, examining our own politics of location in relation to the subjects of our research can shift the terms of our inquiry. This examination is an invitation for us to become more accountable to our inquiries, to the processes of our research, and ultimately to the voices of the margins.

Chandra Talpade Mohanty (1987) elaborates upon and modifies Rich's visions of the politics of location, offering more complex accounts of positionality for researchers. Her examination of feminist scholarship in the social sciences in "Under Western Eyes" (1987) is an indictment of those strains of Western feminist scholarship that reproduced, however "innocently," the altruistic missionary/explorer position. Mohanty's use of the term references "the historical, geographical, cultural, psychic, and imaginative boundaries that provide the grounds for political definition and self-definition" (p. 44). Mohanty argues that in order to resist universalizing oppressions and struggles and to make the discursive operations of power visible, it is necessary to historicize and locate political agency. To neglect attending to the narratives of location based on context and history (to ahistoricize) dismisses the varied accounts of (O)ther as political and social agents (p. 113). Mohanty's explorations suggest that the sheer observations of one's location are not sufficient; rather, there needs to be a congruent examination of the meanings attached to our social identities in historical moments that are of strategic significance. One key insight that Mohanty offers in her critique of hegemonic White feminists is that such forms of scholarship, with their homogenizing tendencies to construct "Third World women" as their object of knowledge, not only relegate and solidify the marginal as Other, but in doing so, consolidate their own locus of power. Through such constructions, and the investments in marginalizing Others, the result is to deny marginalized peoples their political and historic agency (p. 213). Mohanty clarifies her position on generalizations as such: "the arguments are not against generalizations as they are for careful, historically specific generalization responsive to complex realities" (p. 211).

Mohanty suggests several approaches to strategically use our works to combat the multifaceted and multiple localities of oppressions. First, we must resist easy generalizations; we need to avoid being reductive in our constructions and formulations of the Other. By situating and contextualizing ourselves, and ourselves in relation to the subjects of our research, our work can provide strategies for counter-narratives and oppositional politics. As well, by understanding the contradictions in the locations of marginal people within differing structures, we can better devise effective political action. Mohanty's work offers foresight about the ways in which unexamined, un-contextualized assumptions of naturalizing oppressions elide the specifics of difference and obscure and negate solidarity and collectivity. In "'Under Western Eyes' Revisited," Mohanty (2003) raises the concern of privileging privilege: " ... if we begin our analysis from, and limit it to, the space of privileged communities, our visions of justice are more likely to be exclusionary because privilege nurtures blindness to those without the same privileges" (p. 231). As argued earlier, these strategies do not help to make the various modes and operations of power visible; rather, they maintain and solidify hegemonic relations of power. Uncontested, privileging privilege cannot provide us with alternative accounts of justice or the ethical grounds to forge relations for political struggles within our research.

A critical engagement with a politic of location has implications for the relationships formed between researchers and communities, and for the utility and applicability of research as a politicized and active endeavour that interrupts the dominant narratives and textualities of marginal lives. By situating ourselves in history and the contexts of our own multiple locations, we can move toward working through and with differences based on multiple subjectivities. These differences help us uncover the dissimilar and/yet overlapping positions, potentially allowing us to forge solidarity on grounds that reject essentialist categories and demarcate the multiple sites of struggles. Her work also offers insight into the interpretive explanations of research: attending to politics of location empowers research to explore the various interpretations and accounts of the meanings that undergird our findings. Mohanty posits that to attend to the specificities of difference enhances our ability to find the grounds for shared struggles. She writes: "The challenge is to see how differences allow us to explain the connections and border crossings better and more accurately, how specifying difference allows us to theorize universal concerns more fully" (2003, p. 226).

There are some cautionary notes I wish to advance in the use of politics of location in research, for attending to politics of location does not necessarily translate into "better" research or research that has greater methodological or scientific rigour. By inviting researchers to consider politics of location as a serious form of enquiry, to map the ways in which we are socially and historically constituted, intertwined, and intersect with(in) the world and in relationship to subjects of our research, reflexivity requires a resistance to theoretical generalizations and monolithic truth claims. As in the case of politics of location, the idea of reflexivity is not new, especially as a requisite for engaging at various junctures of research. Reflexivity serves as a necessary part of political positioning, where we attempt to "know," but recognize that knowing and knowledge is tentative and tenuous. Reflexivity, then, would be characterized as a skill or practice whereby we "interrogate the truthfulness of the tale, and provide multiple answers" (Minh-ha, 1991, p. 12). In other words, critical reflexivity in a politics of location is guided by and radically holds open through continuous interruptions the "return of [a] difference" (Martindale, 1997, p. 78).

Politics of location has been used to signal and incorporate "what is going on" in the research process; that research is shaped and reshaped according to self-critique, which needs to be embedded in the various steps of research, the chosen methodologies, and in the findings and discussion. The emphasis in this section is to engage in an ongoing enquiry of a politics of location that is continuous, connected, specific, and emerging in any research process as a means of always questioning and queering the thresholds of re-search-ing. Critically inquiring into the reasons for researching particular communities helps elucidate the need to build rapport with, or becoming "up close and personal" with marginal "Others"; accordingly, the question of "why" the proposed research is undertaken becomes crucial to "how" and "if" there is a need to embark with particular research interests. Furthermore, by critically locating ourselves within the relational contexts, constructions, and histories that (re)produce marginal communities, we differently situate ourselves to recognize the shifting and multiple subjectivities of marginal communities, struggles, and the nuances of the asymmetrical relationships (and the implications of these relationships) that we forge.

Using politics of location should not be about enumerating one's categorical list of identities as a researcher, although this may serve as a useful place of entry. Nor is the politics of location meant to serve as an apology at the end of one's research discussion ("the apologetic addendum") as to how and why marginal voices were not represented within the process. By relegating marginal lives to the end of our discussions, or as endnotes, how can marginal narratives and discourses in our research and research findings be centralized? The effect of this "apologetic addendum" is that, on the one hand, it provides nothing other than a "matter-of-fact" account of narratives neglected by the researcher and, on the other, it solidifies the very processes of hegemony. These tokenizing and co-opting gestures are both incompatible and inconsistent with critical theories and practices for they obfuscate the strategic formulations of politics of location. Listing categories can often reinscribe essentialist, homogenizing, and universalizing notions of identity. Such practice assumes a historical amnesia in relation to one's identity and obscures the multiple meanings and knowledges that emerge from these varied locations. This form of listing also implies and presumes that the subjects of research are vastly or strangely different from ourselves, and that the researcher and research subject are socially and politically isolated in relationship to one another, or that we are internally and exclusively coherent entities. Further, categorical listing assumes a fixed, generic, and linear version of identity, which in turn limits our ability to engage with the complex matrix that forms and informs one's critical self-inquiry, resulting in cultural relativism while creating an asymmetric relationship between "Self" and "Other."

Politics of location ultimately can become a reified academic state, where it becomes a tool for cementing fixed hegemonic relations. Paradoxically, it can be intrinsically linked to forging a politics of collectivity with marginal communities. Politics of location can become an excuse for cultural relativism, or a space to deconstruct hegemonic constructions of "otherness." Satya Mohanty (1989) argues, "a simple recognition of differences across cultures" results in "a sentimental charity, for there is nothing in its logic that necessitates our attention to the other" (p. 23). Eschewing cultural relativism interpellates the grounds for attending to the agency and the embodied subjectivities of "Others." Furthermore, politics of location is not an invitation to "make room at the table" for difference, where the shifts of one's body to "accommodate" results in fixing sites of dominance. Suzanne de Castell and Mary Bryson (1996) write: "It is no longer plausible (if it ever was) to 'move over' and 'make room' for the participation of ethnography's traditional 'Others.' The problem isn't a lack of space, it is the kind of space, the kind of place ethnography is, which shapes its ethos and its conditions of occupancy" (p. 2). Politics of location also cannot be seen as a call to plurality, where various inequitable trajectories of power are disguised or dismissed in favour of a relativism that speaks to a "sameness of difference" or "cross-cultural" practices. Politics of location must be understood within a paradigm of transformative potential where connections are sought through struggle when attending to the politics and processes of working with communities. The politics of location is one of many considerations that situate differences, and a recognition that centralizing the constitutive nature of differences garners a place of transforming the contexts in which differences are lived.

In order to avoid the many pitfalls of politics of location, or to ensure that the "endlessness" of contradictory, intersecting, and multiple locations does not become "a pure concept, an end in itself" (Radhakrishnan, 1996, p. 189), we must heed the call to a "politics of accountability" (Razack, 1998). I want to draw attention to accountability to ensure that in stressing the critical need to "interrogate" and deconstruct the markers of privilege, I do not wish to leave an impression that this is sufficient to gain entry into "othered" worlds. Politics of location in and of itself is not necessarily transformative. My emphasis here is to seek ways in which we build in, with, and on the processes of attending to differences within the purview of accountability, our politically ethical responsibilities to communities under/within our gaze. Rosi Braidotti (1994) insists that we need to have accountability to our shared historical conditions. She writes: "Accountability and positionality go together. In emphasizing the importance of accounting for one's own investments ... I have also insisted ... on the need to also take into account the level of unconscious desire and consequently of imaginary relation to the very material conditions that structure our existence" (p. 168). Braidotti furthers her point of accountability with this quote from Caren Kaplan: "such accountability can begin to shift the ground of feminist practice from magisterial relativism ... to the complex interpretative practices that acknowledge the historical roles of mediation, betrayal, and alliance in the relationships between women in diverse locations" (quoted in Braidotti, 1994, pp. 168–169). Of significance here is to elucidate the ways in which we are both historically and contemporarily already implicated in various forms of subjugation. Whether we practise our research from liberatory, critical, and/or radical standpoints, we cannot claim epistemological or ontological innocence, for we are not outside of the conditions, contexts, and positionalities of life and living.

Within research, we must forge and centralize a politic of accountability to communities who are/have been subjects of research. Accountability must be politically and ethically enacted continuously with and in research, an ethic that calls for us to shift, change, or disinherit some of our ideas, practices, methods, and interpretations if we want to sustain politically ethical relationships with marginal communities. The danger of humanistic approaches to research in marginal communities is that they can easily slip to strategies of appropriation, relativism, "equalizing" discourses, and the superficial gestures of inclusion. Responsibility to, and being accountable for, our research requires that we need to be as attentive to process as we are to content. We need to ensure that we do not reproduce patterns and processes of colonization or "epistemic violence" in relation to marginal knowledges. We need to be attentive to how we relate to and with communities, and to engage politics of location continuously in order to forestall the commodification or fetishizing of marginal identities, knowledges, ways of being, and communities. If we are to produce research that benefits marginal communities and promotes justice, we must be accountable to marked privileges by rigorously attending to the politics of transformative methodologies and epistemologies, particularly situated epistemologies.

Pro/Positioning Queer Flexabilities and the Ex-centric Researcher

In order to forge methods of developing and maintaining a stance of a critical researcher, I wish to explore a method of engagement or framework with/in this revisioning of privileged positionality. I want to investigate specific theoretical propositions to visit these altering terrains, specifically, queer flexibilities and the ex-centric researcher guide my explorations. Queer flexibilities provide both a conceptual framework and a theoretical paradigm for critical research, while the ex-centric embodies the performative modes of research. Ex-centricity is thus housed in the theoretical propositions of queer flexibilities. Both queer flexibilities and ex-centricity are offered, not as static models, but as possible stances and positions, and are offered as a means of beginning/continuing a dialogue about the nuanced relationships between researcher and researched communities.

"Queer" surfaced in the early 1990s (its emergence as politicized activism can be traced to groups such as ACT UP and Queer Nation) and gained currency within academia as queer theory. Although queer theory emerged from feminist and gay and lesbian scholarship, queer theory is transdisciplinary given its lack of cohesion to any specific theory or discipline, while retaining sites of engagement and contestations. Queer challenges the assumed coherency and stability of chromosomal sex, gender, and sexual desire and posits that identity is neither fixed nor determinate, but socially constructed and contingent on time and context. Queer theorists often dispute the normalized and regulatory aspects of (sexual) identity, and create competing discourses that embrace ambiguity while resisting attempts at coherency.

So, you ask, what does queer (theory) have to do with research and marginality? I wish to pick up on the relative flexibility of queerness, and attend to Judith Butler's reading of queer as a category that will always be in the flux of "becoming" in its venture to avoid naturalization and homogenization, and to be disruptive of coherent articulations of sex, gender, and desire. Butler writes that queer will "remain that which is, in the present, never fully owned, but always and only redeployed, twisted, queered from a prior usage and in the direction of urgent and expanding political purposes" (1993, p. 228). It is from this definition of queer that I wish to read the strategic position and disrupt the subjectivity of "researcher." I want to explore the political potential of queer politics for research and researchers as offering a possible method of traversing thresholds in order to maintain ethical and political affiliations to our research relationships.

Two markers of queer theory can be useful in deliberating the assumed stability of the researcher. Much like queer theory's attention to disrupting the normative, the naturalized, and the hegemonic, I suggest that the position of the researcher needs to be similarly deconstructed. Thus, queer theory may be used to decentre the very position of the researcher, to renegotiate the elements that "fix" researchers to their identity categories, to question the assumptions of one's research ideas/methodologies, to consider that which is considered outside the norm of research, and to interrogate the trajectories of power and knowledge in using the margins to define multiple central locations. Such understanding of queer requires a stance that is oppositional; it defies attempts at assimilation, co-option, exploitation, and appropriation. Such nonconformity requires particular forms of praxis by researchers, and I would argue that having a politic of opposition enables one to attend to various thresholds, as well as through the many passageways of research. Queer researchers can foster questioning stances that constantly question the normative and the status quo, as well as the institutions and values of "normal" society. Questioning the "normal" requires the excavation of "truths," of reconsidering and redefining existing dominant constructions of marginal communities, and privileging ambiguity or eliding the perceived direction of one's research. This questions our need to anchor and ground our epistemic inquiry within the security of "knowing," and instead replace this certainty of knowing with what David Halperin (1995) describes as "pointing ahead without knowing for certain what to point at" (p. 93), a looking ahead without consolidating the future, a pointing ahead at what might become.

The call to adopt an attitude of epistemic uncertainty is paradoxical to what we come to know academically, where claims to know are cherished, where contributions to cultivating specifics of disciplines are notarized to ensure upward mobility, and, above all, where accumulated knowledges provide the credibility that underpins belonging in the academy. The confusion and chaos borne of knowledge that is continually circulated as being "under construction" (Jagose, 1996) may seemingly undermine the very markers of academic success. Queer flexibilities foreground curiosity, and maintain a stance that is willing not only to critically identify and name oppression, but also seek to understand and dismantle the workings and processes of oppression. Allowing for marginal or deviant knowledges requires a dismantling of inherited and cultivated knowledges, and to explore the nuanced spaces of oppression rather than a mere acknowledgment of difference. How many of us are willing to let go of our ideas, conceptualizations, and methods when we learn something new or different that cannot fit into our previous assumptions? How can research attend to politics of knowledge in order to dismantle ahistorical and apolitical knowledge claims? How can the varied and competing investments in "expert" positions be disrupted? I would suggest that maintaining a queer flexibility is a critical tool in disrupting what and how we know. By embracing a queer flexibility, we are better positioned to let difference live, where we can find pleasures in the ambiguities of multifocaled thresholds. In turn, this openness can create alternative strategies and visions for a radical praxis, where bordered and domesticated claims of knowledge are contested, challenged, decentred in order to engage processes of alteration, regeneration, and transformation. Queer flexibilities incite a desire to find differing thresholds, multiple thresholds so that we continually return to thresholds that disjuncture normative relations.

Queer activists and theorists have paid attention to the articulation, constitution, and modes of analysis of resistance that can provide further insight for transformative research. I engage a queer understanding of resistance to be both relational and oppositional. Consequently, queer resistance can be seen to mobilize in relation to that which constitutes the normative. Following and incorporating a Foucauldian analysis of power and resistance, and in particular the displacement of binary understandings of power (and therefore resistance), the unstable and multiple voices and expressions of power and resistance call for subversive strategies of resistance. Reading queer notions of resistance in relation to research suggests a responsibility to dissenting politics. Researchers must incorporate divergent and diffused locations of resistance where resistance frames the relationship to the kinds of knowledges that researchers seek to centralize. Institutional pressures to focus one's inquiry to the institutional and disciplinary requirements can run counter to emancipatory knowledges and principles. Accordingly, resistance in research processes means revaluing audience, voice, subjectivities, authority, and disrupting and disrespecting any attempts at (re)colonizing knowledges. Furthermore, in queering one's research, one needs to resist assimilationist and co-optive strategies exercised by the dominant to ensure that the very strategies that "define" queer (provisional and contingent, transdisciplinary, subversive rather than regulatory, and so forth) are not reproduced.

The ex-centric researcher is closely aligned to the conceptual spaces of queer flexibilities. Like queer flexibilities, ex-centric researchers stand in defiance of dominant sites of privilege, and are critically engaged in divesting themselves of their centred locations, interests, and agendas. Ex-centric researchers know the value of subjugated knowledges, and promote the scholarly and epistemic worth of texts. Ex-centric researchers also focus on the commitments to relationships and the struggles to create the spaces for ethical dialogue with "Others." Ex-centrics are those who commit themselves to knowing their history, and the ways in which their histories are constituted through others as one of the precursors to forming politically ethical relationships. Most saliently, ex-centrics are drawn to standing outside of the centre, embracing the borderlands of various worlds because ex-centrics do not belong to any one world.

By using the term "ex-centric," I am not suggesting a complete and unequivocal disavowal of academic responsibilities, methods, and processes (even if this were possible or perhaps even desirable), nor am I proposing that we should valorize and romanticize the alienation associated with ex-centric subjectivities. Ex-centricity focuses primarily on process; it is provisional and relational to the borders between various academic sites and communities, and to our own relationship and commitment to our discipline. I want to view ex-centricity as a process whereby we can interrupt the terms of "business as usual" and disrupt the processes that enable the academy to maintain its exclusion of ideas and knowledges that conflict with existing established knowledges. Becoming ex-centric allows for a critical stance that can challenge the reconfiguration and tightening of borders of exclusion and denial, while building solidarity with and commitment to (O)ther communities/identities/spaces.

What are our investments in becoming uncomfortable with academic interests that promote these existing power structures and hierarchies of knowledge? What are the effects or consequences of being relatively discomforted and dislocated from dominant academic ideas, modes of communications, and methods of analysis? How might we critically engage normalizing rhetoric that is a smokescreen for exclusion and isolation of ideas that challenge dominant hierarchies? How can queer flexibilities create possibilities of greater alliances and strengthened relationships between the academy and community groups? What are the possible counterdiscourses produced in the processes of ex-centring? How might queer flexibilities decentre and destabilize established legitimized knowledges? I do not wish to suggest that processes of researching are determined by dominance; rather, I wish to challenge and qualify the ways in which research is influenced by dominance. It is the subtleties of the myriad ways in which researchers and research processes are influenced by historic and contemporary articulations of dominance that are important to attend to, for it is in these subtle spaces that our research can have damaging, lasting impacts on marginal communities. To further delineate the role of the ex-centric, I wish to read three authors who describe their experience of life in the marginal locations between various axes and nexus of power: bell hooks, Gloria Anzaldua, and Edward Said. Outlining the terms that these writers deploy to speak to struggle and resistance is not meant to imply that these are the only writers who situate ex-centricities. Many other writers also trouble and unsettle normative positions in favour of exploring the various ways in which they are a part of and disengage with modalities of power. This includes Patricia Hill Collins's notion of "outsider-within" (2000, p. 11), and Rey Chow's (1993) deployment of the term "diaspora."

bell hooks speaks to the political possibilities of margin, "a space of radical openness" (1990, p. 145) where there is an interplay between struggle and resistance, where she can find the multiple voices and discourses within her. The margin is a place that hooks "chooses" to occupy where the process of revisioning can occur (p. 145). The progression of decentring and choosing the margin is a radical political act. hooks writes that to choose the margins does not mean occupying marginality. Attending to the transformative potential of the margin, hooks characterizes the space of the margins as a radically open and unfolding subject position.

> I made a definite distinction between that marginality which is imposed by oppressive structures and that marginality one chooses as site of resistance—as location of radical openness and possibility.

This site of resistance is continually formed in that segregated culture
of opposition that is our critical response to domination. We come to
this space through suffering and pain, through struggle. We know
struggle to be that which gives pleasures, delights, and fulfils desire.
(hooks, 1990, p. 145)

hooks offers strategy and the necessity of ex-centricity. She refers
to the possibilities of solidarity and collectivity in the fissures between
privileged and marginal communities. Given the privileges of being
in the academy, choosing the margins as one's identification is a
political act. It is important to note, though, that "the academy" is
not a homogenous or equalized site; while it is a privileging site, not
all differences are equal, nor are the borders between academy and
community necessarily rigid and dichotomous.

Gloria Anzaldúa (1988) provides a slightly different look at the
traits of an ex-centric researcher. She speaks to the different worlds
that she intersects; she is the bridge to cultures and identities to build
a new world. In describing bordered identities, Anzaldua writes: "each
world within its own peculiar and distinct inhabitants, not comfortable
in anyone of them, none of them 'home,' yet none of them 'not home'
either" (p. 712). Borderland is the space where one finds comfort in
ambiguity and contradiction, where we eschew comfort and safety to
making ourselves vulnerable to different ideas, thoughts, and ways of
being. To allow ourselves to be vulnerable to shifting means that the
space where comfort is found is no longer comfortable; for shifting
requires seeing that "what" and "who" defines comfort is always
historically and politically implicated. "After I first left home and became
acquainted with other worlds, the Prieta that returned was different,
thus 'home' was different too. It could not completely accommodate
the new Prieta, and I could barely tolerate it. Though I continue to go
home, I no longer fool myself into believing that I am truly 'home'"
(p. 713). The dislodging of hegemonic comfort zones may provide a
different lens and require us to forge a different kind of relationship
with marginal communities. Becoming an ex-centric means trying to
find the pleasures of possibilities in the struggles of positioning oneself
at the intersections of contradictory and disagreeable discourses where
there are penalties to be paid, and where transformational possibilities
lay in creating research that is meaningful and engages social justice.

Edward Said (1994), in the 1993 Reich Lectures for the BBC, talks of
the role and representation of intellectuals. His proposals speak to this

process of ex-centricity through his metaphorical use of the term "exile." He describes the intellectual in metaphorical exile as "disagreeable," who is "happy with the idea of unhappiness" (p. 39), and that this intellectual is not cynical, but appreciates irony and skepticism (p. 45). He defines this intellectual as such:

> ... even intellectuals who are lifelong members of a society can, in a manner of speaking ... be nay-sayers, the individuals at odds with their society and therefore outsiders ... so far as privileges, power, and honors are concerned. [They are in] the state of never being fully adjusted, always feeling outside the chatty, familiar world inhabited by natives, so to speak. (Said, 1994, p. 39)

Said outlines a number of advantages to this standpoint. One such advantage is that this space clarifies the historical processes that shape how things have come to be as they are, and to view situations as "contingent, not as inevitable" (p. 45). Another point that Said makes is that the exiled intellectual is freed from the bonds of conventional measures of intellectualism. He argues that these intellectuals are marginal, and this marginality can offer places of "innovation and experiment rather than the habitual, to innovation and experiment rather than the authoritatively given status quo" (p. 47).

Said's definition of the exiled intellectual offers vision and clarity for the queer ex-centric researcher. His proposals for ex-centricity invite curiosity and allow a critical and questioning stance. This process of ex-centring calls for risk taking and becoming somewhat comfortable with loneliness, for ex-centricity can often be isolating. Ex-centricity is about being disloyal to the reconstitution and reproduction of hegemonic processes and dominant ideology. It is about engaging with the shortcomings of knowledges and maintaining skepticism of truths borne in knowledge.

The passions and visions offered by hooks, Anzaldúa, and Said reinforce the ethic of the politics of location, and speak to the imperatives of the threshold. Each writer stresses the queer knowings of ambiguity, and the pleasures and challenges of ex-centricity. Of significance, hooks's notion of "margin," Anzaldúa's borderland, and Said's notion of "exile" provide a glimpse of a methodology that dislocates the colonizing traversals of thresholds.

Crossing Thresholds

In this chapter, I have strived to and stressed the need to continue to engage with the ongoing debate and dialogue regarding positionality of social work researchers who propose to enter and work with marginal communities. Furthermore, I have endeavoured to suggest that it is not sufficient to consider locating positionality within the fixed categorical limits of "proper[5] research" and a "proper researcher." Rather, I contend that we are always already situated in and in relation to multiple communities and ongoing multiple passageways. Also, I have argued against formulaic (re)presentations of positionality that present researcher subjectivity in Cartesian terms by constructing the researcher in fixed and stable terms, where the Self is all knowable. Instead, reflexivity of positionalities need to be an ongoing critical practice that refuses to accept compulsory and fixed identities, and that challenges the notion that researchers are situated outside of life processes. Integral to such considerations is whether we (re)produce epistemic or colonialist violence in our process of entry or participation in and with marginal communities.

Regardless of whether our concerns are with making visible our conceptual baggage or with ensuring accountable and accessible research, we need to consider whether we are willing to abandon the focus of our research, the methodologies of our research, or the research project altogether. The politics of attending to "finding" any passageways must include the impossibility of entering. As Scheurich (1996) points out, "I fear the arrogance we enact 'unknowingly,' I fear my seeming lack of fear in proposing new imaginaries of validity, even transgressive ones. Perhaps, instead, we (I) ought to be stunned into silence—literally into silence, into a space of emptiness, into the clarity of the unknowing that appropriates no one or no thing to its sameness"(p. 58).

My readings and critiques of positionality are not to be deemed as a rejection or panacea of positionality; rather, I want for us/me to reconsider how we use and deploy politics of identity. Focusing on and interrogating the deployment of positionality permits researchers to explore the ways in which our shifting subjectivities relate to and are complicit with hegemonic power and knowledges. By directing ourselves to the "how," we may also illuminate our struggles to avoid reproducing the very forms of hegemonic powers that we seek to resist.

In suggesting the lens of queer flexibilities and ex-centricities, I am not proposing a "better" method of practising research. My intent is to fracture the notion of "comfortable" and "proper" research, and to strongly insert the compulsory political ethic of disrupting and taking for granted that any of our research attempts and methods are innocent. Decentring positionality may facilitate the necessary skepticism, especially where we feel that we are most honest or transparent in our research. The movement away from established places of knowing, and embarking on/engaging in research as a process whereby we are confounded and dislocated, where there are no easy answers or even "successful" research outcomes, or where we fail to map the start and endpoints of our linear research processes, where we are unable to find language, may indeed be the very knowledge and ultimately the learning we require in representing ourselves.

Notes

1. I am deeply grateful to Proma Tagore and Roshni Narain for their generous and abundant feedback, close readings, and various (inter)ruptions in the writing of this article. Thank you to Peter Cole and Pat O'Riley who beautifully and simply said, "Just write." I would also like to thank Mehmoona Moosa-Mitha and Leslie Brown for their continued and ongoing support and encouragement with my work.
2. Throughout this chapter, I use the term "we." In doing so, I realize the pitfalls and epistemic problems related to the use of this term, especially given that it is often invoked by Euro-centric, Western writers to speak into a universal and homogeneous subject. My use of "we" in this chapter refers specifically to those who identify themselves within the discipline of social work to be social work practitioners and/or researchers, and who may very well embody varied subjectivities. In addition, it is recognition and acknowledgment of the ways in which I am implicated in the various communities I speak of/to, and the relations I have with these communities in different ways.
3. Many thanks to Leslie Feinberg for hir work on creating language that disrupts, challenges, and attempts to move beyond the categorical imperatives of her, he, she, and him. See Feinberg's 1998 text, *Trans Liberation: Beyond Pink and Blue*, published by Beacon Press.
4. At times throughout this chapter, I have used differing forms of the word "other." I have placed brackets around (O)ther to signify that (O)ther can

be read/engaged with in two ways: first, the ways in which representation works to produce and construct "the other," which is not the self. The second reading of (O)ther is as "another" who is *differently* situated in material reality. Also, at moments I have placed quotes around "other" to mean that the "other" is socially constructed, and this construction is both real and fictitious.

5. The term "proper" researcher is used to challenge the unity of identity found within the categorical proper noun of "to be a researcher," and the various processes, investments, and effects of being a "proper researcher."

References

Abu-lughod, L. (1993). *Writing women's worlds: Bedouin Stories*. Berkeley: University of California Press.

Anzaldúa, G. (1988). Bridges, drawbridge, sandbar, or island. In M. Blasius and S. Phelan (Eds.), *We are everywhere: A historical sourcebook of gay and lesbian politics*, pp. 712–722. New York: Routledge.

Anzaldúa, G. (2002). (Un)natural Bridges, (un)safe spaces. In G. Anzaldúa and A. Keating (Eds.), *This bridge we call home: Radical visions for transformation*, 1–5. New York: Routledge.

Bishop, R. (1998). Freeing ourselves from neo-colonial domination in research: A Maori approach to creating knowledge. *Qualitative Studies in Education* II (2), 199–219.

Braidotti, R. (1994). *Nomadic subjects: Embodiment and sexual difference in contemporary feminist theory*. New York: Columbia University Press.

Braidotti, R. (2002). *Metamorphoses: Towards a materialist theory of becoming*. Cambridge: Polity Press.

Brand, D. (2001). *A map to the door of no return: Notes on belonging*. Toronto: Doubleday Canada.

Butler, J. (1993). *Bodies that matter: On the discursive limits of "sex."* New York: Routledge.

Chow, R. (1993). *Writing diaspora: Tactics of intervention in contemporary cultural studies*. Bloomington: Indiana University Press.

de Castell, S., and Bryson, M. (1996). Queer ethnography: Identity, authority, narrativity, and a geopolitics of text. Conference paper, Simon Fraser University.

Dirlik, A. (1994). *After the revolution: Waking to global capitalism*. Hanover: Wesleyan University Press.

Dominelli, L. (1997). *Sociology for social work*. Hampshire: Macmillan Press.

Dominelli, L. (2002). *Feminist social work theory and practice*. Hampshire: Palgrave.

Epstein, L. (1999). The culture of social work. In A. Chambon, A. Irving, and L. Epstein (Eds.), *Reading Foucault for social work*, 3–26. New York: Columbia University Press.

Fuss, D. (1991). *Inside/out: Lesbian theories, gay theories*. New York: Routledge.

Grewal, I., and Kaplan, C. (1994). *Scattered hegemonies: Postmodernity and transnational feminist practices*. Minneapolis: University of Minnesota Press.

Halperin, D. (1995). *Saint Foucault: Toward a gay hagiography*. New York: Oxford University Press.

Haraway, D. (1997). Modest_Witness@Second_Millennium. *FemaleMan©_Meets_ OncoMouse™: Feminism and Technoscience*. New York: Routledge.

Heilbrun, C. (1999). *Women's lives: The view from the threshold*. Toronto: University of Toronto Press.

Hill Collins, P. (2000). *Black feminist thought: Knowledge, consciousness, and the politics of empowerment*. New York: Routledge.

hooks, b. (1990). *Yearning: Race, gender, and cultural politics*. New York: Routledge.

Jagose, A. (1996). *Queer theory: An introduction*. Washington Square: New York University Press.

Kaplan, C. (1996). *Questions of travel: Postmodern discourses of displacement*. Durham: Duke University Press.

Kirby, S., and McKenna, K. (1989). *Experience research social change: Methods from the margins*. Toronto: Garamond Press.

Martindale, K. (1997). Que<e>rying pedagogy: Teaching un/popular cultures. In Suzanne de Castell and Mary Bryson (Eds.), *Radical in<ter>ventions: Identity, politics, and difference/s in educational praxis*, 59–83. Albany: SUNY Press.

Minh-ha, T. (1989). *Woman native other*. Bloomington: Indiana University Press.

Minh-ha, T. (1991). *When the moon waxes red: Representation, gender and cultural politics*. New York: Routledge.

Mohanty, C.T. (1987). Feminist encounters: Locating the politics of experience. *Copyright* 1 (Fall), 30–44.

Mohanty, C.T. (2003). *Feminism without borders: Decolonizing theory, practicing solidarity*. Durham: Duke University Press.

Mohanty, S. (1989). Us and them: On the philosophical bases of political criticism. *Yale Journal of Criticism* 2 (March), 1–31.

Moreau, M. (1979). A structural approach to social work practice. *Canadian Journal of Social Work Education* 5 (1), 78–94.

Morrison, T. (1992). *Playing in the dark: Whiteness and the literary imagination.* New York: Vintage Books.

Narayan, U, and Harding, S. (2000). *Decentering the center: Philosophy for a multicultural, postcolonial, and feminist world.* Bloomington: Indiana University Press.

Radhakrishnan, R. (1996). *Diasporic mediations: Between home and location.* Minneapolis: University of Minnesota Press.

Razack, S. (1998). *Looking White people in the eye: Gender, race, and culture in courtrooms and classrooms.* Toronto: University of Toronto Press.

Rich, A. (1986). *Blood, bread, and poetry: Selected prose, 1979–1985.* New York: Norton.

Said, E. (1994). *Representations of the intellectual: The 1993 Reith lectures.* New York: Pantheon Books.

Scheurich, J. (1996). The masks of validity: A deconstructive investigation. *Qualitative Studies in Education* 9 (1), 49–60.

Soja, E. 1989. *Postmodern geographies: The reassertion of space in critical social theory.* London: Verso.

Webster's New Lexicon Dictionary. (1988). New York: Lexicon Publications.

CHAPTER SIX

SUPPORTING YOUNG PEOPLE'S TRANSITIONS FROM CARE:

REFLECTIONS ON DOING PARTICIPATORY ACTION RESEARCH WITH YOUTH FROM CARE

Deb Rutman, Carol Hubberstey,
April Barlow, and Erinn Brown

Introduction

During the 1990s policy and legislative discourse emphasized citizen involvement in issues ranging from health to social services to the environment. Similarly, government policy and practice documents highlighted youth involvement in the decisions that affected them. In British Columbia, this was reflected in the creation of several youth advisory councils attached to major service agencies and charitable foundations, and in the mandate of various youth- and family-serving organizations such as the Provincial Child, Youth, and Family Advocate (subsequently disbanded), First Call, and the B.C. Youth in Care Network. Yet, while there has been mounting interest in youth participation, little has been written about the experience of youth/non-youth collaboration, and how processes aiming to "involve" youth work out in practice.

This paper shares reflections gained from a research project, guided by participatory action research (PAR) principles, that was co-sponsored by the Victoria Youth in Care Network (VYICN) and the Research Initiatives for Social Change unit (RISC) at the School of Social Work at the University of Victoria. The Supporting Young People's Transitions from Government Care project ran from 1999 to 2001 and took place in Victoria, B.C. The project focused on the experiences of youth leaving government care and aimed to identify and then implement approaches to supporting youth during their transition from care.

Our collective interest in the experiences of youth from care had its genesis in personal relationships as well as the research literature.

April Barlow (the VYICN coordinator) had experience living in care and was passionate about the need for (self)-advocacy, (peer) support, and responsive services, resources, and opportunities for youth in care. Deborah Rutman (the RISC research coordinator) had never lived in foster care; however, she had a long-standing interest in the experiences of youth in transition from care and in participatory action research, and she also had involvement in participatory policy-making processes. Together, April and Deborah considered developing a project about—as well as with and for—youth from foster care.

This chapter highlights our experiences of conducting research that was inclusive of young people from care who had lived expertise of the care system, but who lacked formal research training or education. We offer insights and lessons learned about the careful construction and negotiation of roles, relationships, and power dynamics between adult and youth team members, and about the challenges, opportunities, contradictions, and contributions of this type of participatory approach. We hope that the lessons we have learned may be of value to other researchers and participants in similar projects that share commitments to social justice and anti-oppressive processes.

Participatory Action Research: An overview

Participatory action research rose to prominence in developing countries in the 1970s as a tool for fighting oppression by involving people affected by an issue directly in the research design and process. The thinking and reflection of significant researchers and writers in this field such as Freire (1970) in turn influenced the thinking of researchers and academics in First World countries (e.g., Hall, 1979; Maguire, 1988; Tandon, 1988). PAR in part derives from two other streams of research: action research and participatory research. A comprehensive literature review and analysis of participatory action research and its roots by Potts (1997) outlines the key components, similarities, and unique aspects that exist between action research, participatory research, and participatory action research.

According to Potts, action research does not require participation by the subjects. Professionals usually design both the research and actions. However, action research does incorporate a collaborative approach by involving "clients" in identifying their practical concerns in an immediate problematic situation, and by involving social researchers who have access to authority and funding. In action research, there is an assumption that solutions acceptable to all interested and/or affected parties are possible.

In participatory research, by contrast, no action is specifically required or expected. Professional researchers invite clients to help in undertaking the inquiry, but citizen or client ownership and control over the problem definition is downplayed in favour of a collaborative approach. Participatory research emphasizes useful knowledge and questions the distribution of power and resources. According to Leischner (2002), the common objectives in doing participatory research are for shared ownership, learning, and action. This often pits researchers and clients/subjects against authority and resources; indeed, the solutions to issues that emerge do not have to be acceptable to those who hold power and control over resources.

Participatory action research is more than a particular research design. It represents a philosophical approach that is rooted in social justice. As it is ideally laid out, participatory action research brings together several elements of research—inquiry, learning, critical analysis, community building, and social change. Participatory action research can be defined as "a way of asking questions about important issues in the life of a group or community. People involved in participatory research combine investigation, education and community action to create an empowering movement for personal and social transformation" (Potts, 1997). According to Maguire (1988), participatory research aims at three types of change:

- development of critical consciousness of both researcher and participants
- improvement of the lives of those involved in the research process
- transformation of fundamental societal structures and relationships

Thus, PAR starts with people who wish to research their own lives; they are key to what takes place, and their desire to improve social conditions is paramount. Ideally in PAR the research participants determine the focus of the inquiry, the methods of research, and ultimately the course of action that stems from the knowledge emerges from the research activity; in addition, ideally PAR participants are involved in all aspects of the research.

At the same time, differences between PAR in its ideal or "true" form, and PAR as it can play out in practice, have been noted by PAR researchers and community activists. For example, Leischner (2004) identifies the challenges of having participants be active in all stages of the research, as well as challenges in retaining research participants/ PAR researchers. In Leischner's community-based research, initially 14 women who had been using substances during pregnancy explored the process of their recovery and empowerment; over the course of the two-year PAR project, only four women remained as participant-researchers. Similarly, Potts (1997) points out barriers to and contradictions in PAR when projects are carried out through or in partnership with the university academy. She questions whether academic researchers' own professional needs and agendas, reinforced by the academy's mechanisms for career enhancement, create inherent barriers to the practice of "true" PAR.

Commonalties between PAR and AOP

Since the mid- to late 1980s anti-oppressive practice (AOP) theory and research has gained recognition and prominence in social work education and practice in North America and the United Kingdom. AOP is based on notions of equality, rights and justice, and non-discrimination. Recognizing that multiple forms of oppression are perpetuated daily through language, discourse, societal institutions, and cultural dominance, AOP research is, at its core, about power relations (Potts, 2004). Inasmuch as traditional knowledge is critically questioned and examined, AOP is considered to be a political act. Consequently anti-oppressive practice is seen as "innovative, evolving and contentious" (Hick, 2002).

Both PAR and AOP share the understanding that researchers are knowledge producers and are located within a complex set of social structures. Their identities, motives, and agendas influence the questions they ask, the methods they use, and the conclusions they draw. In other words, the production of knowledge is not an "objective" exercise. Social research often spends time examining the lives and experiences of people who are relatively powerless or marginalized. Typically they have no control over how they are represented in research reports or the type of analysis that is conducted on their lives/information/ experiences. AOP research seeks to develop methodologies that are respectful, ethical, sympathetic, authentic, and anti-discriminatory.

PAR and anti-oppressive research have certain commonalties. While the starting place for each may be slightly different, they are compatible in that both adhere to the belief that research and practice are not value neutral. Moreover, PAR and AOP theorists both believe that research participants must have a role in deciding the research agenda, determining how the research should occur, how the information is to be used, how the analysis is to be constructed, and so forth. In other words, the research participants are partners rather than "subjects."

However, AOP generally starts with those who are already in positions of power—those engaged in research, for example—and challenges the practitioner or researcher to continually question his or her "location" in terms of beliefs, values, identity, and power, as well as to identify ways in which he or she perpetuates those power imbalances. As such, the "location" of the researcher is continuously examined and recognized as an integral part of the research process.

Within PAR not as much emphasis is placed on the "location" of the researcher. Rather, there is an assumption that the researcher and the "researched" are closely allied—if not one and the same—and would not have engaged in this particular type of research without having developed a critical consciousness of power dynamics within society, including that of the researcher's own position within society. As such PAR ideally starts with those who are without power and asks what kind of knowledge they are interested in generating, and to what end. Even in circumstances wherein the research inquiry is generated by academics, PAR would still require that "subjects" be fully involved in determining the course of the inquiry and the actions that follow.

Because of the project team's familiarity and experience with PAR projects (relative to anti-oppressive research), we were guided by PAR principles in the Supporting Young People's Transitions from Government Care project. At the same time, the project clearly had commitments to social justice (a shared PAR and AOP principle), not only in its aim to improve the lived experience of youth in and from foster care—a highly marginalized group—but also in terms of how we worked together as a project team.

Project Origins and Development

In 1997, April Barlow (co-coordinator of the Victoria Youth in Care Network) and Deborah Rutman (research coordinator of the Research

Initiatives for Social Change unit at the School of Social Work, University of Victoria) engaged in several discussions regarding issues affecting youth leaving care. April described her experiences of leaving care:

> My social worker pointed me in the direction of the income assistance office and that was the extent of my "preparation" for exiting. I wanted to explore and expose the experiences of youth from care. My hope was that ideas of how to improve the transition process could be identified from young people's experiences, and that implementation of these ideas would enable others to have a better exiting experience than I had myself.

In addition, April's informal consultations with several youth from the Victoria Youth in Care Network suggested that they too were interested in issues affecting youth in transition from care.

A component of April and Deborah's early meetings was to seek out and examine the research literature on young people's experiences of exiting care. They discovered that the Canadian literature on youth's transitions from care was very scant, although April and the VYICN had recently completed a study with youth in and from care that contributed to this knowledge base. The existing literature revealed, however, that young people exiting government care often faced a number of challenges (Barlow, 1997; B.C. Task Force on Safeguards for Children and Youth in Foster or Group Home Care, 1997; Raychaba, 1988; Victoria Sexually Exploited Youth Task Force, 1997). These youth typically lacked financial support; emotional support in the form of someone who cared about how they are doing; and practical skills such as grocery shopping, meal planning, budgeting, searching for and finding safe housing, decision making, and self-advocacy. As well, youth faced numerous health issues such as inadequate food/nutrition, unsafe shelter, substance misuse, violence, emotional/mental health problems, sexually transmitted diseases, pregnancy, and difficulties in accessing health/dental services.

The literature also demonstrated that youth leaving care are expected to establish their own households *earlier* than their peers who grow up with their parents. Whereas the average age for leaving home is in the mid-twenties (Martin, 1996), the reality for youth in government care is a total loss of support provided by their public "parents" the day they turn 19 years old. Some youth, who end up in care only "temporarily," often find themselves living on their own even earlier. April, for example, found herself living in a motel on income assistance and going to school at age 17.

In sum, youth in care—who, it should be recalled, generally come from poor, marginalized families, and who themselves often live with disability and the consequences of trauma—are asked to do more sooner, and typically with few internal and external resources. The literature thus supported April and Deborah's belief that issues for youth leaving care needed attention and action in line with social justice principles. The literature also furthered our desire to examine the experience of leaving care, to involve youth in/from care as co-researchers as well as research participants, and to do something with the results of the research study (i.e., to engage in a specific action strategy that could be carried out as a part of the project). Thus, a PAR fit best with our personal and research goals.

Pursuit of Funding

Interestingly, little is typically written in the PAR literature about PAR projects' funding and how issues associated with seeking out and obtaining funding relate to the projects' development and implementation. Yet, the obvious reality is that with the exception of researchers whose income needs are already met (most often through tenure-stream positions within the university academy), researchers/activists involved with PAR projects require financial compensation for their time. In the case of our project, although Deborah was affiliated with the University of Victoria School of Social Work, she received no salary support from the university; thus, her participation with the project needed to be funded. Similarly, although April received part-time income through the Victoria Youth in Care Network, funding to support her participation in the project was required. Moreover, participation in the project by youth in/from care and/or other community researchers—as project staff and/or in other capacities—needed to be supported financially.

In terms of funding sources, however, Deborah and April quickly discovered that few Canadian funding bodies (outside of charitable foundations) were willing to provide salary support to community-based researchers. Overall, funding agencies were set up according to the premise that research took place within a university context, and thus the only salaries that would be required (and thus were permitted according to agency guidelines) were those of university students working as research assistants.

One of the few exceptions in terms of the above was the B.C. Health Research Foundation.[1] The foundation provided salary support to community-based researchers. Moreover, in the mid- to late 1990s, the foundation expanded its focus beyond laboratory-based research and clinical trials/intervention projects and introduced a community-based research program that espoused participatory research principles. At the same time, the foundation remained a conventional funding body with standard requirements for accountability and research design. For example, although community-based organizations could sponsor a research project, partnerships with universities or other traditional research centres were, in practice, required even if this requirement was not stated in the funding guidelines. As well, the foundation required an elaborate project proposal, framed in the discourse of professional researchers, which spelled out in detail the research plan, data collection methods and instruments, and all budget line items. (Of course, specifying these types of details in advance is in itself antithetical to a PAR approach, in that PAR maintains that the research activities need to stem from an evolving process determined by the research participants.) Nevertheless, from Deborah and April's perspectives, the B.C. Health Research Foundation was the most appropriate funding source to pursue, and they began work on a funding proposal.

Based on our conversations with the staff of the funding body, we knew that the project proposal needed to be framed in traditional research terminology[2] (or at least our chances of funding success would increase significantly if we used "proper" language), and thus that the proposal needed to be written primarily by those with the most traditional research experience (i.e., not by youth in/from care themselves). At approximately this time, a second experienced researcher, Carol Hubberstey, who was community based and who also knew both April and Deborah professionally and personally, joined in the discussions and expressed interest in the project and proposal development. Although Carol had not lived in care, like Deborah she was interested in issues affecting youth from care and also had experience working with participatory policy development processes. Deborah and Carol thus took the lead in proposal development, and April collected and reviewed the relevant literature and liaised with youth in/from care to determine their interest in the project and their ideas about possibilities for youth involvement.

Project Overview and Proposal Development

Through the proposal development process, we (i.e., April, Deb, and Carol) conceived the project as having the overall goal of using a participatory process to identify and implement ways of improving young people's preparation for and experiences of leaving government care to live on their own. The project was viewed as having two interconnected stages. In Stage One, youth participants would recount their stories of leaving care and identify their support needs; caregivers, government, and community-based service providers also would identify issues and needs of youth in transition from care. Based on the Stage One findings, in Stage Two, the project team would then organize, implement, and evaluate a strategy to support youth.

During our proposal writing, we also agreed that the project needed to be based on guiding principles that enshrined our belief in a collaborative and participatory process. As a result of these discussions, we agreed that the project would be based on the following principles:

- The project must use a collaborative process with opportunities for involvement by youth, community, and government.
- The project needs to provide opportunities for youth in care or recently from care to be involved in guiding and participating in the project.
- There must be an action component wherein ideas for supporting youth leaving care are tried out.

We also set out that the project objectives were to provide youth in/from care with opportunities to do the following:

- voice their experiences of the transition from care process
- strengthen peer support through sharing their experiences and involvement in action planning and implementation
- develop and/or augment a variety of skills, including analytical and critical thinking, problem solving and consensus building, writing, and independent living skills
- work collaboratively with government and community service providers to identify and implement a strategy to improve young people's transitions from care

These principles and project objectives were included as part of the funding proposal, and guided our thinking during project planning and implementation.

As we conceptualized it, the project design included an active, ongoing role for youth. For example, we envisioned that youth would be part of the advisory committee and the project team. Those on the advisory committee would be paid an honorarium; those on the team would be paid a salary. Based on our brainstorming as well as ideas received from members of the Victoria Youth in Care Network, we identified in our project proposal a variety of possible types of involvement for youth. These included:

- researcher/consultation facilitator
- participant in consultations
- assisting in recruiting youth participants
- assisting in and/or jointly doing the data analysis
- producing articles on the project for relevant newsletters
- participating in implementation team(s)
- providing leadership/mentoring in action stage
- participation in evaluation of activity

In the end, although the project proposal articulated the project's objectives, potential roles for youth, anticipated data collection methods, and budget, we successfully argued that it was not possible to lay out in advance the nature of the Stage Two strategy for supporting youth in transition from care. In the spring of 1999, we were thrilled to learn that the project was awarded funding by the B.C. Health Research Foundation. In hindsight, it is interesting to speculate whether we would have been successful had we argued—in keeping with PAR principles or ideals—that the research process (including the processes in which youth were involved and/or had ownership of) could not be specified in advance. Ironically, perhaps, the University of Victoria's human subjects committee required even more detailed information regarding the project's data collection methods and instruments—that theoretically shouldn't be specified in advance in PAR—than did the funding agency. For example, in an ideal PAR project we would not have been able to specify in advance the interview questions with youth or say how those interviews or questionnaires would be carried out. However, we were required to provide this information to fulfill the ethics approval process at the university.

Project Implementation: An Overview

Advisory Committee

When the project commenced, the team was comprised of April, Deb, and Carol. The initial team recruited youth from care, community-based service providers, as well as policy and front-line staff from the Ministry for Children and Family Development (MCFD) to form an advisory committee for the project. The advisory committee provided guidance to key aspects of the project, including: confirming the importance and potential contributions of the project to the community; helping to recruit participants for stages One and Two; confirming research interview questions and processes in Stage One; providing input on and helping us select potential strategies to implement in Stage Two; and providing input on our draft Stage One and Stage Two reports.

Project Team

Shortly after the formation of the advisory committee, youth from care were recruited to join the project team. Our budget enabled hiring three youth on a part-time basis of up to 10 hours per week (at $15 an hour, roughly double B.C.'s minimum wage at the time) to form an overall six-member team. In keeping with our understanding of PAR, we sought to create a project team that had diverse and complementary strengths, skills, and life experiences. However, also in keeping with PAR, a mandatory criterion was that the youth had experienced living in and leaving care. Youth project staff were recruited through advertisements in youth-friendly centres, in a weekly alternative magazine, and the Victoria Youth in Care Network newsletter and the Southern Vancouver Island Foster Parents newsletter. Youth were asked to submit a one-page letter describing:

- why they were interested
- how they could contribute to the project
- what they hoped to get out of participating
- their contact information and number(s)

Several youth applied and the project team, using the following questions as a guide, interviewed them all:

- What attracted you to the job?
- How did you hear about it?
- What is your experience with teams?
- How have you sorted out conflict?
- What is your experience or connection with being in care?
- How do you see that as contributing to what you would bring to the project?
- What was your experience of leaving care?
- What is your understanding/idea of what this job entails?
- Do you have any ideas about research activities you might be want to look into?
- Have you had experience as a mentor or being mentored? What was that like?
- Can you commit to this job until next April?

From this selection process three youths, all women between the ages of 19 and 23, were hired. One had previous connections with the Victoria Youth in Care Network and was thus known to April, Carol, and Deb, but the other two youth had no connection to either the project or the Youth in Care Network. Of these, one was attending university and one was just finishing a community work project. All had experienced living in government care; one came into care as a toddler, and two came into care as teenagers.

Youth Involvement

There were several distinct types and levels of youth involvement. The youth who were employed by the project were very involved in the project in a variety of ways (as is described below). Several other youth from the Victoria Youth in Care Network participated in the project's advisory committee; however, beyond attending those meetings, they really had little involvement in project activities. In addition, although a few youth who participated in the research interviews subsequently became advisory committee members or expressed interest in keeping abreast of project activities, the reality was that most of these youth did not stay connected with the project following the research interview. In this respect our experiences parallel those described by Leischner (2004).

Nevertheless, during Stage One, primarily through their roles on the project team, youth participated in nearly all facets of the project, including the following:

- *Stage One research:* Youth took leadership for revising the interview guide and consent form; conducted research interviews with youth in/from care and service providers; and transcribed the interviews and collaboratively analyzed the data.
- *Evaluation of the participatory action research process:* Youth took leadership for developing an evaluation framework for the research process, for facilitating the project team's group evaluation of Stage One, and for developing problem-solving and conflict-resolution mechanisms for Stage Two.
- *Writing:* Youth prepared the flyer for recruiting youth participants as well as articles for youth-to-youth newsletters on different aspects of the project, and collaboratively drafted sections of our Stage One report and other written products.
- *Liaising with government in relation to youth policy development:* Youth took initiative to participate in consultations with the Ministry for Children and Families to provide written feedback on MCFD's draft *Practice Standards for Youth Services,* and participated in MCFD's provincial consultations regarding policy and program planning to improve youth's transitions from care, and participated in the B.C. Federation of Youth in Care Network's conference on behalf of the project.

In Stage Two, our youth project team members continued to assume crucial roles, including the following:

- recruiting youth participants
- developing the peer mentoring and life skills training materials and workshop schedule
- co-facilitating the workshops
- presenting/leading most of the workshops
- mentoring and providing peer support to youth workshop participants
- assisting in the design and undertaking of the Stage Two evaluation
- collaboratively drafting sections of our Stage Two report

Doing the Stage One Research: Data Collection and Analysis

Youth participants shared their stories of leaving care via in-depth, face-to-face interviews, which were carried out as guided conversations. We interviewed a diverse sample of 20 young people ranging in age from 16–26, including 10 youth who had recently left and two who anticipated leaving in the near future. Twelve of our participants were female; eight were male; two self-identified as being Aboriginal; and five were young parents. We also interviewed six youth-serving community-based practitioners, three foster parents/caregivers, and six youth-serving Ministry for Children and Family Development workers in order to explore their experiences of engaging in supportive practice with youth in transition from care (see Rutman et al., 2001 for a discussion of the project's research findings).

We almost always employed a team approach to data collection, whereby one of the youth researchers paired up with an adult member of the project team to conduct an interview. This facilitated learning and mentoring and also ensured that there was back-up support, particularly if the interview resulted in disclosure of highly sensitive or emotionally charged information.

Interviewing, transcribing, and data analysis occurred over the course of many months. The team elected to engage in data analysis as a collective activity, which involved reading the transcripts numerous times; identifying and discussing the "units of meaning" and then the key themes as a group; sorting, connecting, and analyzing these themes into separate topic areas (e.g., "supportive practice for foster parents"); and identifying the implications of our findings for Stage Two of the project (the implementation of a doable strategy), as well as for policy and practice.

Internal Evaluation of Stage One

In late spring 2000, we undertook an internal evaluation of our first year/Stage One. This was prompted in part by our work in planning and thinking through the potential roles of project team members in Stage Two. It was also prompted in part by one of the young adult team members who took the initiative to design a process for the team to reflect on our experiences and engage in self-evaluation. We also were committed to tracking the lessons we had learned from the Stage One research, and we wanted to document these lessons. While this process occurred organically within the project, in hindsight we appreciate that reflexivity is consistent with PAR and AOP principles as well as good practice.

Our internal evaluation process was spearheaded and facilitated by one of the youth team members, who devised a framework, based on our various Stage One activities, through which we first individually and then collectively described and appraised our work processes as a team. Through this team evaluation, we thus identified: what had worked well during Stage One; what the project's challenges were during Stage One; and what we might strive to do differently during Stage Two. Next, we used a similar framework to individually complete a self-evaluation in which each team member reflected upon her or his own personal contributions, challenges, and interests; these reflections were used to guide our (self)-assignment of roles during Stage Two. Finally, through the internal evaluation process, we recognized that we needed to develop decision-making and conflict-resolution processes as a project team. Accordingly, we developed a framework for decision making and conflict resolution at a team meeting in July 2000.

Planning for and Doing Stage Two: Peer Mentoring and Life Skills Training

Stage Two of the project was designed to build on the work and findings of Stage One by pilot testing at least one strategy designed to support the transition from government care.

An analysis of the interviews conducted in Stage One yielded several possible strategies. A forum was held in April 2000; its purpose was to select a strategy to pilot test. The forum included members from the advisory committee for the project, other community leaders, youth who had participated in the interviews, and project staff. The idea of holding a forum to inform decisions regarding the next stage of the research was consistent with PAR principles in that the forum engaged people who were affected by the issues in decision–making. One of the primary considerations in selecting a strategy was that it needed to be feasible within the context of the existing resources, staffing, and locale.

Based on the forum, the strategy that was selected was a peer mentoring and life skills workshop series that would be co-facilitated by young people who were part of the project team (April Barlow and Erinn Brown). Our purpose in Stage Two was twofold: To help support youth in their transition from care by offering peer-supported, independent living skills and peer mentor training; and to create a cohort of trained peer mentors who would then be available in the community for youth currently in care.

The two co-facilitators had prior experience of living in care and thus knew first-hand some of the challenges facing youth leaving care. In addition, they had some experience with group facilitation. Perhaps most importantly, though, by having the young adult members of the project team take on the co-facilitation role, they were in a position to act as role models for the youth participants.[3]

Eight youths participated in the workshops. Six were female, two were male, and they ranged in age from 17–20. One of the youth was parenting an infant, one self-identified as being Aboriginal, and one was a visible minority. Most youth were in the process of completing their high school; as well, several held part-time jobs. Three of the participants were in the Ministry's Independent Living[4] program and had been living on their own, though often with roommates, for at least several months. Three participants were still living in foster care and two were living on their own and receiving income assistance.

Stage Two Evaluation: Youth Participants' Evaluation of the Workshops and Team Members' Evaluation of the Stage Two Process

We were committed to learning from the experience of piloting the workshop series. As well, the youth participants completed written evaluations, based on one-page evaluation forms, after each workshop session. An evaluation focus group was held with the youth participants upon completion of the workshops. In addition, a joint evaluation interview was conducted with the two young adult workshop co-facilitators, carried out by the adult members of the team. Finally, all team members wrote out their reflections on Stage Two processes and lessons, which informed the production of the Stage Two report.

Challenges and Contradictions, Opportunities and Contributions

Given the length and multifaceted nature of the project, it is probably not surprising that we encountered both bumpy patches along with periods of smooth sailing in our project's process. In hindsight, a number of our rough spots were akin to the kinds of challenges or conundrums noted in the PAR research literature, particularly with regard to balancing PAR "ideals" with the potentially competing requirements of a funding body, university, and multiple professional regulatory bodies. As well, upon reflection, the process-related challenges that arose in our project may have come as a result of our naive or inadequate assumptions about PAR and the practice of PAR with marginalized youth. Below, we reflect on the dilemmas we encountered as well as our successes in carrying out a project with youth in/from care guided by PAR principles.

Issues of Power and Location within the Work Environment

Based on the principle that in PAR everyone is working, researching, and learning together, we assumed that undertaking PAR with marginalized youth meant that we would strive to create a work environment in which there was input from all team members, everyone's ideas were valued as having merit, and that no one person would have sole power and authority over decision making. Our attempts to create such a work environment failed to take into account that differences in responsibility, authority, power, knowledge, and life circumstances did exist. For instance, three team members were named in the project proposal and presumably could not be dismissed from the project, while the other three members were employees who presumably could get fired. Thus, try as we might to disregard or mask our locations within the project, our power differentials were inherent from the beginning. As a result of our self-evaluation process midway into the project, this became more explicit. Recognizing that this was the case was somewhat of a relief to the whole team because it allowed for more honest discussions and clarity about our various roles within the team.

Another difference among team members was how much accountability each team member held. For example, Deborah was ultimately accountable to both the B.C. Health Research Foundation and to the Office of Research Administration at the university. As such she was regarded as the "voice of authority" on matters pertaining to conduct of the research (e.g., doing the interviews and analyzing the data). As well, both Deb and Carol were members of professional associations with established practice-related accountabilities. By contrast, the youth team members felt more accountable to their own community of youth from care and, in one instance, to street youth.

Despite these differences, the team made decisions jointly and created a joint work plan. We found that the downside of not assigning roles was that we did not create and did not have a consistent, agreed-upon process to deal with problematic issues. Thus, while the different types of accountability were managed within this structure, there were instances of role strain that had to be addressed.

For example, we realize that the lack of assigned job duties, time sheets, and concrete, day-to-day tasks affected team members differently. Ironically, perhaps, this lack of structure created significant challenges for the youth team members in particular as they were less used to working in such a loosely structured environment where they were expected to get their work done, but without a lot of direct supervision. For one youth team member, these struggles were exacerbated by the fact that she had few internal or external resources to fall back on, even relative to the other young adult researchers. This made it difficult for her to cope with the expectations she felt from the rest of the team to be at work or to follow through on her assignments. In the end, this youth was fired from the project largely because the other two youth team members were unhappy with both her limited presence and contributions, which they felt were lacking relative to their own level of effort and productivity.

Taking our assumption about PAR one step further, initially we believed that equality in all project decision making was both feasible and a main priority. Shared decision making was challenging, in that it was highly time consuming. We had to allow time to discuss, argue, and debate items, which then affected the timeliness of accomplishing some tasks. Nevertheless, for most matters, except those relating to personnel, shared decision making was valued and worked well in that it allowed everyone to fully explore the issues, to provide input, and to be comfortable with the direction of the project.

Our commitment to shared decision making was eventually modified to not include personnel matters. For example, in the situation described above in which one of the youth team members had great difficulty in meeting the team's collective expectations, Deborah and Carol were initially reluctant to be seen as imposing their "higher authority" on the situation. They tried to find ways to accommodate the youth team member and retain her on the project. The other two youth team members, by contrast, were most affronted by the situation. They believed that Carol and Deb should have been quicker to take action in identifying and resolving the situation (i.e., by firing the staff member). In the end, the team jointly decided that personnel decisions needed to be made by the person with the designated authority and accountability within the university setting; however, those decisions were largely vetted and supported by the whole team.

Another dimension of our assumption that doing PAR meant working non-hierarchically was our belief that the development of the research process should emerge from the group. These beliefs seemed connected to a central tenet of PAR: that research conducted and driven by oppressed people in communities should have the same legitimacy and status as research conducted within the academy. Thus, Deb and Carol initially shied away from "training" the young adult team members in "credible" research methods. Yet all of us were aware that certain ways of doing research were understood to have more credibility than others (or at least credibility within the professional/academic research community). After we completed several research interviews and collectively concluded that the data we were getting were below par, we recognized that we all needed to know and consistently use certain approaches in data collection and analysis. For example, in analyzing our own research practice, we discovered that the youth members of our team tended to use our interview guide as a questionnaire, which elicited less information. As well, when it came time to transcribe the interviews, some team members summarized the interviews, while others transcribed them verbatim. Our process for working through this issue was to spend considerable time in team meetings to discuss the various ways the interviews could be conducted and then transcribed, along with the benefits or limitations of each approach. This ultimately led to a consensus among the team as to how best to proceed, as all team members wanted the project to have credibility as a research project (indeed, the consensus that the team arrived at was in keeping with standard research practices for qualitative data gathering and analysis). Thus, through the time-consuming discussions leading to consensus, we managed to reconcile the potentially competing goals of PAR: credibility vs. consciousness raising. However, to be clear, this was done at the expense of expediency!

Participation

Initially we assumed that we'd be able to find certain times to meet as a team, and that team members would all be available to meet at some point during the day, Monday to Friday. The team agreed to hold regular weekly meetings to help ensure that the project was on track. However, because everyone's positions on the project were part-time, all team members held other jobs/contracts. Having multiple jobs/projects affected team members differently. For the young adult team members, their additional jobs had set hours. By contrast, Carol and Deb had contracts that were more flexible, albeit with set deadlines and deliverables. All of this made finding a common meeting time problematic. Moreover, one youth held several jobs, which meant that her availability was quite circumscribed. As such she wanted to hold team meetings on weekends or in the evenings during the week. This did not work for three of the team members who had families, including one young adult team member with children who had a carefully constructed parental sharing arrangement. To complicate scheduling further, this young mother was not able to afford after-school child care and therefore could meet only between 9 a.m. and 2 p.m. We might have been able to adapt to this circumstance by having the project pay for child care whenever team meetings were scheduled after school hours, but this possibility did not come up, in part because the team member who held multiple jobs was available only after 5 p.m., which was an impossible time for team members with families.

We share the minutiae of this story in order to make the point that, in the interest of involving youth from care as co-researchers, i.e., one of our social justice goals, we struggled to maximize participation of youth from care for more than two years. Ultimately the young person with multiple jobs chose on her own to leave the project at the end of the second year, reducing the team to two adults and two young adult members.

Another challenge for the team was that the limited resources of the project budget meant that we were unable to adequately provide resources to facilitate the participation of all team members. In hindsight, it was an oversight on our part not to have requested resources to purchase computer equipment for the project. This meant that all team members had to either possess or have access to personal resources such as a computer, printer, fax machine, and so forth. Alternatively they needed to be able to get to the research office in the School of Social Work, where such resources were available. The university was not as accessible to those in the project team with limited funds who had to rely on public transportation and/or were not comfortable in the academic environment. Eventually Carol was able to provide a spare

172

computer and printer for the research office (which was downtown in a central location), which alleviated some of tension.

Striving to Enable Participation ... While not Recognizing that Team Members Might Need Additional Support to Participate

As noted above, our assumptions about egalitarian work environments led us to overlook the need for creating structure and supervisory relationships. Inherent in this was our assumption that all team members could take initiative in doing tasks and work with minimal structure; our team approach also presumed a high level of interpersonal skills (i.e., in problem solving, exchange of ideas, analysis, group process, and so forth) among all team members.

These were high expectations; indeed, they were expectations we probably did not realize we held at the outset of the project, as they were in large part the way that Deb, Carol, and April worked in their other projects. These expectations were, moreover, not realistic for all team members. A couple of the youth team members had difficulty with what they perceived as a lack of direction. One may have been used to and needed a structured and highly supervised work environment for employment success.

Finally, in keeping with PAR principles, we expected and assumed that youth from/in care would be interested in the project either in a volunteer capacity (for which they would receive an honorarium) and/or as paid members of the project team. We now believe that it was unfair to expect that youth from care could volunteer on a regular or ongoing basis, and that this expectation did not reflect their real life circumstances and needs with regard to self-sufficiency and survival. Furthermore, volunteering one's time tends to be more of a middle-class activity as it is easier to volunteer when one is secure in the knowledge that other basic needs in life are already taken care of. Ongoing youth participation needed to be funded on a wider scale than we made provision for in the project.

Expecting youth involvement over the course of several months or years also does not recognize the often transient and uncertain nature of young people's lives. At the same time, once the "participatory relationship" is defined by regular receipt of an honorarium/salary, accountability to the funder becomes a tangible reality within the project, along with the team's expectations for (youth) participants'

173

contributions and commitment. As well, receiving payment from the project (which had to be documented through the university's accounting department) potentially negatively affected those youth who were receiving income assistance because their income assistance would be reduced by the same amount.

Opportunities and Contributions

Having described the numerous challenges we encountered, there also were many ways in which the project not only followed PAR and AOP principles but also made contributions to social justice (albeit on a small scale).

The youth researchers who remained on the team often stated that they were cognizant from other work-related experiences that the project provided them with a decent wage. Indeed, the salary offered through the project was significantly higher than what youth earned in their other jobs. Not only did the youth note the difference in wages, they also commented from time to time on the work environment being different and more respectful than in their other employment experiences. For example, one person worked in the restaurant/ nightclub industry, which, in her experience, did not pretend to create a decent work environment and paid her in cash only. There were stretches of time when she did not receive payment. Another young adult team member supervised access visits between parents and their children, where she was expected to follow orders, but had no other meaningful input into the way in which the work was constructed or how the parents/children were treated. Both were low-paying jobs.

Our aim was to create and maintain a respectful atmosphere wherein everyone's contribution had value and all team members had equal opportunity to explore their skill sets and take the lead or provide direction to the project. This was unlike their previous or current work experiences and was invaluable to helping the teamwork through tensions mentioned previously.

The project also provided valuable learning experiences for youth who had been in care. In Stage Two, the team decided to create a series of life skills workshops that would help youth begin to prepare for leaving care. Two young adult team members designed these workshops, based on a combination of their own interests and experiences, along with input from youth participants in the workshops. The workshops were designed so that others could easily modify or adapt them to their own needs and circumstances. In designing the materials for the workshops, April and Erinn were very creative in drawing upon their own experiences and knowledge of life as youth living in care or about to be living alone, and in soliciting the ongoing input from youth participants about what they wanted to do and how they wanted to learn. April and Erinn facilitated the workshops together; they prepared for this in part by attending a workshop on group facilitation (paid for by the project).

Youth were also involved in writing all reports and the Life Skills Workshops Facilitators' Guide. For some with more limited writing experience and skills, writing was a challenge, especially writing more academically oriented publications, including reports to the funders. Nevertheless, all team members were given the opportunity to draft and/or provide feedback on drafts of all project reports, articles, and so forth, and all team members contributed to final products. (At the same time, participating in the writing was not a requirement imposed on team members.) Team members who were most comfortable and interested in writing (regardless of age and location within the team) generally wrote first drafts, while everyone provided ample feedback and participated in discussions about our products during team meetings. In addition, after the completion of the second workshop series, the young adult co-facilitators worked together to write and edit "Stepping Stones: Life Skills Workshops for Youth Leaving Care: A Facilitators' Guide." This involved a significant amount of time, as they had to decide on a format and layout for the guide, locate references and materials, and also refine the resources that they had created for individual workshops.

Youth gained computer skills, including desktop publishing. Through the course of creating the facilitators' guide, the young adult team members gained and/or had an opportunity to enhance their computer-related skills in desktop publishing, editing, formatting, and use of software.

Finally, several youth (all youth who expressed interest) participated in the project's advisory committee and were provided with an honorarium for doing so. They provided input into the design of our project, advised on practical matters, and were recognized for their lived expertise in relation to foster care issues. Youth's participation on the project's advisory committee also facilitated their involvement with the B.C. Federation of Youth in Care Networks. Moreover, on several occasions our youth advisory committee members were invited to participate in or provide feedback on other ministry initiatives, such as the drafting of the youth policy framework. Youth appreciated these opportunities in which they assumed the role of expert rather than the role of client.

Conclusions

At the end of our project, we came to the conclusion that while social justice goals can be achieved through participatory action research projects, the location of the project can determine the extent to which these goals are achieved. For example, pure PAR may be more achievable within a peer model framework wherein the imperative and initiative for the inquiry are really coming from the grassroots level and the thrust is not so much research as it is community development and ownership of the knowledge.

We also found that it is difficult to achieve broad-scale social justice goals in a research project without continuous review of principles of AOP at an individual/team level. We had to work within the constraints of the funder and research expectations, but could have addressed some of the practical day-to-day issues differently such as child care and structure of the work. At the same time, we did in a small way achieve social justice goals because the young adult team members earned a better wage than they received elsewhere and were able to explore and expand their skills and knowledge in several areas.

At the same time, continuously looking at relationships through the lens of AOP misses the complexity of relationships—power, class, privilege, or other such dynamics did not drive all of our interactions. Personality conflicts were present too as were challenges associated with our own lives, and these factors cut across age, class, power, and so forth. Working as we did allowed us to focus on the same goal and not cleave ourselves apart on the basis of our differences. While we may have missed opportunities to address imbalances, on the whole we developed respectful and caring relationships that helped us to talk through tense moments. As a result, on many occasions we were able to challenge each other's assumptions and to learn from each other as a result.

It is unclear what influence we (i.e., all members of the project team) had on the youth who participated in the workshops, as we were unable to maintain contact with them once the workshops/project ended. However, it is unlikely that what we did changed their circumstances much. For those who were living in government care, availability of resources and support continued to dwindle. At the same time, in terms of the political context, a change in the provincial government resulted in increasingly more stringent rules regarding accessing services or income assistance. Thus, youth in and from care continued to have to do more with less, and in this regard, the project most likely failed to achieve social justice for the group members. However, it did provide them with a reasonable honorarium for their participation (both in the research interviews and in the life skills workshops) as well as a completion bonus at the end of the workshops series, and to the extent that this gave the youth a small amount of financial relief, then we did achieve something worthwhile. Also, some youth received direct one-to-one help with some crucial areas of their lives, such as applying for income assistance or education courses.

And what about the project team (i.e., the young adults and adults who signed on for this experiment in working together)? Our postscript to this chapter is that in June 2003 we received a three-year grant from the National Crime Prevention Centre to follow what happens to a sample of youth once they exit from foster/government care, particularly in relation to their social relationships, involvement with the criminal justice system, education, and employment. We also are examining how policies and programs can help or hinder successful transitions from care. Although our current project does not profess to be guided by PAR principles, our approach to working together has carried on from the "Supporting Young People's Transitions from Care" project. And we continue to challenge each other's assumptions and beliefs on an ongoing basis! As well, on a personal note, four years after the first project started, one of the young adult team members decided to get her degree in social work, the other decided to complete Grade 12, and Carol and Deb continue to bring PAR and social justice principles into their other research and contracted projects. To researchers interested in PAR projects and processes, we offer these final words: Despite the challenges of doing PAR within traditional academic environments, there is much to be gained by taking them on, not the least of which is the potential for consciousness raising within the walls of the academy! Moreover, there is much to be gained by bringing certain hallmarks of an AOP approach into PAR processes, especially reflexivity by the project team and participants. Making time for ongoing reflection and critical analysis, including how the project is or is not adhering to its principles, is essential for good research practice and, in turn, for social justice outcomes.

Notes

1. The B.C. Health Research Foundation was disbanded in late 2000, but funding for our project was provided for its full term, from April 1999 to June 2001.
2. From our informal conversations with a member of the BCHRF adjudication committee, we were also aware that the committee was primarily comprised of researchers who valued and had expertise in traditional, quantitative, objective health services research. While BCHRF was attempting to expand the types of projects it funded, it was our impression that the people who were making the decisions were nonetheless unfamiliar with community-based research using qualitative and/or non-traditional methodologies.
3. Our Stage Two report (available through the authors) provides an in-depth discussion of: Stage Two workshop planning; participant recruitment; involving youth in the planning process; workshop topics and format; having food as a part of the process; peer support/mentoring by the workshop co-facilitators; and working together as a young adult/adult team. Also see D. Rutman, C. Hubberstey, A. Barlow, E. Brown, Supporting Young People's Transitions from Care, *Canada's Children … Les Enfants du Canada* 8 (Winter 2001), 27–31.
4. In British Columbia, Independent Living is a program to "help youth in care, age 16 and older, become independent" (Ministry for Children and Family web site). Youth need to obtain permission from their social worker to participate in the program. Through the IL program, a youth receives funds for rent and food, a bus pass, and a clothing allowance.

References

Barlow, A. (1997). *Victoria youth in care network: Options for action.* Victoria: Victoria Youth in Care Network.

B.C. Task Force on Safeguards for Children and Youth in Foster or Group Home Care. (1997). *Report of the Task Force on Safeguards for Children and Youth in Foster or Group Home Care.* Commissioned by the Minister for Children and Families, Province of British Columbia.

Dominelli, L. (2002). Group interventions and collective action. In L. Dominelli, *Anti-oppressive social work theory and practice*. New York: Palgrave Macmillan.

Freire, P. (1970). *Pedagogy of the oppressed*. New York: Continuum Publishing.

Hall, B.L. (1979). Participatory research: An approach for change. *Convergence* 9 (2), 24–32.

Hick, S. (2002). Anti-oppressive practice: Challenges for social work. *Critical Social Work* 2, 1–5.

Leischner, C. (2002). Oral presentation. FAS, power, and relationships. 6th National Health Promotion Conference, April, Victoria, B.C.

Leischner, C. (2004). Participatory action research. Virtual presentation on PAR, March 17, 2004. Also see: "Participatory Evaluation" at www.nfhs-ph.org

Maguire, P. (1988). *Doing participatory research: A feminist approach*. The Centre for International Education. Amherst: University of Massachusetts Press.

Martin, F. (1996). Tales of transition: Leaving public care. In B. Galaway and J. Hudson (Eds.), *Youth in transition: Perspectives on research and policy*, pp. 99–106. Toronto: Thompson Educational Publishing.

Potts, K. (1997). What is participatory action research? Unpublished paper.

Potts, K. (no date). Paradigms and power: Social change and anti-oppressive approaches to research. Course syllabus, University of Victoria, B.C.

Raychaba, B. (1988). *To be on our own with no direction from home: A report on the special needs of young people leave the care of the child welfare system*. Ottawa: National Youth in Care Network.

Rutman, D., Barlow, A., Alusik, D., Hubberstey, C., and Brown, E. (2003). Supporting young people's transitions from government care. In K. Kufeldt and B. McKenzie (Eds.), *Child welfare: Connecting research, policy and practice*, 227—238. Waterloo: Wilfrid Laurier University Press.

Rutman, D., Barlow, A., Hubberstey, C., Alusik, D., and Brown, E. (2001). *Supporting young people's transitions from government care: Stage one report*. Victoria: University of Victoria.

Tandon, R. (1988). Social transformation and participatory research. *Convergence* 21, (2/3), 5–15.

Thompson, N. (2001). *Anti-discriminatory practice* (3rd edition). Basingstoke: Palgrave.

Victoria Sexually Exploited Youth Task Force. (1997). *Report of the sexually exploited youth task force of the CRD*. Victoria: City of Victoria, Community Development and Leisure Services Department.

CHAPTER SEVEN

WIFE RENA TEARY

Rena Miller

Personal Experience and Institutional Ethnography

Several years ago, while I was in the middle of a graduate program in social work, my husband, Jim, became suddenly and fatally ill. A Vietnam veteran and war resister, Jim was diagnosed with a deadly form of cancer connected to previous Agent Orange exposure. I withdrew from my academic courses and, with our two sons, cared for him at home until he died. During these four brief and rapid months, while I was preoccupied by practical details and struggling to understand what was happening, I also discovered myself as a relentless observer.

At this time I did not think of myself as a researcher, but as a practitioner who was obliged as a graduate student to do research. In the process of writing my thesis—and even more acutely in the process of preparing this chapter—I became aware of these early observations as the very beginning of my research into my own experience. In this process I mentally noted, filed, and speculated upon my own and others' reactions and behaviour. My encounters with the community palliative care system were particularly intriguing and sometimes troubling to me, especially in the context of my graduate studies. In one course, for example, I had critiqued a particular palliative care intake and assessment form, which was used with me (or perhaps it would be more accurate to say *on me*) as a client six months later.

I was particularly puzzled by the way in which we were frequently encouraged to utilize more services than we were requesting; this seemed odd for a health care system allegedly on a shoestring budget. My initial speculation was that the workers who interacted with us were not accurately perceiving us as strong, intelligent, and well-supported people. When I decided to research my own experience for my thesis, with the strong support of my supervisor, past moments of puzzlement became the entry points to my inquiry. Thus, I set out to explore what was happening along this "line of fault," the gap between my lived experience as the wife of a dying person and my experience as a recipient of palliative care.

This line of inquiry fit perfectly with institutional ethnography, a methodology developed by Canadian sociologist Dorothy Smith. Institutional ethnography is located within the constructivist paradigm, which assumes that all knowledge is socially constructed, and the social organization of knowledge approach, which links subjective experience through social action to the outside world. In this approach, even though experience is considered central to knowledge, "there is more to knowing than studying experience" (Campbell, personal communication, November 1996). Unlike some interpretive methodologies, the intent is to understand how everyday experience is inextricably bound to relations of dominance and subordination (Smith, G., 1995) rather than to interpret experience in a way that elevates subjectivity or illuminates individual motivations. This satisfied my preference to use my own experience as the site of my research as well as my commitment to analyzing and explaining it in political terms.

As a social work practitioner and educator, I have long-held political commitments to feminism, social justice, and resistance to oppression. Daughter of a union organizer, I joked that Marxism was the religion of my childhood, but had never relinquished my particular family values. Institutional ethnography fit well with my commitments. It required me to begin with lived experience (in this case my own), uncover how this experience happened the way that it did, and how it was shaped and organized by what Dorothy Smith (1987) calls "regimes of ruling"—in this case the social relations of bureaucratic public health care systems. My purpose was to produce an analysis that would intentionally subvert rather than support existing regimes of ruling and domination.

The primary resource for my inquiry was my own experience as I lived, remembered, and recorded it. As I lived it, I was intermittently puzzled by certain experiences and reflective about them. Three weeks after Jim died, I started to write a narrative account of the four months of his illness. I did not know at that time what I wanted to do with this narrative, but I knew that I wanted to write about it in some way.

While I was writing the narrative account, I was clearly aware of the therapeutic aspects of this activity. I had used journals before as a tool for making meaning of my experience, though I could only manage a few feeble entries during Jim's illness. But as I wrote about the past, the present kept breaking into the story as commentary, reflection, and emotional expression, and I thought of the whole process as part of my mourning.

When I first considered using my own experience as research "data," I had some doubts about its academic propriety. The notion that I could create my own data and then analyze it challenged the hegemonic belief that objectivity, neutrality, and distance are essential components of legitimate research. Having to some degree internalized this belief, I anticipated members of my thesis committee suggesting that I was too close to my data, but this never happened. Although I later came to understand the extent to which institutional ethnography has had to struggle for a place within social research, at the time it was not a marginal methodology, but a life preserver that offered me a congruent and affirming means to organize and analyze my experience. This "life preserver" was thrown to me at a critical time in my academic process by my thesis supervisor, the institutional ethnographer Dr. Marie Campbell. I initially sought her out to talk about my moments of puzzlement; her response helped me to reframe these moments as research questions. I was also fortunate to be in a graduate program in which feminist, constructivist methodologies were taught, and in which marginalized researchers—mostly women doing women's work—were encouraged to explore alternative methodologies, and to see their own experiences as legitimate sites for research. This support and legitimization allowed me to resist the doubts instilled by dominant ideas about research and knowledge production.

I wanted to understand more fully what it was that resulted in my shrugging off most professional palliative care help like an ill-fitting jacket. What I discovered was my resistance to being transformed into an object of professional work by the complex interactions of discourse, documents, and organizational practices. Each shapes and is shaped by the other to construct the palliative care patient and family as a multiproblem situation requiring the services of a multidisciplinary team. It became clear to me that the interests being served in this process are primarily those of the organizations involved. The resulting necessity to explore power relations along the line of fault between discourse and experience fit well with my intention to practise from

183

an anti-oppressive standpoint as a researcher, a teacher, and a social worker.

Wife Rena Teary: Setting the Context

In utilizing my personal experience for research, I decided to pay particular attention to those moments that I recorded or remembered as jarring or confusing in some way, as these represented the clash between discourse and lived experience that served as the entry points to my analysis. In addition and in contrast to my journal, I analyzed the *Palliative Care at Home Manual*, and material from Jim's care file at the regional health office, obtained through freedom of information procedures.

It was my observation that community care for dying people was organized around *Palliative Care at Home*, produced by the Victoria Hospice Society. The manner in which a home care nurse issued this document to us led us to nickname it the "Holy Binder." I obtained a photocopy of this manual, which included several forms that seemed significant to the organization of palliative care, and I also requested a copy of Jim's files from the local community health unit, asking for files from both Home Nursing Care and Long-Term Care. When the package arrived in the mail, I was actually surprised at how much was there—32 pages of file material, including pages from the B.C. Cancer Agency and a private home health care agency.

When I first looked through what I was now beginning to think of as "data," I noticed myself described as a "very supportive, caring wife," Jim as "intelligent, insightful man. Self-determining ++," and our situation as "Close family. Devoted wife, sons. Many good friends, neighbours offering support." The guilt that I have frequently felt in pursuing my research question attacked me once more. How, after reading this, could I have the perception of not being seen for myself or truly heard by community health professionals? Was researching my own experience just another way for me to unleash my anger at the "system"? Then I remembered that the social worker who wrote the latter two comments was the same person who, in the same encounter, advised me to go away for the weekend by myself even though she recorded Jim's prognosis as four to eight weeks to live (in fact he died three weeks later). The data then became even more mysterious to me, revealing that the worker had both a realistic idea of

Jim's prognosis, and a realistic idea of our family and living situation. That she strongly advised me to go away for the weekend *anyway* and have a home support worker(s) look after Jim seemed contradictory. Her recommendation to me was not immediately apparent anywhere in the files.

I had to work hard with and against guilt as I pursued my research. I experienced guilt frequently enough to think of it as a perverse research associate whose objections I had to overcome. As I reviewed aspects of palliative care in the community, I found myself feeling guilty for being critical of particular individuals or services, just as I had felt guilty for my negative reactions to professionals during Jim's illness. Guilt told me that the negative feelings that resurfaced as I worked on my data, which ranged from annoyance to irritation to anger, were merely symptoms of my grieving process. Guilt suggested that my research was not research but actually a therapeutic exercise in "working through my anger" and that this was inconsistent with academic standards that I wanted (and needed) to meet. Again I surprised myself with the extent to which dominant ideas about objectivity, which I consciously rejected, were embedded in my personal conceptualization of acceptable research subjects and methods.

Guilt also constrained me from talking about my work with other graduate students, many of whom worked in the same programs that I was critiquing. When I did become involved in discussion of what I was doing, I sometimes encountered defensiveness, or perhaps guilt told me I was making people defensive. Even though I tried hard not to criticize individuals, I was quickly silenced by some reactions, such as "Others need these services" and "You were in a privileged position," neither of which I was disputing. I was well aware of the privilege conferred by our personal relationship with our physician, for example, and our well-developed support system, both of which allowed me to not need the services I was critiquing. But I was also still very close to Jim's death, and in my grieving process, silence was often more sustainable than argument.

Guilt also motivated me to dig deeper into the data—my memories, the documents—in order to argue back against it. I wanted to understand how ruling relations not only organized the practice of the workers but also the way in which I experienced their practice. I often looked for parallels in my own life as a social worker. In this way I tried to turn the tables on guilt, exploring guilt itself as data. Paying attention to the context in which guilt arose became an important part of my analysis, providing additional insight into the social construction of palliative care patients and palliative care practices.

Wife Rena Teary: The Data

One example of the many ways in which my interaction with Home Nursing Care (a community health care program) was organized by documents is contained in a form used by the nurses to record their work. Reflecting on this document's problem focus, I came to recognize the significance of the nurse's recording of an interaction involving myself, Jim, and the palliative care nurse. The form required that the nurse find and record manageable problems. Through using the methods of institutional ethnography, I developed an analysis of how the nurse's recording constructed Jim and myself as "problems" to which palliative care work processes had to be applied. Based on this analysis, I contended that the nurse's work process, organized around the discovery and documentation of problems, was oriented to organizational interests rather than ours. As a social worker myself, I can speculate that these organizational interests might involve the demonstration of accountability and objectivity. While I recognize that the nurses were conducting their work competently and professionally, indeed using the very concepts and language that I found in the palliative care literature, this resulted in my feeling objectified by being treated as a problem with a solution. This document-driven, problem-focused approach fits comfortably within the medical model and the palliative care discourse, and may well have fit within the needs of the organization. The only place this world of manageable problems did not fit was the world of our house and the experience we lived there.

I found ample evidence of the problem-building process in the document that is the focus of this example, a form with the printed title "Open Flow Sheet," a document used by home care nurses to record their visits and telephone contacts with us. The document's "openness" appears to relate to its use as a shared communication tool by various staff members. Each one who had contact with us contributed notes to the same document. As a flow sheet, the document seems to work by providing an overall sense of the flow or progress of the team's work from contact to contact. It consists of a grid of squares or boxes. Six vertical columns to the right are each headed by a handwritten indication of the date and time of the contact. Typed assessment numbers and problem names head the horizontal columns. The home care nurse then writes comments in each box, documenting the visit or telephone contact. At the bottom are boxes for the visit number and the nurse's signature. On the flow sheet used with our family, four different signatures appear on the two pages of the form, covering three visits and nine telephone calls.

The nurse, through this form, is led to structure each contact with the palliative patient around problems. Every comment she makes relates to a specific "problem name"; presumably she is being asked to describe the parameters of the problem. This fits with my conceptualization of the palliative care discourse as problem-saturated. While this may be considered a feature of the medical model generally, an extra urgency exists around palliative care. I describe this as an effort to resolve the irresolvable by breaking down the process of dying into a set of manageable problems.

My experience as one of the objects of this work begins to make sense when overlaid by the grid of the "Open Flow Sheet." The first visit, by Nurse B., was our after-hours intake meeting when we received the "Holy Binder." The second visit, by Nurse V., was in response to my request for assistance with a pressure sore Jim had developed on his coccyx after three days in hospital. Nurse V.'s notations for the visit suggest that describing our situation in terms of problems was a stretch. She commented on the other "problems" listed in a way that seemed to indicate that they weren't really problems. For example, under "Feelings & Attitudes," she wrote: "Cheerful, wife and client managing care at present." There seems something ominous about the phrase "at present," as if it forecast a future inability (which never actually materialized).

After V.'s visit there were two telephone contacts by our "regular" nurse, N. Nurse N. questioned me about each of the problem areas and wrote comments such as "[coccyx] dry and healing?"; "wife says things are stable"; and finally, "would like HNC visit Mon. a.m. to assess." What I remember about these two phone calls was N. saying that she "really should" have a home visit with us, since she was our regular nurse and she hadn't met us face to face. I distinctly recall her telling me that the visit would take about an hour. I don't think I requested it, but she may have asked me something like "Would you like me to come on Monday morning?" to which I must have replied in the affirmative. Perhaps it seemed inescapable. My clear memory of the visit as an event that N. required was translated in the official record into a statement that I would like a visit. This translation relates directly to the dependence of her work on the existence of manageable problems. In this instance, I see the nurse reconstructing our interaction into a formulation that is both ideologically correct and organizationally relevant, one in which we have the problem for which we require her professional assessment and intervention. If I had declined visits and insisted that there were no problems, perhaps there would be no work to be done on us. Would this create an organizational problem for the nurse on whose caseload we fell?

N.'s visit took place on February 20, 1995. I wrote about it: "She stayed for about an hour, which was way too long for Jim, who actually got a bit testy with her towards the end." I remember sitting on the couch with N., Jim facing us in his easy chair, as she worked her way down the checklist. Now that I know she was looking for problems to record, her persistent gentle probing and sad, compassionate gaze are more understandable to me. The column on the flow chart that represents this visit includes as categories "Medication: done—see med list"; "Skin Integrity: Healed"; "Pain Control: MS contin 30 mg. BID"; "Signs & Symptoms: Abd. more distended"; "Elimination, Voiding & B.M.: Reg, with colase." So far, no "real problems" had been identified. Finally, under "Coping with ADL" (activities of daily living), N. found a problem to report: "Wife Rena teary. She has requested counselling."

Somewhere in our conversation, I had asked N. about the services available through Hospice. It was not convenient for me to attend the weekly caregivers' support group, and I wondered about other groups. I was also looking for an individual counselling session, assuming, as a counsellor myself, that this would be helpful to me. I mentioned that I had telephoned Hospice, asking for a counselling appointment over two weeks previously, and that I hadn't heard back. It's possible I became teary at this stage of N.'s visit, though I didn't record that in my journal. What I wrote about crying was that I seemed to cry frequently for days at a time, so much so that I reminded myself of Alice in her sea of tears. This was followed by a dry, arid, empty period of several days. Being teary, in my view, was not a problem but a welcome relief from the emptiness, and a regular means of expression—part of what my sons called the "new normal." It was not how I would have primarily characterized myself, yet it was how N., who needed problems to record and work on, characterized me. The recording of the problems fixed us more securely within the framework of the palliative care discourse and the requirements of the organization, making it possible for us to become her "work" within the problem context.

During this visit and afterwards, N. worked on the problem of "Wife Rena teary" in several ways. In the immediate moment, she encouraged me to express my emotions. This type of intervention was rated by families of terminally ill patients as "least helpful" in one study I reviewed (Weatherill, 1995, p. 51), and was similarly unwelcome to me. She also began to look through the *Palliative Care at Home Manual* for the information I was seeking about groups. "It's on a page with a flower," she repeated several times while leafing through the manual. Jim and I sat patiently waiting for her to complete this task, which we could just as easily have done ourselves. In the end the task was futile; the "page with the flower" was not to be found, though N. used a good portion of her hour with us searching for it. This was not the way in which we would choose to spend our very precious and limited time, and Jim later referred to this incident derisively when refusing further visits from N. "I don't need her over here looking for the page with the flower," he said.

At the bottom of the column of problems, under the heading "Report to Doctor," N. wrote: "PC to Hospice. Dr. to visit tonight." I assume that the first part of this comment, the phone call to Hospice, was also work performed by N. on the problem of "Wife Rena teary." This work fit with her role as the coordinator of our care, a role sanctioned for home care nurses throughout the palliative care literature and discourse. N., having successfully located and identified a problem, performs work on this problem, both directly on me, and indirectly through her phone call to Hospice. I suspect that this telephone call motivated the subsequent call I received from a Hospice counsellor to make an appointment. In the recording of my next contact with N., a telephone call one week later, she notes at the bottom, "Wife to see Hospice counsellor." The manageable problem of "Wife Rena teary" has been thus documented and resolved, even though it was not a problem and not resolvable in the world of my experience.

Conversely, N. only faintly alluded to the part of the visit that I reacted to most strongly and wrote about in my notes in her final comment, "Dr. to visit tonight." My journal reads:

> N. was very keen that we should fill in and sign the "Do Not Resuscitate Order." This was a form at the back of the Palliative Care Manual. We'd been told by everyone not to call 911 if anything happened to Jim, unless we wanted the paramedics to undertake life-saving measures. They had to do this unless a DNR order was

signed and waved in their faces. We were told to call Hospice instead where a Palliative Response Team was available after hours ... but N. kept going on about the DNR order and how important it was. She said that if many different people were in the house providing care, someone might call 911 by mistake. We said we would discuss it with Dave [Jim's G.P.] when he made his home visit that night.

When Dave showed up, he told us that N. had called him at his office to inform him that we hadn't yet signed the DNR order and suggest that he encourage us to do so. It pissed us all off that she called Dave "behind our backs."

"What do you need her for?" Dave asked me. Jim had already made it clear that he didn't need her for anything, and didn't want her to come over.

I said that I wanted somebody to see Jim, look at him, on a regular basis.

"Why? What do you think she'll see?" Dave was soft-spoken but insistent.

"I don't know ... how he's doing ... if he needs anything ... "

"He isn't going to need anything that he can't tell you about himself," Dave said. "Or if he can't tell you, you'll see for yourself what he needs. You don't need to bother with the DNR order if you don't need the nurse, and you don't need the nurse—you've got me."

This was very affirming. Dave convinced me that I could manage without N., without the Palliative Response Team, and without Long-Term Care. This was a big relief to Jim, and it allowed us to keep our home full of people who loved us, and not people who were working on us.

It is interesting that this aspect of the visit and follow-up, which was so significant to me, becomes invisible in N.'s account. "Dr. to visit tonight" is noted, but there is no record of a "PC to Dr." or of the DNR order itself. Perhaps this is because of the difficulty in assigning the event to any of the predetermined problem categories. Perhaps N. did not perceived it as a "problem," but somehow it was subsumed into the part of her work that was neither documentable nor recordable. After all, as a friend familiar with the forms pointed out to me, the boxes to write in are quite small, so the nurse has to be selective in recording. Our perception that N. was "harping" on the DNR order and "tattling" on us to the doctor was selected out in favour of the problem of "Wife Rena teary."

To Jim and me, the significance of the "harping and tattling" was that it resulted in our declining further visits from Home Nursing Care for the foreseeable future. We perceived the behaviour that N. probably saw as so routine that it wasn't necessary to record as intrusive and disrespectful. It is only since I have researched the palliative care literature that I have begun to understand this behaviour differently. I see now that N. was fulfilling her role as the coordinator of the multidisciplinary team, which is itself a standard, almost institutionalized, model of service. Our brief experience of being the objects of such teamwork threatened us with the loss of self-determination and decision-making power. I wrote in my journal: "Dave's not a team player, he wants to be the kingpin—and I'm glad." I was fortunate that both Jim and Dave were so sure that "the old-fashioned way is best"; without Jim's quiet strength and Dave's unconditional support, I might not have been as assertive as I needed to be in declining further visits from N., as well as other palliative care services.

N. continued to work on the problem of "Wife Rena teary" through two subsequent telephone contacts. On March 6 she started a new "Open Flow Sheet," in which she omitted some of the previous categories, and added "General Status" and "Family Coping" as problem names. In the latter box she observed on March 6: "Rena's OK but shows stress. Seeing E. [Hospice counsellor] today. Jim doesn't want more people." One week later, March 13, she wrote, "Rena feels better seeing E." These notations are puzzling to me except as a representation of work performed to solve a manageable problem of her own construction. I first of all wondered how I "showed stress" over the telephone. Guilt—familiar companion of my research—tempted me to dismiss this query as semantic quibbling. After all, there was no doubt that I was under stress, which was probably evident in my voice. Consulting my daybook, I saw that March 6 was not only the day of my counselling appointment with E., but also the day that we were setting up a hospital bed in the living room. Jim had become too weak to climb steps, and we had to make the difficult decision to move downstairs. He would sleep in the hospital bed, and I would use a foam mattress on the floor; it was a wrenching loss for both of us to be unable to sleep together. No wonder I was "stressed."

Reviewing the "Open Flow Sheet," I realized that what was jarring to me about "Rena's OK but shows stress" was its total separation and distinction from the issue of the hospital bed. In the very first problem category, ADLs, N. wrote on March 6, "Hospital Bed being set up," an entry that is physically separated from "Family Coping," the very last problem category listed. Nothing links them together on the flow sheet, and my perception remains that "Hospital Bed being set up" was entered as a solution to the manageable problem of Jim's declining strength. To me, "Hospital Bed being set up" was a problem: a separation foreshadowing the impending and final separation, and thus an integral part of the huge, irresolvable problem of Jim's dying. There's something belittling about seeing this graphically reduced to separate manageable bits in the "Open Flow Sheet," something that seems smug and self-serving about the tidy solutions provided for these constructed problems.

The final resolution to "Wife Rena teary" is the entry, "Rena feels better seeing E." Looking at this entry, I once again feel bemused at the way my experience has been altered and disguised. First of all, I found it a challenge to get to see E.; as already pointed out, I made two phone calls and N. made one before she contacted me. After our appointment at Hospice on March 6, E. went on holiday, and though she did give me her home number, I didn't use it. I did not meet with her again until after Jim's death; I wasn't "seeing her regularly" as suggested by N.'s note.

I wrote in my journal about the appointment with E. that "it was good to have a place to just cry unreservedly without making myself stop too quickly … usually when I start to cry with my friends, they start to cry too and then my impulse is to stop sniffling and pat them on the back." I am sure that "Rena feels better seeing E." resulted from N.'s invisible questioning. At the end of an interview that otherwise elicited comments such as "Wife managing"; "No problem"; "No change"; and "Will pc if problems," I must have replied politely and positively to her questions ("Yes, I saw E. Yes, I feel better now"), and though I can't confirm this through my memory or notes, I suspect that she reached me at a non-teary moment. This allowed N. to wrap up the problem she had identified. There was no more work for her to do, although there were four more telephone calls before Jim's death, three from N. and one from Nurse W. Almost nothing is recorded on the flow sheet from these calls except "No problems" — this despite Jim's steady decline in strength and rapidly approaching death! This painful irony illustrates the way in which the palliative care discourse, the "Open Flow Sheet," and the nurses' work practices interact to construct the situation from the standpoint of the intervener — the palliative care system — in terms of manageable problems only.

I asked Jim, after my appointment with E., whether he would like her to come to the house to talk with him. I said that she was a pleasant and interesting woman, a social worker, who had a great deal of experience being with people who were dying. Perhaps she could answer some questions for him. Jim smiled and said quietly, "I'm not very interested in what happened for other people. I'm content for this to be my own unique experience." I am thankful that we were able to live out our own unique experience, the last one we would share outside the bounds of memory. My examination of the "Open Flow Sheet" confirms my intuitive knowledge about the impact that community health care services could have had on this experience, like capturing a delicate, fragile being by forcibly restraining it, altering and distorting its shape.

Wife Rena Teary: Analysis

Recently, I heard a palliative care doctor being interviewed about research he was undertaking into the spiritual needs of dying people. He said that he had been inspired to do this work by one of his patients with AIDS, a well-known writer and director who had thanked him for all his help, saying that he now had to involve himself in a spiritual journey that did not require the doctor's professional skills. The doctor realized that he indeed knew nothing about his patients' spiritual needs, and decided to research this by interviewing dying persons about their spiritual needs, so that professional interventions in this area could be developed by palliative care teams. He did not seem to understand the way in which his research negated rather than supported the message from his patient. Dorothy Smith's (1987) article, "The Social Construction of Documentary Reality," describes in detail the kind of documentary processes that I experienced in my encounters with community palliative care services. Although not describing the same bureaucratic organization, her analysis of documents and the textually mediated work of professionals provide insights into my own experiences with palliative care. Smith points out that reporting and recording practices are a socially organized method of constructing knowledge and that though these practices are "decisive to its character, their traces are not visible in it" (1987, p. 257). Techniques of eliciting information by using questions or other strategies structure the account in definite, though invisible, ways. Further, Smith argues that the social relations embedded in these structuring procedures, and in documentary reality itself, are those of ruling and domination. While it seems unpleasant—almost transgressive—to think about the helping efforts of N., E., and B. as exercising ruling and domination, it would seem that in order for us to use their services, we would have had to let their documentary reality overcome and manage our lived experience. Documentary reality was organized by social relations whose relevances originated elsewhere—in an office down the street, a very different world from the one I experienced in my home. These organizational relevances, while not immediately apparent during our interactions, were in part revealed to me as I studied the recording of their work. As Smith says, in reference to the collection of demographic data by hospitals, "how their practice intersects with the lives of those they treat and the character of their practice, constitutes that birth (or that sickness or that death) very differently from how it is constituted by those for whom and to whom it happens" (1987, p. 265).

Jim's dying was constituted by the palliative care system as its work, and the work was constituted as the resolution of a set of manageable problems. The "Open Flow Sheet" was an instrument of this construction and the nurse its active agent. The three visits and nine telephone conversations with home care nurses ranged in my perception from satisfactory to irritating. While I was aware of my resistance to using more services, it was only when I began to study the documents that I realized I had been resisting the objectification that results from being absorbed into the system. I saw how the palliative care literature, and other aspects of the discourse of palliative care that were active in popular culture, established and supported the problem orientation of the organizational document, and how both discourse and its textual manifestation directed the work of the nurse. This work is defined as the identification and resolution of the multiple problems assumed to be experienced by dying people and their family caregivers. We may also assume that the performance and documentation of this work must be articulated to the organization's systems for control and accountability.

In our experience of this process, the intertextuality of discourse, document, and work practices resulted in N.'s construction of a problem—"Wife Rena teary"—that was not a problem to us, as well as her construction of a solution—"Hospital bed being set up"—that was deeply problematic to us. This distortion of our lived experience to fit a context constructed by discourse and organization seemed even more objectifying to me as I read and re-read the file than it had at the time I lived it when my energies were preoccupied. What both Jim and I were intuitively resisting was the loss of autonomy that comes from being turned into a problem and worked on. Shaken to our roots by uncontrollable events that were changing everything for us, we resisted being reconstructed as a set of manageable physical and emotional problems to be solved by the multidisciplinary team.

Conclusion

What I learned from my research, especially my analysis of the data, has influenced me both personally and professionally. While this is only a part of the life-changing learning that I experienced in Jim's dying, it is the part most relevant to my practice as a social worker. I began my research from the standpoint of my lived experience, the irritation and disappointment with community palliative care professionals that signalled a clash or disjuncture between my world and theirs. The guilt that accompanied my criticism of their work practices recurred as I analyzed the social organization of the documents. Later, in reflecting on the process, I realized that guilt was in part inspired by my sense of the nurses and social workers involved as skilled and compassionate professionals. I knew that they were trying to help me, and the guilt was for being "ungrateful." However, my study and analysis of the documents showed me how workers' efforts were mediated by a discourse-driven organizational process that could be seen to objectify the recipient of services.

My analysis also helped me to see how the textually mediated process of helping constructs the workers involved as much as it does the clients or patients. This bridged the gap between my sense of most workers as competent and caring, and my overall experience of being objectified and misinterpreted. The organizational and discursively constructed constraints and limitations on the worker's practice may result in her own conscription as an agent of a process that I have described as both colonizing and objectifying. A process that is unable to address individual situations in any meaningful way can overwhelm the worker's caring and helpful intentions. My experience as a recipient of service, and my reflections on that experience, have greatly deflated my previously held assumptions about people's need for professional helping, as well as further developing my ideas about the value of such professional help. These ideas, whose influence on me preceded Jim's illness by several years, have had a profound impact on the way I work; my personal experience as an object of helping has strengthened and anchored my beliefs. As I engaged in my research, I thought about the many ways in which professionals create their work by defining people's lives in terms of problems to which they—the professionals, the multidisciplinary team—also have the solutions (Ferguson, 1984; Mueller, 1995). I realized how I too construct my clients according to particular organizational contexts in a way that benefits me at least as much as them.

I try to remember now that there is no escape from the very real effects of our intervention in people's lives as a researcher, teacher, or social work practitioner. I need to be able to acknowledge to people when I am engaged in a practice that objectifies them, such as writing assessment reports. Transparency may reduce client confusion, but does not reduce our complicity in objectifying practices. As a social work educator, I try to present students with similar questions for them to ponder, rather than formula-like solutions to the dilemmas of helping work. I'm aware of the risk involved in seeing any method, technique, or even way of thinking as a solution to the dilemmas of professionalized helping. We may come to believe that we have found a way of doing helping work that is not objectifying to people, that if we have the correct political perspective and the latest technology of questioning, we are not complicit in ruling processes. This would be a mistaken belief. It is important that students understand their co-optation into these practices as both the inevitable result of employment in the bureaucracy of caring and as an identifiable and resistible force.

As for research, I now understand this as part of my everyday life rather than confined to laboratories and libraries. Dorothy Smith and Marie Campbell, among others, showed me how to deconstruct the social relations of lived experience, and to analyze how they were shaped by dominance in order to resist dominance. I am aware and honoured that other graduate students have seen my thesis as a useful example of this process. My thesis also circulates, much less actively, within the Home Nursing Care program. My commitment to link my personal experience to social action led me to meet with the director of the program, a fellow graduate student. She accepted my thesis copy with thanks, engaged in brief discussion, and never contacted me again. However, several years later I heard that it remains in the resource library and that nurses have recommended it to one another.

196

While the reductions and cutbacks in all health care services since my experience have preoccupied the attention of workers and the public, I still think that it's important that this counter-narrative of palliative care be told.

References

Ferguson, K. (1984). *The feminist case against bureaucracy*. Philadelphia: Temple University Press.

Miller, R. (1997). Manageable problems/unmanageable death: the social organization of palliative care. Unpublished master's thesis, University of Victoria.

Mueller, A. (1995). Beginning in the standpoint of women: An investigation of the gap between *cholas* and "women of Peru." In M. Campbell and A. Manicom (Eds.), *Knowledge, experience and ruling relations*, pp. 96–107. Toronto: University of Toronto Press.

Smith, D. (1987). *The everyday world as problematic: A feminist sociology*. Toronto: University of Toronto Press.

Smith, D. (1990). *The conceptual practices of power: A feminist sociology of knowledge*. Toronto: University of Toronto Press.

Smith, G. (1995). Accessing treatments: Managing the AIDS epidemic in Ontario. In M. Cambell and A. Manicom (Eds.), *Knowledge, experience, and ruling relations*, pp. 13–18. Toronto: University of Toronto Press.

Victoria Hospice Society. (1993). *Palliative care at home*. Victoria: Victoria Hospice Society.

Weatherill, G. (1995). Family care when the patient is dying. *Caring Magazine* (April), 50–53.

Additional Institutional Ethnography Resources

Campbell, M., and Manicom, A. (Eds.). (1995). *Knowledge, experience and ruling relations*. Toronto: University of Toronto Press.

Campbell, M., and Gregor, F. (2002). *Mapping social relations: A primer in doing institutional ethnography*. Aurora: Garamond Press.

CHAPTER EIGHT

THE VIEW FROM THE POSTSTRUCTURAL MARGINS:
EPISTEMOLOGY AND METHODOLOGY RECONSIDERED

Susan Strega[1]

> The master's tools will never dismantle the master's house.
> —Audre Lorde

> The master's house will only be dismantled with the master's tools.
> —Henry Louis Gates, Jr.

These alternative visions, separated by gender and by almost a generation, offer some insight into the quandaries and dilemmas faced by researchers from the margins and scholars who share a social justice agenda. The goal of destroying the master's house necessarily leads researchers into the question of how best to go about doing so. The research "tools" that might be employed in this endeavour are not just particular methods of data collection and analysis, but the methodologies that frame these methods, and their epistemological and ontological foundations. The researcher who asks herself at the inception of a research project the following questions is asking about the ontological and epistemological foundations of her work: How can I best capture the complexities and contradictions of the worlds, experiences, or texts I am studying? Whose voice will/does my research represent? Whose interests will it serve? How can I tell if my research is good research? For researchers concerned with social justice, the answers represent not just methodological choices, but choices about resistance and allegiance to the hegemony of Eurocentric thought and research traditions—the master's tools.

From my position as a marginalized researcher who is committed to furthering social justice in my work, there are compelling reasons to resist using the master's methodologies. For more than 30 years, I have been an activist involved with, among other causes, anti-racism and the elimination of violence against women. In all of the years that I have been concerned with these problems, I have heard and read a great deal of explanation about them, much of it regarding how these problems might be solved or at least ameliorated. The research that I have read has encompassed both quantitative and qualitative methodologies, and has claimed to prove a number of theories about how these problems have arisen and how they might be solved. I would contend, though, that none of the research to date, nor the programs and policies it has engendered, has made significant radical change in the world. Thus, like Lorde, I have come to the position that we must use different tools if we wish our research to further social justice goals because I believe that there is a relationship between producing knowledge or meanings about the world and the actual practice of doing research.

In this chapter, I take up and support Lorde's contention in two ways. First, I critique the existing "tools" of traditional social science research by examining their ontological and epistemological foundations, explaining how and why most challenges to mainstream approaches have failed, and discussing whether traditional social science can or ought to be transformed. Secondly, I take a critical look at the progressive possibilities of one methodology—feminist poststructuralism—that I believe offers a useful approach for those seeking a social justice orientation in their research. As I will explain, feminist poststructuralism requires that researchers examine power and how it operates through discourse and subjectivity. Through this examination, more effective means of resistance to inequity and injustice may be uncovered.

Ontologies, Epistemologies, and Social Justice

The ontologies and epistemologies of different research traditions are the foundations of how knowledge about "social phenomena" can and should be acquired: each has different ideas about what should be studied, why and how it should be studied, how it should be analyzed, how it should be assessed, and what ought to be done with research results. As O'Connor notes, "these ideas are not simply theoretical musings, they have pragmatic and ethical relevance" (2001, p. 155).

200

An ontology is a theory about what the world is like—what the world consists of, and why. Another way of thinking about ontology is to think of it as a world view. The world view of the researcher shapes the research project at every level because it shapes a researcher's epistemological foundation. An epistemology is a philosophy of what counts as knowledge and "truth"; it is a strategy by which beliefs are justified. Epistemologies are theories of knowledge that answer questions about who can be a "knower"; what tests beliefs and information must pass in order to be given the status of "knowledge"; what kinds of things can be known. All research methodologies rest on some ontological and epistemological foundation.

Marginalized researchers and researchers committed to social justice, concerned with the inability of traditional research methodologies to bring about social change or further social justice efforts, challenge not only research methods, but the ontological and epistemological foundations of these methods. As critical race scholar Ladson-Billings (2000) notes, taking up this challenge can be difficult:

> How one views the world is influenced by what knowledge one possesses, and what knowledge one is capable of possessing is influenced deeply by one's world view. The conditions under which people live and learn shape both their knowledge and their world views. The process of developing a world view that differs from the dominant world view requires active intellectual work on the part of the knower, because schools, society, and the structure and production of knowledge are designed to create individuals who internalize the dominant world view and knowledge production and acquisition processes. (Ladson-Billings, 2000, p. 258)

The hegemony of the dominant world view is more than one way to view the world; it is successfully positioned as the most legitimate way to view the world. The existence of non-Western, non-Eurocentric world views that are not founded on a hierarchical dualism, which posit that both existence and knowledge are contingent on others, and/or on the world and other living entities, have important implications for researchers. For example, some Indigenous peoples define the basis of knowledge as connection: everyone and everything in the world is connected, and understanding these connections is the beginning of knowledge. The Afrocentric world view "Ubuntu," or "I am because we are" also suggests a knowledge based in relationship (Ladson-Billings, 2000).

Most of us who have been educated in Europe or North America have been socialized into a Western or Eurocentric ontological and epistemological frame. The foundation of Eurocentric thought is Enlightenment epistemology. The Enlightenment is the period in European thought when the demarcation between science and non-science was established, and when "science" and "knowledge" began to have the same meaning. This division between scientific knowledge and all other types of knowledge is hierarchical; science is the "best" kind of knowledge, superior to various forms of unreliable and unverifiable non-scientific knowledge, such as philosophy, folklore, mythology, poetry, old wives' tales, and oral traditions. Within Enlightenment epistemology, there is only one "true" path to knowledge: the application of rigorous scientific methodology by a rational, neutral, and objective subject to the study of an object clearly positioned outside of himself. Thus, only science is considered capable of producing "truth."

Science becomes truth, or "verifiable knowledge" through the stringent application of various tests. These verification methods include observation, mathematical calculation, experiment, and replication. Only propositions that can be empirically tested and replicated (by competent scientists) can be considered "objective truth." The application of rigorous scientific methods that derive from mathematical logic ensures objectivity, neutrality, and the absence of bias. Objectivity is achieved by separating the "knowing subject" from the "object of knowledge," can only be achieved through the application of reason, and therefore can be applied only by those who are rational. The scientific method I have described, which was first applied to the study of the natural sciences and has been more recently applied to the social sciences, allegedly brings about the discovery of knowledge unattached to ideology or to power. Because scientific knowledge is free of bias, it has been positioned as the only kind of knowledge that can be relied upon for tasks that require prediction and control, such as the making of law and policy.

Indigenous scholars, critical race theorists, and feminists have all raised important questions about producing knowledge within Enlightenment epistemology, and the positioning of science as the "best" kind of knowledge, asking the following: Who is entitled to or allowed to create meanings about the world? What criteria are used to decide what constitutes valid truth? How do gender, class, and race factor into this? As Tuhiwai Smith points out, "research [is] a significant site of struggle between the interests and ways of knowing of the West and the interests and ways of resisting of the Other" (2001, p. 2). The idea that there is only one path to truth, that its discovery is guaranteed by objectivity and the rigorous pursuit of a scientific methodology by a rational subject, disguises both the gendered, raced, and classed nature of this discourse and its privileging of White, upper/middle-class masculinity. The scientific method not only guarantees truth, but positions only men (or those who act like them) as capable of finding the truth—there is a particular (White) male way of thinking that is critical to scientific method. As Usher notes:

> a commitment to reason, perspectiveless truth, objective and [allegedly] neutral forms of knowledge, separation of the subject from the object of knowledge are all commitments to the production of [White] male theory in which reason surreptitiously defines itself by excluding categories associated with femininity [and marginalized peoples]—subjectivity, the emotions, desire and specificity. (Usher, 1997, pp. 46–47)

Such critiques point out that Enlightenment epistemology rests on a dualistic foundation, in which qualities such as rationality, reason, objectivity, and impartiality are privileged over and opposed to irrationality, emotion, subjectivity, and partiality. The claim that only rational, objective, and abstract thought can lead to truth is a specifically White masculine claim. It rests on a hierarchical system of dualisms between White male and coloured (classed) female, in which the White male element is privileged over the coloured (classed) female element. This dualism is everywhere in Western/Eurocentric thought, and it is always oppositional and hierarchical, never neutral. It "maintains its position by its capacity to define itself as a universal standard against which the subjective, the emotional, the aesthetic, the natural, the (coloured, classed) feminine must be judged" (Usher, 1997, p. 45).

The Enlightenment, in Eurocentric history, also marks the beginning of the "modern" era, and Enlightenment epistemology is thus sometimes known as "modernism." After the Enlightenment, the experimental scientific method became the research norm, the means by which knowledge could be "legitimized." Thus, in order to position their research as legitimate, those working in the emerging field of "social" science also adopted this approach. Enlightenment epistemology (or modernism) informs both quantitative and qualitative social science methodologies, and continues to instruct both quantitative and qualitative researchers. While both qualitative and critical social scientists have critiqued modernism's epistemological foundation, rarely have they challenged it. Moreover, I would contend that their attempts to be objective in a subjective kind of way have reinforced the position of the experimental scientific method as the gold standard against which all ways of discovering knowledge continue to be assessed.

The defining characteristics of modernism include the notion that knowledge can be (and is, if the rules are followed) objective, impartial, innocent in intention and effect, and neutrally discovered; that there is only one true method by which knowledge is acquired; and that knowledge can be discovered by a rational subject who is distanced from its object of investigation and who can separate herself or himself from emotions, personal self-interests, and political values in creating innocent knowledge. Information gathered by other methods, and by researchers who socially and politically locate themselves, fails to attain the status accorded to knowledge. Knowledge has both status and function; in modernism, it is seen as a tool that can be used to satisfy needs and to control the physical and the social environment. Human life is said to improve in a progressive fashion through the discovery, acquisition, and application of knowledge. The advancement of the human condition is thus both "natural" and the inevitable result of the accumulation of this "pure" knowledge.

While feminist critics have stressed gender as the fundamental dualism in Enlightenment thought, another and equally important hierarchical division, that of race, also lies at its foundation. The connection between "light" and knowledge lies within the word "Enlightenment" itself, and provided for the explorers and slaveholders of Enlightenment times (and for those in centuries to come) a rationale for conquering and subjugating the "dark" peoples of the world. Today it provides a rationale for the continuing project of colonializing and assimilating people of colour into White, Western ways of knowing, being, and doing. As Tuhiwai Smith notes:

> [r]esearch is one of the ways in which the underlying code of imperialism and colonialism is both regulated and realized. It is regulated through the formal rules of individual scholarly disciplines and scientific paradigms, and the institutions that support them (including the state). (Tuhiwai Smith, 2001, p. 8)

The irrational is fundamentally associated not just with the feminine, but also with darkness, whether darkness of night or darkness of skin, and, further, to its association with "magical," "superstitious," and irrational ways of knowing. Thus, the dominant pattern in Enlightenment epistemology is a hierarchical, gendered, raced, and classed dualism, an asymmetrical division in which the White and male side is valued over the dark and female side.

Modernist Methodologies

Methodologies are the theoretical and conceptual frameworks within which research as a practice is located; they offer a theory and analysis of how research could or should proceed. Enlightenment epistemology is the foundation for three major methodologies in the social sciences: positivism, qualitative methodology (interpretivism), and critical social science. These modernist approaches all embrace humanist values, share a belief in progress, and posit that the meaning of social phenomena can be discovered, albeit by different means.

Positivism assumes the existence of a rational, Enlightenment subject that can recognize truth and distinguish it from falsehood by the application of reason. It is positioned as not only the best way but also the only way to discover social science "truth." Other, inferior approaches might yield information (anecdotal evidence, personal experience, stories, and traditions), but this information will not be seen as reliable as that discovered by "science." Positivist explanations must be provable and contain no logical contradictions—a fact, though provisional, is still a fact, and if people disagree about facts, further use of measurement and further observation can and will confirm one version of the facts over another. Criticism of a "fact" that has been derived from the application of positivist methods can be and is dismissed as inappropriately imposing subjective judgments or irrationality—that is, personal opinions. Other research methodologies—other ways of arriving at "facts"—are also dismissed as irrational, illegitimate, biased, and opinionated.

Both qualitative and critical researchers have questioned the value of quantitative methodologies for investigating social phenomena and human behaviour. They question whether the allegedly objective measures applied to the study of the natural sciences can or should be applied to study in these areas. Qualitative methodologies, or interpretivism, search instead for understandings rather than facts about the social world and social beings. These methodologies include a variety of approaches, such as grounded theory, hermeneutics, phenomenology, case study, narrative analysis, ethnography, and institutional ethnography. Neuman and Kreuger define qualitative research as "the systematic analysis of socially meaningful action through the direct, detailed observation of people in natural settings in order to arrive at understandings and interpretations of how people create and maintain their social worlds" (2003, p. 78). Some interpretive methodologies (such as grounded theory) are more closely aligned with positivism, while others (such as institutional ethnography) are located within a critical or social constructivist paradigm. Each methodology has slightly different definitions for what constitutes data, how data should be gathered, and how data should be analyzed. All share the goal of understanding social life and discovering or revealing how people create meaning in natural settings: What do their words and actions mean to the people who engage in them? How do people define and understand what they are doing? What is relevant? What do they believe is true?

The intention of doing interpretive research is to give those who read the research a feel for others' social reality by revealing or illuminating the meanings, values, interpretive systems, and rules of living they apply. For interpretivism, "truth" has been found if the researcher's description and conclusions make sense to those who are being studied (and others like them), and if it allows others to understand this reality. The researcher's theory or description is accurate if the researcher conveys a deep understanding of how those who are being studied think, feel, believe, reason, and see reality. Reality is about the meaning that people create in the course of their social interactions; the world is not about facts but about the meaning attached to facts, and people negotiate and create meaning. In interpretivism, facts are context-specific actions that depend on the interpretations of particular people in a social setting. The social context of actions and words is a critical piece of qualitative research. Understanding the "reality" of an experience or process or phenomenon is contextual and must be grounded in the experience of those who have had the experience or process or phenomenon. Rich, "thick" description brings a deeper, more complex understanding.

Although many qualitative researchers believe that a value-free science is impossible, they are nonetheless instructed to (and often attempt to) bracket their "assumptions." The task for the researcher is to notice, acknowledge, and be reflexive about what her biases and values are, and hold these separate from the data ("bracketing") in order to correctly interpret the material being gathered. Reflection and analysis of the researcher's own thoughts and feelings are considered not only an important part of research but also an indication of interpretivism's ability to be as rigorous in its methods as positivism, and thus an equally legitimate means by which to generate knowledge. These attempts to redefine objectivity to, as Con Davis says, "do the police in other voices" (1990, cited in Lather, 1993, p. 674), have failed to dislodge the hierarchical dualism of Enlightenment epistemology, in which positivist social science continues to be the standard against which all other methodologies are evaluated. Hekman suggests that such attempts "to redefine or even to perfect objectivity will not succeed in displacing the epistemology that relegates women and the social sciences to an inferior role" (1990, p. 96). Advocating for the interpretive position has served, by its insistence that qualitative methodologies are equally valid, to simply reinforce the dualism that constitutes them as inferior.

Critical social scientists are, in some ways, more allied with a positivist than an interpretive research stance. While they critique the value orientation of Enlightenment epistemology, they also generally believe that there is a "reality" that can be discovered. Where they differ from positivists is in believing that reality is shaped or constructed by social, political, cultural, and other forces. Facts are not neutral, and therefore require an interpretation from a value or ideological position. Thus, sites of conflict, contradiction, and paradox are the best places to research because they can reveal what "true" reality is underneath its surface presentation.

Critical social science not only acknowledges its value position, it takes the stance that some values are better than others, and makes an explicit commitment to social justice. It rejects positivism and interpretivism as not being about changing the world. It accepts that knowledge is power, and challenges researchers to think about whether they want to support or challenge existing power structures. Many critical social scientists contend that while positivism works in the service of the existing power structure, interpretivism fails to acknowledge these structures, leading to individualizing social problems rather than seeing them as a function of inequitable social relations.

Critical social scientists critique existing social relations in order to transform them. The agenda of critical social science is to uncover myths, reveal hidden truths, and help people change the world for themselves. It involves two steps: accurately describing reality, and then applying that accurate description to suggest or undertake action. In critical social science, this is called "praxis": explanations are valued when they help people to understand the world and take action to change it. "Research as praxis" (Lather, 1986) is emancipatory social science that is intended to redress structural inequalities and challenge the claim that research can or should be value neutral. This theory of research recognizes the historically, socially, and culturally constituted nature of knowledge.

From a critical perspective, research must be about empowering the marginalized and promoting action against inequities. Questions about the relationship between the researcher and the researched are highlighted, as is the question of whose voice(s) the research (re)presents. Critical social science asks questions, exposes hypocrisy, and investigates social conditions to encourage grassroots action. It is concerned with empowerment and/or emancipation of those marginalized by society or in a particular sphere of society. It is avowedly and clearly political in intention and in process. The meaning that people make of situations is important, but there are real, observable structures to be discovered — these "unseen forces" are what the critical social scientist is interested in. Despite its commitment to social justice, critical social science relies on Enlightenment epistemology through its continuing commitment to the idea that "reality" can be uncovered. Thus, it implicitly continues to support hierarchical dualism and the inequities it engenders.

Significant challenges to the privileging of positivism have come from feminism. Historically, feminists deployed their efforts along three strategic courses. First, they dared to attack positivist science on its own terms, critiquing the methodology by accusing it of falling short of "good" scientific practice, and also by suggesting that some of the presuppositions of the scientific approach may be flawed. But, as Hekman notes:

> If the canons of scientific method as they have been defined by the dominant tradition since Bacon are inherently sexist, then adherence to these methods, no matter how rigorous, will not produce results that will fundamentally alter the sexist character of scientific discourse. (Hekman, 1990, p. 124)

A second strategy, primarily employed by liberal feminists, demands that women be allowed entry "into the sphere of rationality as it has been defined by men" (Hekman, 1990, p. 40). This approach accepts the definition and the privileging of the rational Enlightenment (White, male) subject and seeks to earn that privilege for women by demonstrating that women can become like men. Feminists from Mary Wollstonecraft through to recent second wave feminists have suggested that if women are allowed the same educational and life chances as men, they too can become "rational subjects" capable of "creating knowledge." By erasing their difference from men, women can abandon the inferior status of "Other" and thus women too can achieve "the Truth that is accessible to the ideally rational man" (Hekman, 1999, p. 91). Some people of colour have also embraced this position, and it is this thinking that has largely informed affirmative action programs. But, as Catherine MacKinnon (1987) has pointed out, equality between sexes and races is predicated on the ability of "Others" to successfully emulate the qualities valued and exhibited by White men, and meet standards developed and set by them, and thus leaves the hierarchical dualism at the heart of Enlightenment epistemology intact.

A third feminist route has involved accepting the dualism as an accurate or semi-accurate reflection of the "essential" natures of men and women while attempting to privilege "woman's nature" by valorizing "essential" feminine qualities (such as intuition) and women's ways of knowing (such as "experiential" knowledge). This strategy has included both the idea of complementarity (that men and women represent "two halves of a whole," and that both ways of "knowing" the world are needed), and the radical feminist suggestion that feminine qualities and values are superior, and should be embraced by all, men and women alike. For example, feminist theorists Mary Daly (1978) and Susan Griffin (1982) suggest that "male" qualities such as rationality and distance must be displaced by the womanly attributes of intuition, irrationality, and emotionality. But through accepting rather than repudiating an essential female "nature," such a position reinforces a hierarchical dualism. As Hekman points out, "much as we might laud the 'feminine' values the radicals proclaim, these values will continue to be viewed as inferior until the dichotomy itself is displaced" (1990, p. 41). Further, the radical feminist position has been critiqued by women of colour and some lesbians, who have noted that this stance fails to account for differences within the category "woman," while reversing and thus maintaining a dualistic hierarchy of difference. It also fails to contend with the symbiotic relationship between sexism and racism through which racism sustains and rearticulates sexism, and sexism sustains and rearticulates racism.

Given the sexual and racial violence and inequity that structure the world, the Enlightenment contention that "truth" can be discovered, and that such discoveries provide for progress, is seductive. Part of what is so alluring in the possibility of discovering incontrovertible "proofs" that sexism and racism are wrong is that it allows women and others on the margins to locate this assessment outside of themselves, and thus avoid the retribution that is deployed against those who take moral and political positions that name these injustices and notice that (White, privileged) men benefit from them.

It is also difficult to challenge Enlightenment epistemology because "the belief that coherent political action must be grounded in absolutes is deeply rooted in feminist as well as modernist thought" (Hekman, 1990, p. 186). The roots of feminism, like those of many emancipatory struggles such as the civil rights movement, lie in an Enlightenment discourse of rights, equality, freedom, and justice, and various strains of feminism have seized upon these ideas in particular ways, attempting to make them serve feminist campaigns. Even Marxist or socialist feminism, which rejects most liberal feminist and liberal humanist ideology, is an emancipatory movement, rife with rights rhetoric and having at its foundation a dualism and a belief in absolutes. But, as a number of feminist and critical race theorists (MacKinnon, 1987; Razack, 1998; Williams, 1991; Young, 1990) have pointed out, the rhetoric of rights and equality masks substantive inequality because it fails to account for differences.

Enlightenment epistemology inscribes a hierarchical dualism that inevitably positions women and other marginalized peoples as inferior. This ascription of inferiority lies at the core of the justification of racial subjugation, violence, and structural inequities. Tuhiwai Smith positions resistance to dominant epistemology as a matter of survival for Indigenous peoples: "To acquiesce is to lose ourselves entirely and implicitly agree with all that has been said about us. To resist is to retrench in the margins, retrieve what we were and remake ourselves" (2001, p. 4). In a similar fashion, Hekman notes that "feminists cannot overcome the privileging of the male and the devaluing of the female until they reject the epistemology that created these categories" (1990, p. 8). The dualism must be rejected, the epistemology abandoned, the hierarchy displaced, and the entire project of "the search for the one, correct path to truth" (Hekman, 1990, p. 39) must be refused. "An epistemology that defines women as not fully rational, moral or even human cannot simply be repaired to allow women a new status. It must be rejected outright" (Hekman, 1990, p. 59).

At the same time, as women of colour have made clear, researchers must find an epistemological position and methodologies that can make sense of differences. Research must locate itself within an epistemology of "truths" rather than "Truth" because "Truth" has failed to account for racialized epistemologies, women's ways of knowing, and other subjugated knowledges. As Usher states, "anything short of a rejection of the rationality and dualisms of Enlightenment thought and the research methodologies which derive from it, will not prove a successful strategy" (1997, p. 44).

These are not abstract philosophical issues. The epistemological foundation of methodology prescribes what good research involves, justifies why research is done, gives a value base to research, and provides ethical principles for conducting research. The failure of Enlightenment-based methodologies to challenge what Ladson-Billings calls the "status quo relations of power and inequities" (2000, p. 263), and their basis in racist and sexist thought, means that marginalized researchers must challenge, discard, or transcend this epistemology, and locate themselves within an epistemological foundation of multiple and partial perspectives. For some marginalized researchers, including myself, an alternative lies at the intersection of radical feminism and poststructuralism.[2] I believe that this methodology breaks with Enlightenment epistemology and can be usefully appropriated for the political purposes of researchers concerned with social justice. At the same time, I acknowledge that methodological choices are complex, and that we may, for various reasons and at various times, continue to use mainstream methods. In these situations feminist poststructural ideas can, I believe, help researchers push their methodologies to encompass social justice concerns.

Poststructural Possibilities

Poststructuralism seeks to displace Enlightenment epistemology by challenging "the fundamental dichotomies of Enlightenment thought, dichotomies such as rational/irrational and subject/object" (Hekman, 1990, p. 2). Feminisms, despite their differences, challenge the fundamental dualism of Enlightenment epistemology, that of masculine/feminine, and some strains of feminism have allied with subjugated knowledges to dispute the hierarchy of light/dark. Hekman contends that "feminism and postmodernism are the only contemporary theories that present a truly radical critique of the enlightenment legacy of modernism" (1990, p. 189). Both poststructuralists and radical feminists "reject both the notion that knowledge is the product of the opposition of subjects and objects and that there is only one way in which knowledge can be constituted" (Hekman, 1990, p. 9). Through the development of theories such as feminist standpoint (Harding, 1987; Hartsock, 1987) and the sociology of knowledge (Smith, 1990), feminist researchers have pointed out the role of the social, the experiential, and the discursive in the construction of knowledge. Similarly, poststructuralists have advocated an understanding that all knowledge is contextual, historical, and, penultimately, produced by rather than reflected in language.

Poststructuralism's interest in language, and particularly in the constitution of language as discourse, resonates with feminist understandings of how language shapes women's lives. Second wave feminists have taken up the language question in many ways, including through research (Hollway and Featherstone, 1997; Kitzinger and Thomas, 1995; Walkerdine, 1986), critique (Penelope, 1990; Spender 1980), and attempts to invent a "women's language" (Daly and Caputi, 1987; Haden Elgin, 1984). Many theorists, among them French feminists such as Irigaray (1985) and Cixous and Clement (1987) believe that women's oppression is rooted in language. Hekman offers this summary of their position: "Phallocratic language offers women only two options: either they can speak as women, and, hence, speak irrationally, or they can enter the masculine sphere of rationality and speak not as women but as men" (1990, p. 42).

While I acknowledge that poststructuralism offers an important and necessary modification to the essentialism of White, Western feminism, I find myself asking Sneja Gunew's (1990, p. 13) question: "Do feminists have any use for a body of theory which has largely misrepresented and/or excluded women?" I also note Finn's observation that "you cannot 'doctor' these theories [Western philosophical theories such as poststructuralism] with respect to women and at the same time save the theory" (1982, cited in Hekman, 1990 p. 7). Is the pre-eminence of poststructuralism's challenge to modernism just another way in which "male-defined models of knowledge and ways of gaining access to knowledge [continue to] prevail" (Gunew, 1990, p. 21)? I would suggest, for example, that many of the insights that poststructuralism offers about language and discourse echo those already proposed by feminist and critical race theorists such as Brossard (1988), Hill Collins (2000), Penelope (1990), Spender (1980), Williams (1991), and Wittig (1992). As Ladson-Billings (2000) notes, African American scholars such as W.E.B. Du Bois and Carter Woodson challenged Enlightenment epistemology at about the same time as critical scholars of the Frankfurt School, but they remain largely unacknowledged outside of critical race scholarship. In interrogating "the conditions of knowledge production by means of which certain kinds of truth or science came to appear as 'legitimate' at the same time that certain specific groups were authorised to articulate these truths" (Gunew, 1990, pp. 20–21), I must notice that theories about the pervasiveness of language's role in dominance and subordination, and the links between knowledge and power, have acquired a new legitimacy since their "authorization" by White male theorists such as Foucault. Poststructuralism's refusal to engage with or acknowledge the legacy of critical race theorists and radical feminists makes its appropriation by those on the margins problematic because this refusal implicitly restates the Enlightenment idea that only certain kinds of minds (White, male, privileged) can make theory. Tuhiwai Smith (2001) suggests that poststructuralism and postmodernism are convenient inventions of Western intellectuals that reinscribe their power (and right) to define the world.

Thus, although Hekman believes that poststructural, Foucauldian "analysis also suggests the possibility of the creation of a discourse that does not constitute itself as inferior" (Hekman, 1990, p. 21), it seems that such a discourse cannot be created by those who *are* "inferior"—women and other marginalized people—or perhaps it is that we cannot be credited with the creation of such a discourse. Feminists and other holders of subjugated knowledge such as Indigenous scholars and critical race theorists have for some time been delineating "ways of knowing" and of researching that challenge Enlightenment epistemologies and methodologies. Thus, it is difficult to believe Hekman's contention that "postmodernism involves a crisis of cultural authority" (1990, p. 13) when the poststructuralist challenge to authority resides primarily in the hands of White, privileged men. I am also conscious, as a lesbian, that the partnering of feminism and poststructuralism is for the most part an alliance between White (heterosexual) women and White (heterosexual) men that disprivileges people of colour and lesbians.

The poststructuralist position that there is not one "truth" but multiple "truths" has, as I noted, offered a means by which to theorize and account for differences. But the insistence on multiple perspectives has also been criticized as poststructuralism's fatal political flaw. If all truth claims are perspectival and partial, how then can the truths we uncover through the methodologies of feminist poststructuralism provide us with a rationale for political action? Feminist standpoint theory, which also understands knowledge as contextual, historical, and discursive, privileges the perspective of women. Similarly, women of colour, seeing danger in the notion that all visions are equal, have insisted on the epistemic privilege of the oppressed (Hill Collins, 2000; Narayan, 1988). But Hekman declares, from a poststructuralist perspective, that the vision of the oppressed is not any closer to "reality": "If material life structures consciousness, if the different experiences of different groups create different realities, then this must hold for the oppressed as well as the oppressor" (1999, p. 34). But I would locate myself with Ladson-Billings (2000), who posits that while the view from the margins "is not a privileged position, it is an advantaged one" (p. 271).

Hartsock's contention "*both* that reality is socially and materially constructed *and* that some perceptions of reality are partial, others true and liberatory" (cited in Hekman, 1999, p. 31, italics in original) inevitably leads to the question of who has the right to decide, and on what basis, what is "true and liberatory"? Alternatively, if there are many truths and many paths to "truth," as poststructuralism insists, and none of these is to be privileged along gender or racial lines, we are left unable to speak the following "truth": we live in a system of domination and subordination that differentially benefits (most) White men over (most) women and (most) people of colour, and that privileges the Western world over the rest of the globe. What epistemology, what methodology, will allow us to speak truth to the power of White men's dominance?

Despite my hesitations about feminist poststructuralism, I have made an (uneasy) alliance with it in much of my research work. Having earlier noted the futility of both quantitative and qualitative efforts to redress the nature and extent of social injustice and structural inequalities, I make this alliance in part because I agree with Hekman's declaration that "we must first alter the criteria of what it makes sense to say before we can proclaim another 'truth' and expect it to be heard" (1999, p. 137). I also locate myself here because I believe that we must unapologetically challenge the epistemologies and methodologies that dehumanize and depersonalize those on the margins, and justify social injustice and inequality on the basis of our difference from the ideal White, heterosexual male Enlightenment subject. I do not have a definitive answer as to which epistemologies and methodologies will best serve the cause of social justice, but I suggest that feminist poststructuralism raises useful questions about knowledge, power, truth, difference, and the constitution of the self, and thus contributes to the developing dialogue about anti-oppressive research. In the remainder of this chapter, I will discuss three key concepts in poststructural research (discourse, power, and subjectivity), and then conclude with some thoughts about a poststructural approach to evaluating research.

Discourse

"Discourse" is a term that is widely used and variously interpreted. In its modernist conception, discourse is usually used to apply to talking, or to a way of talking, to partition off a circumscribed area of discussion, as in "the discourse about the economy," or to delineate the manner in which a topic is discussed, as in "scientific discourse." Such usage is directly related to an understanding of language as transparent and expressive, and of words as representative of or signifying the objects or concepts to which they refer. Discourse, in this conception, is also understood to be functional, having necessarily arisen to allow for the possibility of discussing a particular topic. Any curiosity about "where words come from" or "what words mean" (beyond their dictionary definitions) is, in this understanding, a purely etymological concern and thus, "the social and ideological 'work' that language does in producing, reproducing or transforming social structures, relations and identities is routinely 'overlooked'" (Fairclough, 1992, p. 211). Transformations in language and the development of new discourses are ascribed to progress or the need to develop new and more "accurate" words to describe new discoveries, understandings, or areas of interest. Thus, language and discourse are dissociated from power and ideology and instead conceptualized as "natural" products of common sense usage or progress. Enlightenment epistemology positions the individual sovereign subject as the originator of meaning, able to both convey and control meaning by the "correct" selection and arrangement of words. However, women's ability to *be* a subject and authorize language or discourse has been complicated by the hierarchical dichotomy of Enlightenment thought, which has positioned her as "object" due to her imputed inability to be rational. People of colour have been similarly positioned through allegations about their intellectual inferiority.

There have been a number of challenges to understanding language and discourse as transparent, functional, and progressive. Structuralists such as Saussure argued that language is socially and historically specific and that the meaning of words is constructed rather than pre-existing (1974, cited in Featherstone and Fawcett, 1995). Althusser described language as a social product that reinforces and reproduces ideology; as a Marxist, he was particularly concerned with how it is instantiated through "ideological state apparatuses" such as educational institutions and the church (Althusser, 1984).

Feminists and other marginalized groups have explored the complex relationships that exist among power, ideology, language, and discourse in some depth. While the second wave of feminism is usually characterized as primarily concerned with the material conditions of women's lives under patriarchy, it also produced a voluminous literature on women's subjugation through language and various discourses. For example, linguist and radical feminist Julia Penelope (1990), in *Speaking Freely: Unlearning the Lies of the Father's Tongue,* dissects in detail what she describes as PUD: the patriarchal universe of discourse. In addition to examining how the inferiority of women, lesbians, people of colour, and the disabled, and the concomitant superiority of White, heterosexual, able-bodied men is constructed through language and discourse, Penelope also maps the discursive processes through which the marginalized unintentionally participate in constructing their own subjugated identities. Other analyses of language and discourse produced by second wave feminists examined academic discourse (Russ, 1983; Spender, 1980); psychology (Broverman, 1970; Weisstein, 1971); theology and medicine (Daly, 1978); violence against women (Walker, 1990); and moral theory (Gilligan, 1982). Critical race theorists such as Hill Collins (2000), Razack (1998), Said (1993), and Trinh (1989) have taken up the construction of race and racism through language and discourse in diverse ways. For example, Sherene Razack (1998) has delineated how the liberal, humanist discourse of justice, rights, and equality simultaneously masks and constructs relations of domination and subordination along lines of gender, race, and class.

Although the significant break with modernist ideas about language and discourse is generally attributed to poststructuralists, I believe that the writings of feminist and critical race theorists also challenge these ideas. They consider, in varying ways, how language both serves and masks ideology. They suggest that, rather than describing reality, language constructs and constitutes "reality" insofar as we can apprehend, understand, and describe events and experiences only through the words, language, and discourses that are available to us. Further, they propose that the availability of words, language, and discourse is produced and constrained by factors unrelated to the need for accuracy or to "natural," progressive developments. They suggest that these factors are related to history rather than progress, and to the workings of power and ideology rather than necessity. Finally, in various ways these writers begin to interrogate the idea that we are ideally unitary, rational beings through questioning the notion that we can originate and control meaning by our choice of words and concepts. As Wittig (1992) points out, our minds are also colonized territories.

Poststructuralist researchers go beyond an interest in the workings of particular "discourses" to focus on the all-encompassing nature of discourse as the constructor and constituter not just of "reality" but also of our "selves." This last idea clearly demarcates the break with Enlightenment epistemology's idea of the rational, meaning-making subject and the modernist conception of the self, for poststructuralism posits that "our existence as persons has no fundamental essence, we can only ever speak ourselves or be spoken into existence within the terms of available discourses" (Davies, 1991, p. 42). Among poststructural theorists, Foucault is most associated with the poststructuralist understanding of discourse, and his various understandings most inform my own, albeit as a feminist I have some caution about appropriating his work. Foucault's writings are not definitive on the subject of discourse as his own ideas about it reflect various conceptions. In his early work, *The Archaeology of Knowledge* (1972), Foucault described discourse as the principal organizing force of all relations and offered "archaeology" as a methodology by which discourse could be exposed and explored in terms of *how* it functioned rather than *why* it functioned. He also accepted the existence of some relations as "extra-discursive," or outside the discourse, and suggested that the relationship between discourse and the extra-discursive could be mapped or articulated.

As a feminist, I am interested in both discourse and in noticing the connections or articulations between discursive relationships and the "extra-discursive." This is, I think, a point where the feminist standpoint insistence on articulating women's experience *as* knowledge comes to bear, for our current knowledge of male violence toward women is in part dependent on women speaking what was previously unspoken. Alternatively, where Foucault's discourse theory is so interesting to me is in its curiosity about how experience enters into, or is barred from entering into, what counts as knowledge.

Foucault's other writings offer a range of meanings for discourse, "treating it sometimes as the general domain of all statements, sometimes as an individualizable group of statements, and sometimes as a regulated practice that accounts for a number of statements" (Mills, 1997, p. 6), but always relating it to the way in which, at historically specific points, language, power, and social and institutional practices coalesce to produce particular ways of thinking, understanding, being, and doing. Foucault was particularly interested in the relationships between power, knowledge, discourse, and "truth," and *Power/ Knowledge* contains an often-quoted description of this relationship:

> Each society has its regime of truth, its "general politics" of truth: that is, the types of discourse which it accepts and makes function as true; the mechanisms and instances which enable one to distinguish true and false statements, the means by which each is sanctified; the techniques and procedures accorded value in the acquisition of truth; the status of those who are charged with saying what counts as true. (Foucault, 1980, p. 131)

In this understanding of discourse, knowledge and power are inseparable and are both productive of and constraining of "truth"; in Foucault's understanding, power is so co-extensive with knowledge that only an expression such as "power/knowledge" can describe it. He also saw this as a recursive relationship in that discourse also produces power/knowledge and what may be understood to be "truth" at any particular time. Knowledge is not "discovered" but is a product of discourse and power relations, a discursive struggle over which (and whose) perspective or understanding emerges as the one that "counts," the one that has the power to organize relations. Ramazanoglu (1993, p. 21) offers this interpretation of Foucault's understanding: "There is no single truth ... but many different truths situated in different discourses, some of which are more powerful than others."

However, as Weedon notes, most discourses "deny their own partiality. They fail to acknowledge that they are but possible versions of meaning rather than 'truth' itself and that they represent particular interests" (1997, p. 94). Discourse does this through how it organizes and constitutes inclusions and exclusions, by noticing and valorizing some forms of knowledge while obscuring and devaluing other forms of knowledge. Discourse organizes social relations as power relations while simultaneously masking these workings of power. It is instantiated not only in texts, speech, and institutions but also in the constitution of relationships and of the "self." Mills offers this definition: "[a] discourse is a set of sanctioned statements which have some institutionalised force, which means that they have a profound influence on the way that individuals act and think" (1997, p. 62). Sanctioning is primarily discursive but is also extra-discursive and occurs in a number of ways, for example, through what various media present or represent as "reality"; through what is taught; and through the penalties that are imposed for attempting to circulate an unsanctioned discourse. For example, the psychiatrist Thomas Szasz (1970), who has suggested that a biologically based understanding of mental illness is a myth that masks psychiatry's function as an instrument of social control, has been ridiculed and vilified by his colleagues for these ideas. As Usher notes, "not only does a discourse permit certain statements to be regarded as the truth but the rules which govern a discourse also determine who may speak, what conventions they need to use and with what authority they may speak" (1997, p. 48).

Hegemonic or dominant discourses and subjugated or illegitimate discourses are produced by processes such as the sanctioning, including, excluding, valuing, and devaluing of certain concepts, ideas, language, and words. Earlier I described the continuing dominance of Enlightenment epistemology in shaping our understanding of what "knowledge" is and how it can be produced, referring to positivism as the gold standard by which knowledge claims are assessed, and the positioning of the rational White, male subject as the ideal knower. Those discourses that reflect, promote, and ally with the discourse of Enlightenment epistemology are thus most able to both conceal their partiality and position themselves as "the truth." But processes of exclusion make even dominant discourses vulnerable. As Hekman suggests, "the gaps, silences and ambiguities of discourses provide the possibility for resistance, for a questioning of the dominant discourse, its revision and mutation" (1990, p. 189). They also provide the terrain on which alternative, oppositional, and counter discourses might emerge.

Subjugated knowledges and the possibilities of other "truths" that might break the hold of hegemonic discourse are of particular interest to feminists and critical race theorists because of the role that dominant discourse has in rationalizing the inequitable position of women and people of colour. Feminism has, for example, looked to women's experience as a source and guarantor of knowledge, as that experience was shared in consciousness raising and then became the focus of research through various qualitative methodologies and the promotion of feminist standpoint theory. While a great deal of information has been acquired in these ways, most women's lives are not substantially different now than they were before these efforts; as McNeil notes, "the more we know about patriarchy, the harder it seems to change it" (1993, p. 164). This conundrum brings me to a consideration of a concept central to poststructuralist theory and regarded with much hesitation by those on the margins—subjectivity.

Subjectivity

Enlightenment epistemology inscribes a subject/self that is autonomous, rational, neutral, unitary, and abstracted from its context. Liberal humanism, rooted in Enlightenment epistemology, posits a subject/self that has agency: this self is "self-conscious," in control of itself, and capable of and required to create an identity from an allegedly unlimited range of choices. As I discussed earlier, these understandings of the subject are fundamentally gendered; the qualities associated with this Enlightenment, humanist self are those qualities associated with "man." There have been three challenges to this notion of the self from feminists and scholars of colour. One has been to insist that women and people of colour can also become "rational subjects" through producing themselves as invested with the qualities of the rational, modernist subject—becoming like White men. One of the complications of this notion is that unless we are to insist that women and people of colour consciously and persistently make choices that are not in their own interests, it fails to adequately account for people's suffering under White patriarchy. "The structural and institutional oppression of women disappears behind the belief that if I, as a rational sovereign subject, freely choose my way of life on the basis of my individual rational consciousness which gives me knowledge of the world, then I am not oppressed" (Weedon, 1997, p. 81).

The material fact of oppression in the midst of the modernist, humanist conception of the self has spawned various analyses that purport to explain this contradiction. Structuralism, Marxism, and feminism have all proposed the existence of "false consciousness," the notion that an individual can be, and sometimes is, deceived into complicity with oppression and will therefore unintentionally think and behave in ways that harm her self. The corollary to this notion is that our consciousness can be "raised" or undergo a process of "conscientization" (Freire, 1973) that will diminish our complicity with the external forces that oppress us. Alternatively, feminist and humanist psychology has suggested that the complicity of women and people of colour, their "bad choices," results from the damage inflicted on their psyches through living under oppression and might thus be resolved through therapeutic interventions. Thus, we are encouraged to accept that "the political is personal" and abandon our insistence that "the personal is political." A return to rational agency is thus dependent on our exposure to and acceptance of analyses, generated by those more aware or advanced than us, about the ways in which we are oppressed and participate in our own oppression. Whether pursued through conscientization, consciousness raising, or therapy, this approach has been unsuccessful in materially changing the conditions of most people's lives under White patriarchy.

Another challenge has involved problematizing the Enlightenment subject by valorizing rather than discarding "essential" attributes such as emotionality and relationality, positing a complementary subject that can be valued equally with (or, as some theorists suggest, more highly than) the rational, White male subject. Thus, women's choices are not "bad" or "unconscious," but related to their womanly nature. In this analysis, oppression will disappear as essential female qualities, and therefore the women who embody them are more valued in the world. Similarly, some contributions of Indigenous peoples, notably their spiritual practices, and contributions of people of colour, notably their creative and artistic endeavours, have been positioned as equal in importance to the ideas of those who are dominantly located. These strategies have also failed.

The third way, which involves discarding the rational, unitary (Enlightenment) self altogether, has thrown some of those interested in pursuing this possibility into an often uneasy alliance with poststructuralism. Poststructuralists, and perhaps especially Foucault, reject the notion of an autonomous, essential self who freely chooses. For Foucault, the self/subjectivity is an *effect* of discourse: historically and socially situated, constituted, and constructed in discourse and discursive practices. In poststructuralism, subjectivity is unstable, "precarious, contradictory and in process, constantly being reconstituted in discourse each time we think or speak" (Weedon, 1997, p. 32), rather than stationary or evolving in a progressive or unified way. This understanding of subjectivity leads to an alternative reading of "choice"; in Davies's analysis, "choices are understood as more akin to 'forced choices' since the subject's positioning within particular discourses makes the 'chosen' line of action the only possible action, not because there are no other lines of action but because one has been subjectively constituted through one's placement within that discourse to *want* that line of action" (1991, p. 46). Such an analysis is appealing because it allows us to see and understand how and why we are being complicit without pathologizing it or attributing it to an underdeveloped consciousness. The latter are essentially "dependent" positions that leave the marginalized relying on an external other or an external process by which we might either resolve our pathology or come to a higher level of consciousness.

But the poststructuralist position poses some quandaries, not the least of which is that the decentred, unstable, contradictory poststructuralist subject sounds suspiciously like the emotional, irrational, inferior (dark) female subject of Enlightenment epistemology. Such a subject can be easily dismissed. Feminists and other marginalized peoples have also noted that the call to "abandon the subject" comes at a time when the marginalized have just taken up the project of theorizing their selves/ subjectivity. Fortunately, some feminist poststructuralists have proposed alternative and, I think, politically useful ways to think about our selves, our choices, and our complicity while still maintaining a sense of agency.

Davies suggests, for example, that "agency is never freedom from discursive constitution of the self but the capacity to recognise that constitution and to resist, subvert and change the discourses themselves through which one is being constituted" (1991, p. 51). This acknowledges that our choices are constructed for us through discursive practices, and that we can choose only from these discursively constituted choices, but suggests that it is our understanding of these options that guides conscious choices of how we position ourselves. When there are no alternatives available that do not in some measure harm us, choosing the construction that is least harmful can be reconceptualized as a strategy of resistance. Another choice, which is common to those who occupy already devalued subjectivities, is to position oneself as "different from" others who occupy the devalued subjectivity while at the same time accepting the general devaluing of the subjectivity. Thus, a gay person might describe himself as "gay but not promiscuous," or a single mother on welfare might describe herself as different from "other welfare moms." The idea that we are choosing from a range of circumscribed choices allows us to more accurately assess the possibilities for resistance, although these may be on a small scale. Understanding our subjectivity and the range of subjectivities available to us brings not just the possibility of choice but an increased awareness of the mechanisms by which our selves, our subjectivities, are created, disciplined, and under surveillance. In Davies's words:

> To conceive of agency once the male/female dualism is abandoned is to think of speaking subjects aware of the different ways in which they are made subject, who take up the act of *author*ship, of speaking and writing in ways that are disruptive of current discourses, that invert, invent and break old bonds, that create new subject positions that do not take their meaning from the genitalia (and what they have come to signify) of the incumbent. (Davies, 1991, p. 50)

Feminists and other marginalized theorists are also justifiably concerned that accepting the idea that our selves, our subjectivities, are constituted solely as an effect of discourse means that we must abandon knowledge generated from the experiences of women and subjugated others. Having lived so long in a world in which (White, heterosexual, able-bodied) men define their experience *as* reality, it has been critical for women and subjugated others to explore our "realities." Feminist standpoint theory and the notion of epistemic privilege (Narayan, 1988) have been critical in helping the marginalized move beyond exploring their realities to interrogating and theorizing them. These theorists are as insistent as any poststructuralist that knowledge is situated and perspectival, and that there are multiple standpoints from which knowledge is and can be produced, but they do not agree with many poststructuralists' contention that all accounts are therefore equally valid. Rather, they contend that "starting research from the reality of women's lives, preferably those of women who are also oppressed by race and class, will lead to a more objective account of social reality" (Hekman, 1999, p. 45).

While I am hesitant to position either the possibility or the pursuit of "objectivity" as a good move, I have noted my belief that the "view from the bottom" is fuller and often more accurate, at least with certain proscribed areas. As Fine has noted, "in colonizing relations ... dominant-subordinate relations, subordinates spend much time studying the Other" (1998, p. 146) because our survival depends on doing so. For example, I know a great deal about what (White, heterosexual) men think, feel, and imagine about lesbians in particular and the world in general because my economic, academic, and, too frequently, my physical survival has depended on this knowledge and on my concomitant ability to be silent about it. I would also contend, since I have had it frequently demonstrated to me, that most (White, heterosexual) men know little about what lesbians think, feel, and imagine about (White, heterosexual) men in particular and the world in general, although they apparently feel free to speak as if they do. I have essentialized here because I want to make the point that, in the context of the system of domination and subordination in which we live, the marginalized cannot and must not completely abandon the knowledge of our experience.

Alternatively, positioning experience *as* knowledge fails to take into account that experience is also structured by discourse: we can only understand, apprehend, or explain our experience within the discourses and subjectivities that are available to us, so I think that as researchers, we must seek to understand how experience and therefore the knowledge that arises from it are constructed. We must also consider the function of particular constructions of subjectivity, experience, and knowledge in discursively constituted power relations. As Haraway points out in her critique of feminist standpoint theory, "women's experience is constructed. Like every other aspect of our lives, it is apprehended through concepts that are not of our making" (cited in Hekman, 1999, p. 49). The only language through which we can describe our experiences is constituted in the discourses available at each historically specific moment. Do women experience domestic violence, family violence, violence against women, or male violence against women, and what are the consequences of each interpretation? Or are women experiencing essentially "normal" relations between men and women, and what are the consequences of experiencing or interpreting or knowing this as "normal"?

As these conflicting and contradictory choices suggest, "individuals are both the *site* and *subjects* of discursive struggle for their identity" (Weedon, 1997, p. 93, italics in the original). I suggest that everything we do or do not do, say or do not say, write or do not write signifies our compliance with or resistance to what Weedon has described as the "dominant norms of what it is to be a woman" (1997, p. 83). The range of subject positions available to women also turns on dimensions of race, class, age, ethnicity, dis/ability, sexual orientation, and cultural background. The relative power or powerlessness of different subject positions is structured in and through discourse and the social or power relations inherent in it. Each positioning has its own consequences and effects; as Weedon notes, "forms of subjectivity which challenge the power of the dominant discourses at any particular time are carefully policed. Often they are marginalized as mad or criminal" (1997, p. 87), or as both. Our "selves," our subjectivity, are not acted upon by discourse, but are instead an effect of discourse, and thus an effect of power.

Power

The poststructural understanding of power differs from both modernist and most feminist understandings of power and power relations. For Foucault and many other poststructuralists, power is understood as something that is circulated and dispersed throughout society rather than being held exclusively or primarily by certain groups. This is an alternative reading to the understanding that it is the state, and powerful groups that the state supports and that support the state, which have and impose power. From a poststructuralist perspective, "power is a form of action or reaction between people which is negotiated in each interaction and is never fixed and stable" (Mills, 1997, p. 39). Thus, power is exercised and relational rather than merely oppressive or repressive. The individual, or the individual "subject," is not acted upon by power but is positioned in power. For example, the selves/subjectivities available to gay men and lesbians have undergone many transformations over the past century as they have been developed within various discourses even in the midst of many oppressive and repressive state initiatives.

The notion that there is no ultimate determining factor related to power (such as race, class, or gender) and no ultimate holder of power (such as the state) often makes poststructural ideas about power an anathema to researchers concerned with the very real and material structural inequalities that exist in society. But I believe that when poststructuralism is informed by the progressive politics of feminism or critical race theory, it has more to offer those who want their research to make radical change in the world than do analyses based on hierarchies of oppression, which inevitably pit those on the margins against one another. Feminist poststructuralism allows for a process of analysis that can take all of these factors, and how they relate to one another, into account. If, as Foucault suggests, "power is tolerable only on condition that it mask a substantial part of itself. Its success is proportional to its ability to hide its own mechanisms" (1981, cited in Weedon, 1997, p. 117), then analyses directed at uncovering these mechanisms and delineating how they operate within us and in the minutiae of our daily existence present us with better rationales for resistance than do universal and essentialist theories, which both obscure difference and require massive mobilization to bring about change. Gunew suggests that "it may well be quite misleading to think of power as consisting of a centre and a periphery and may be more productive to think of power as a network which operates everywhere in contradictory ways and can therefore be strategically resisted everywhere" (1990, p. 23).

Foucault offered two other ideas about power that can be usefully appropriated for social justice research. One is that there is a recursive and intimate relationship between knowledge and power. From a Foucauldian perspective, knowledge is never disinterested or neutral, but both produced by and productive of power. "Power and knowledge directly imply one another: there is no power relation without the correlative constitution of a field of knowledge, nor any knowledge that does not presuppose and constitute at the same time power relations" (Foucault, 1979, cited in Usher and Edwards, 1994, p. 87). Thus, knowledge disputes are also power struggles, and power struggles are also about which/whose version of knowledge will prevail.

Another useful idea has to do with disciplinary knowledges and the role of these knowledges in producing internally disciplined individuals. In *Discipline and Punish,* Foucault delineates the shift in societal governance from mechanisms of external surveillance and punishment meted out on the body of the wrongdoer to the present situation in which individuals, guided by disciplinary knowledges such as psychiatry, psychology, and education, police themselves. As Usher and Edwards note, "when discipline is effective, power operates through persons rather than upon them" (1994, p. 92). All disciplinary discourses contain instructions for how to be, think, and do. In Foucault's interpretation, "Power is reproduced in discursive networks at every point where someone who 'knows' is instructing someone who doesn't know" (Gunew, 1990, p. 23). While the possibility exists that we can, if need be, be externally disciplined—those defined as "mad," for example, are still routinely locked up—the internalization of disciplinary knowledges is generally effective and, in fact, eagerly pursued: sections of bookstores, and sometimes entire bookstores, are now devoted to "self-help." As "self-discipline" is embraced, the repressive and coercive aspects of power are obscured, and when self-discipline needs shoring up, those expert in disciplinary knowledges (psychiatrists, psychologists, social workers, university professors) offer further instruction. Engaging in research as a practice of resistance requires challenging these instructions and the ways that they shape our research projects and us as researchers. Usher advises that "the researcher should develop a self-reflexive stance toward his/her own relation to their research: she/he must be accountable for her/his own cultural prejudices and disciplinary allegiance and be alert to how these implicate themselves in the choices made in research practice" (1997, p. 53).

All of the poststructural ideas that I have discussed—discourse, knowledge, power, and subjectivity—also come into play when research—and the researcher who has produced it—is assessed and evaluated. As I have noted, traditional social science has been structured around epistemological assumptions about who is best suited to produce "knowledge," how it should be created, and how it ought to be evaluated. The poststructuralist rejection of the Enlightenment epistemological frame requires that researchers also develop different evaluation mechanisms. Working in transgressive methodologies requires that we develop transgressive standards by which to assess our endeavours.

Evaluating Methodologies from the Margins

My suggestions for how research from the margins might be assessed must start with acknowledging the difficulty of steering a course between the conflicting demands of personal, political, and community commitments and the academic and professional "standards" to which we make ourselves subject if we choose to pursue our work within the academy and other mainstream structures. As Ladson-Billings notes, "[m]echanisms for scholarly recognition, promotion, tenure and publication are controlled by the dominant ideology. [The marginalized] are simultaneously being trained in this dominant tradition and trying to break free of it" (2000, p. 267). Often our research must be constructed in certain ways so that we can obtain "approval" for it from various authorities, notably academic institutions, funding bodies, and government and agency officials who control access to funds, documents, and research participants. While feminists, critical race theorists, and Indigenous scholars have managed to open space in the academy, particularly in the social sciences, our historical and critical awareness of the role of research in the lives of the marginalized makes us aware that these institutions are also deeply implicated in maintaining and rationalizing inequities. For researchers committed to social justice, these can be confounding issues. As Foucault notes, "it is always possible that one might speak the truth in the space of a wild exteriority, but one is 'in the true' only by obeying the rules of a discursive 'policing' which one has to reactivate in each of one's discourses" (1981, p. 61).

Under the dominant paradigm of positivism, quantitative research measures of rigour and validity are the gold standard through which "proof" is established and research is assessed. Qualitative research has attempted to make the case that it is as good as quantitative research through offering any number of "alternative" measures through which it might be evaluated; for example, Denzin and Lincoln position triangulation as "an alternative to validation" (1998, p. 4). But because the very use of the word "alternative" indicates a continuing allegiance to the notion of epistemological guarantees, such alternative measures must be discarded by researchers whose methodological stance positions "truth" as multiple, partial, and perspectival.

Nonetheless, it is necessary to provide some criteria that allow the reader to make connections between our analyses and the worlds, texts, people, and experiences that we write about. I believe we must start by discarding standard measures of rigour and validity, in either their quantitative or qualitative guise, as evaluative criteria. The dictionary definition of "valid" is instructive here: "valid implies being supported by objective truth or generally accepted authority" (*Merriam-Webster's*, 1993, p. 1304). We must ask what use the notion of validity is to research that discards the notion of objective truth and researchers who wish their work to be valuable to those who are neither accepted nor accorded status as authorities. As Cameron has noted about feminist attempts to position their work as "rigorous" and "valid," "[t]his is a game that no one engaged in what Gill (1995) calls 'passionately interested inquiry' can win, and it is not clear to me why feminists should want to play" (1998, p. 970).

I would suggest three standards by which we might assess feminist poststructural research; these ideas might also be useful for researchers working in other methodologies who appropriate some poststructural methods. First, we must assess the political implications and usefulness of what we produce for progressive, anti-oppressive politics in marginalized communities. Deyhle and Swisher (1997), in their discussion of Native American research, call this "social justice validity." Thus, the standards and needs of the community in which the research is being conducted become a critical piece in evaluation. Our work must therefore be reconstructive as well as deconstructive. Secondly, we must ask ourselves not just "about whom?" but also "for whom?" Tuhiwai Smith, discussing Indigenous methodology, believes that the results of our studies must be "disseminated back to the people in culturally appropriate ways and in a language that can be understood" (2001, p. 15). I believe we must ask, in essence, whether we have managed to "speak truth to power" in accessible languages and formats.

Finally, we must measure the extent to which we have been reflexive, including the extent to which we have considered our own complicity in systems of domination and subordination. Hill Collins (2000) suggests we must adhere to an ethic of caring and personal accountability as researchers. From my perspective, reflexivity and complicity are also political concerns; I note Lal's comment that "a reflexive and self-critical methodological stance can become meaningful only when it engages in the politics of reality and intervenes in it in some significant way" (1996, p. 207). Reflexivity is a critical measure for a number of reasons. It highlights rather than obscures the participation of the researcher in the research process. It makes clear that interpretation is taking place, and by implication calls into question the alleged neutrality and objectivity of other research/researchers, thus offering an important political and methodological challenge to standard research practices. By implication, it also calls into question whether standard means of assessing rigor and validity are the "proper" or best means by which to assess research. The measurement of reflexivity lies in the extent to which we consider our assumptions, lay out our processes of inquiry, and consider our "effect" on the research. But while we need to locate ourselves and continuously interrogate our perceptions, these matters of self-location and reflexivity must not take centre stage. While our positionalities as researchers must be noticed, questioned, and taken up, they ought not to be the purpose or focus of our work, for the simple reason that this is unlikely, on its own, to contribute to political change. Reflexivity must not be the sole focus of our research: the reader must still learn more about the puzzle or experience being analyzed than about the researcher.

Complicity is an important criterion for me as a feminist, grounded as it is in my belief that patriarchy continues to exist because women support it, to a greater or lesser extent, through their own complicity. Resisting complicity is complicated by the ability of discourse to "account for" such resistance. Regina Austin makes the observation that her insights have been met with the response that:

> you are too angry, too emotional, too subjective, too pessimistic, too political, too anecdotal and too instinctive ... I suspect that what my critics really want to say is that I am too self consciously black (brown, yellow, red) and/or female to suit their tastes and should "lighten up" because I am making them very uncomfortable, and that is not nice. (Austin, 1989, cited in Fine, 1998, pp. 143–144)

While I am not vulnerable to such dismissals on the ground of race, my location as a lesbian is likely to have the same effects. But my positionality must also be acknowledged because it is my location, in part, that affords me the luxury of speaking what most heterosexual women do not dare to say or "know."

Penalties for failures in complicity are both commonplace and familiar to feminists: tenure denied, employment lost, or funding withdrawn. Walker (1990) discusses at length how the Canadian women's movement relinquished its determination to characterize battering as "men's violence against women" once faced with being denied state support for transition houses and counselling services. More strenuous refusals to be complicit, such as the case of Aileen Wuornos, a sex worker who killed her abusive customers in self-defence (Chesler, 1994), provoke more severe consequences; Wuornos was executed in 2002. Despite the human rights victories of recent years, most women in academia, heterosexual and lesbian, know and fear the power of being labelled a lesbian/dyke/man-hater/feminazi. We also fear that our work might be dismissed; as Mills points out, "[e]ven if your research work is factually accurate or insightful, if it does not accord with the form and content of particular disciplines it is likely to be disregarded or to be regarded as non-academic or popular" (1997, p. 69).

All of these situations "instruct" the marginalized in complicity, and yet complicating and challenging complicity is essential for creating political change. As Mills has noted, "all knowledge is determined by a combination of social, institutional and discursive practices, and theoretical knowledge is no exception. Some of this knowledge will challenge dominant discourses and some will be complicit with them" (Mills, 1997, p. 33). Thus, a critical measure by which our work needs to be assessed is the extent to which we are complicit with or challenging of dominant discourses.

While acknowledging that "truth is plural and relative, historical and particular" (Hekman, 1999, p. 24), we must nonetheless manage to justify the particular "truths" at which we arrive. Are the questions we pose as a result of our research interesting, challenging, and different from those that are usually asked? Finally, in a world in which the violence of the dominant toward the marginalized is at one and the same time the context for daily life and a set of invisible facts, have we managed to "make strange that which appears familiar, and make familiar that which appears strange?" (Hekman, 1999, p. 138).

Notes

1. This chapter owes much to Pat Usher, at the University of Southampton, who challenged me to deepen my understandings of both feminism and poststructuralism.

2. There has been much discussion about whether "poststructuralism" and "postmodernism" are synonyms, or whether they in fact represent different concepts. For the purposes of this thesis, I have conflated these terms and, except when I am citing the work of other authors, use "poststructuralism."

References

Althusser, L. (1984). *Essays on ideology.* London: Verso.

Brossard, N. (1988). *The aerial letter.* Translated by Marlene Wildman. Toronto: Women's Press.

Broverman, I. (1970). Sex-role stereotypes and clinical judgments of mental health. *Journal of Consulting and Clinical Psychology* 34 (1), 1–7.

Cain, M. (1993). Foucault, feminism and feeling: What Foucault can and cannot contribute to feminist epistemology. In C. Ramazanoglu (Ed.), *Up against Foucault,* 73–96. London: Routledge.

Cameron, D. (1998). Gender, language and discourse: A review essay. *Signs: Journal of Women in Culture and Society* 23 (4), 945–973.

Chesler, P. (1994). *Patriarchy: Notes of an expert witness.* Munroe: Common Courage Press.

Cixous, H., and Clement, C. (1987). *The newly-born woman.* Translated by B. Wing. Manchester: Manchester University Press.

Daly, M. (1978). *Gyn/ecology.* Boston: Beacon Press.

Daly, M., and Caputi, J. (1987). *Wickedary.* Boston: Beacon Press.

Davies, B. (1991). The concept of agency: A feminist poststructural analysis. *Postmodern critical theorizing—social analysis series* 30, 42–53.

Denzin, N., and Lincoln, Y. (1998). *Strategies of qualitative inquiry* (2nd edition). Thousand Oaks: Sage.

Denzin, N., and Lincoln, Y. (2000). *Handbook of qualitative research.* Thousand Oaks: Sage.

Deyhle, D., and Swisher, K. (1997). Research in American Indian and Alaska Native education: From assimilation to self-determination. *Review of Research in Education* 22, 113–194.

Fairclough, N. (1992). Discourse and text: Linguistic and intertextual analysis within discourse analysis. *Discourse and Society* 3 (2), 193–217.

Fairclough, N. (1996). Technologisation of discourse. In C. Caldas-Coulthard and M. Coulthard (Eds.), *Texts and practices,* pp. 71–83. London: Routledge.

Featherstone, B., and Fawcett, B. (1995). Oh no! Not more isms: Feminism, postmodernism, poststructuralism and social work education. *Social Work Education* 14 (3), 25–43.

Featherstone, B., and Fawcett, B. (2000). Setting the scene: An appraisal of postmodernism, postmodernity and postmodern feminism. In B. Fawcett, B. Featherstone, J. Fook, and A. Rossiter (Eds.), *Practice and research in social work: Postmodern feminist perspectives,* pp. 5–23. London: Routledge.

Fine, M. (1998). Working the hyphens: Reinventing self and other in qualitative research. In N. Denzin and Y. Lincoln (Eds.), *The landscape of qualitative research: Theories and issues,* pp. 130–155. London: Sage.

Foucault, M. (1972). *The archaeology of knowledge*. London: Tavistock.

Foucault, M. (1978). *The history of sexuality: An introduction* (Vol. 1). Translated by R. Hurley. New York: Pantheon.

Foucault, M. (1980). *Power/knowledge: Selected interviews and other writings, 1972–1977*. Colin Gordon (Ed.). New York: Panthon.

Foucault, M. (1981). The order of discourse. In R. Young (Ed.), *Untying the text: A post-structuralist reader*, pp. 48–68. Boston: Routledge and Kegan Paul.

Foucault, M. (1995). *Discipline and punish: The birth of the prison* (2nd edition). Translated by A. Sheridan. New York: Vintage Books.

Freire, P. (1973). *Pedagogy of the oppressed*. New York: Seabury Press.

Gill, R. (1995). Relativism, reflexivity and politics: Interrogating discourse analysis from a feminist perspective. In S. Wilkinson and C. Kitzinger (Eds.), *Feminism and discourse*, pp. 165–186. London: Sage.

Gilligan, C. (1982). *In a different voice*. Cambridge: Harvard University Press.

Griffin, S. (1982). *Made from this earth: An anthology of writings by Susan Griffin*. New York: Harper and Row.

Gunew, S. (1990). *Feminist knowledge: Critique and construct*, pp. 13–33. London: Routledge.

Haden Elgin, S. (1984). *Native tongue*. New York: DAW Books.

Haden Elgin, S. (1987). *Native tongue II: The Judas rose*. New York: DAW Books.

Harding, S. (1987). *Feminism and methodology*. Bloomington: Indiana University Press.

Hartsock, N. (1987). Rethinking modernism: Minority vs. majority theories. *Cultural Critique* 7, 187–206.

Hekman, S. (1990). *Gender and knowledge: Elements of a postmodern feminism*. Cambridge: Polity Press.

Hekman, S. (1999). *The future of differences: Truth and method in feminist theory*. Cambridge: Polity Press.

Hill Collins, P. (2000). *Black feminist thought* (2nd edition). New York: Routledge.

Hollway, W., and Featherstone, B. (1997). *Mothering and ambivalence*. London: Routledge.

Irigaray, L. (1985). *Speculum of the other woman*. Translated by Gillian Gill. Ithaca: Cornell University Press.

Kitzinger, C., and Thomas, A. (1995). Sexual harassment: A discursive approach. In S. Wilkinson and C. Kitzinger (Eds.), *Feminism and discourse*, 32–48. London: Sage.

Ladson-Billings, G. (2000). Racialised discourses and ethnic epistemologies. In N. Denzin and Y. Lincoln (Eds.), *Handbook of qualitative research* (2nd edition), pp. 257–277. Thousand Oaks: Sage.

Lal, J. (1996). Situating locations: The politics of self, identity and "other" in living and writing the text. In D. Wolf (Ed.), *Feminist dilemmas in fieldwork*. Boulder: Westview Press.

Lather, P. (1986). Research as praxis. *Harvard Educational Review* 56 (3), 257–277.

Lather, P. (1993). Fertile obsession: Validity after poststructuralism. *Sociology Quarterly* 34 (4), pp. 673–693.

MacKinnon, C. (1987). *Feminism unmodified*. Cambridge: Harvard University Press.

McNeil, M. (1993). Dancing with Foucault: Feminism and power/knowledge. In Ramazanoglu, C. (Ed.), *Up against Foucault: Explorations of some tensions between Foucault and feminism*, pp. 147–175. London: Routledge.

Merriam-Websters Collegiate Dictionary (10th edition). Markham: Thomas Allen and Son.

Mills, S. (1997). *Discourse*. London: Routledge.

Minh-ha, T.T. (1989). *Woman, native, other: Writing postcoloniality and feminism*. Bloomington: Indiana University Press.

Narayan, U. (1988). Working together across differences: Some considerations on emotions and political practice. *Hypatia* 3 (2), 31–47.

Neuman, W., and Krueger, L. (2003). *Social work research methods: Qualitative and quantitative approaches*. Boston: Allyn and Bacon.

O'Connor, D. (2001). Journeying the quagmire: Exploring the discourses that shape the qualitative research process. *Affilia* 16 (2), 138–158.

Penelope, J. (1990). *Speaking freely: Unlearning the lies of the fathers' tongue*. Elmsford: Pergamon Press.

Ramazanoglu, C. (Ed.) (1993). *Up against Foucault: Explorations of some tensions between Foucault and feminism*. London: Routledge.

Razack, S. (1998). *Looking white people in the eye: Gender, race, and culture in courtrooms and classrooms*. Toronto: University of Toronto Press.

Russ, J. (1983). *How to suppress women's writing*. Austin: University of Texas Press.

Said, E. (1993). *Culture and imperialism*. New York: Knopf.

Smith, D. (1990). *The conceptual practices of power: A feminist sociology of knowledge*. Boston: Northeastern University Press.

Spender, D. (1980). *Man made language*. London: Routledge and Kegan Paul.

Szasz, T. (1970). *The myth of mental illness*. New York: Harper and Row.

Tuhiwai Smith, L. (2001). *Decolonising methodologies: Research and Indigenous peoples*. Dunedin: University of Otago Press.

Usher, P. (1997). Challenging the power of rationality. In G. McKenzie, J. Powell, and R. Usher (Eds.), *Understanding social research: Perspectives on methodology and practice*, pp. 42–55. London: The Falmer Press.

Usher, R., and Edwards, R. (1994). *Postmodernism and education*. London: Routledge.

van Dijk, T. (1996). Discourse, power and access. In C. Caldas-Coulthard and M. Coulthard (Eds.), *Texts and practices*, pp. 84–106. London: Routledge.

Walker, G. (1990). *Family violence and the women's movement: The conceptual politics of struggle*. Toronto: University of Toronto Press.

Walkerdine, V. (1986). Post-structuralist theory and everyday social practices: The family and the schools. In S. Wilkinson (Ed.), *Feminist social psychology: Developing theory and practice*, pp. 57–76. Milton Keynes: Open University Press.

Weedon, C. (1997). *Feminist practice and poststructuralist theory*. Oxford: Blackwell.

Weisstein, N. (1971). Psychology constructs the female. In V. Gornick and B. Moran (Eds.), *Woman in sexist society*, pp. 207–224. New York: Basic Books.

Williams, P. (1991). *The alchemy of race and rights*. Cambridge: Harvard University Press.

Wittig, M. (1992). *The straight mind and other essays*. Boston: Beacon Press.

Young, I. (1990). *Justice and the politics of difference*. Princeton: Princeton University Press.

CHAPTER NINE

HONOURING THE ORAL TRADITIONS OF MY ANCESTORS THROUGH STORYTELLING

Qwul'sih'yah'maht
Robina Anne Thomas

It's July and again I find myself in the backyard, cleaning and preparing fish for canning, freezing, and smoking. There is this moment where I stop, smile, and remember my Grandmother. As a child I used to watch her work on fish. She was an incredible woman, and I think she would be so proud of me, proud that I have learned the skills necessary to take care of my own fish processing! I wonder why it is still so important that my Grandmother would be proud of me. Why, after all of these years, does what she might have thought still matter? It matters because she was a mentor and teacher. Simply by thinking of these questions, I can hear her voice telling me stories. She tells me why it is important to process fish this certain way. She reminds me how important fish was to her and how it was the main staple of their diet. She talks about how at one time the fish stocks were so plentiful and how the stocks were becoming depleted to that point where access to fish was very limited. And, oh yes, I can hear her remind me that it is so wasteful to throw out the heads and tails when you could brew up the best fish head soup. How I hated the sight of that soup or, more specifically, the thought of fish heads (eyes and all) floating in that tasty broth. And, even though she is in the Spirit World, her voice and stories are still with me. I feel blessed by the Creator that she shared these stories.

Traditionally, storytelling played an essential role in nurturing and educating First Nations children. I used to only half listen to the talk of my Grandparents, Aunties, and Uncles and think that I probably would not have this type of "idle chat" with my children. I now realize the wisdom that made up those stories. Now, as a parent and educator, I am always sharing these important stories that I once thought insignificant.

In fact, not only do I share these stories but also I now understand that they are vital to the survival of First Nations peoples. As with the voice of my Grandmother, these stories leave us with a sense of purpose, pride, and give us guidance and direction—these are stories of survival and resistance. In what follows, I will continue to tell stories. I will look at storytelling as a research methodology as well as discuss the joys and challenges of storytelling as a research methodology.

My story about storytelling begins at a community college in Victoria, B.C.—Camosun College. It was my first year of postsecondary education and I had chosen to do an interview-based essay for my final English assignment. All my life, I had heard family and friends abstractly chat about "residential schools," and I wondered what exactly residential schools were. What happened there? And, how did they come to be? I took this opportunity to learn a bit more about residential schools. I remember that my friend Alex Nelson always made reference to St. Mike's. I decided to ask him if he would talk to me about his experience at St. Mike's for this assignment. Alex agreed.

Alex's story devastated me. He shared his experiences at St. Michael's Residential School in Alert Bay, B.C. Today, I cannot remember the specific details of his story, but the sense of trauma I experienced remains absolutely clear. As well, the sense that this experience was not a thing of the past, but continued to play itself out in Alex's everyday life was abundantly clear.

After hearing Alex's story, I got down to the business of writing my assignment. I felt anxious—that feeling we get when we discover a hidden family secret, but even bigger, a Canadian secret. How is it that this incredibly important person was sent to a place like this? How is it that I, now pursuing my undergraduate degree, knew nothing about these places? Why? Why didn't more people know Alex's story? This was a story that needed to be told.

Years later, while doing a graduate degree in social work, it was time for me to begin my thesis. I was still on my journey of understanding residential schools. Because three generations of our family had attended Kuper Island Residential School, I knew I wanted to research this particular school. Kuper Island, one of the pristine Gulf Islands on the east coast of Vancouver Island, is in the heart of Coast Salish territory. Coast Salish is an anthropologically/linguistically defined area from the southern tip of Vancouver Island to the southwestern region of B.C. As a Coast Salish woman (my Grandmother was Snux'ney'muxw, my Grandfather was Sto:olo, and I am Lyackson through marriage, all of Coast Salish territory), understanding the impact of this school located on our traditional territory was significant. Another reason I wanted to research Kuper Island Residential School was because I believed the stories about that place needed to be told.

As my writing process always seems to go, I learned more from doing things wrong than from doing them "right" the first time! There was a time when I was quite anxious to get my thesis proposal done so that I could start the research. Through my research class I had begun my thesis proposal. I am not absolutely sure, but I think I was initially proposing to do some kind of qualitative phenomenology. I finished my first proposal and set up an appointment with my thesis supervisor. As supervisors do, she asked me why had I chosen this and why that, and on and on. As our appointment went on, she finally asked me one last "why" that I simply could not answer. After a moment of silence (and verging on tears), I looked up at her and said, "All I ever really wanted to do was tell stories." And she replied, "Well, why don't you tell stories?" This is where, for me, storytelling as a research methodology began.

"Storytelling in the Spirit of Wise Woman: Experiences of Kuper Island Residential School" (2000), my graduate thesis, uses storytelling as the methodology through which to look at the experiences of three former Kuper Island Residential School students. Although the school has since been torn down, the memories of it remain. The thesis was undertaken to shed light on the devastating and catastrophic legacy of the residential school system in Canada. Residential schools have been the single most devastating event to affect First Nations peoples since contact. Day-to-day, many former students continue to live out the horrific impact of these schools.

For guidance and direction, again I draw upon the voices of my Grandmothers. They lived, they acquired wisdom, and they were all survivors of their experiences—they had much to share. As I began to ask what is in a story, I once more listened for the voices of these Wise Women for examples.

Nana:
"When I was just a young girl, we used to live right over there," Nana pointed to the land on the downtown side of the Ellice St. Bridge. "One Christmas Eve, my Mother, Father, brothers, and sisters were going to my Uncle's place for dinner. It had snowed so much that day that it seemed like it took us hours to get to their

place. They lived down where Uncle's Johnny's place is now. You know, it used to snow lots in those days, not like now."

Grama:

"I am so proud that you are practising some of our old ways," my Grama said. "What is Dylan's name?" "Qwulthelum," I told Gram. "And Paul, what is his name?" "Pahyahutssen." "Did they have the Sxwaixwe dancers there?" "No, Grama they didn't." "Our family is from the masked dance, you know. I remember years ago, when I was young, when we went to the winter dances, sometimes there would be 20 or more dancers there. Someone told us once that one of my Uncle's masks was in a museum in Europe or England or someplace like that."

Amma:

"Amma, why don't you just throw out those old socks?" "Oh, because that would be such a waste. The tops of the socks are perfectly fine, only the feet need to be replaced. I have wool and know how to knit. Why throw the whole sock away?"

What is in a story? Are these simply words? Grandmothers reminiscing? Are they rich with teachings? Wilson states that:

> The intimate hours I spend with my grandmother listening to her stories are reflections of more than a simple educational process. The stories handed down from grandmother to granddaughter are rooted in a deep sense of kinship responsibility, a responsibility that relays a culture, an identity, and a sense of belonging essential to my life. (Wilson, 1998b, p. 27)

I agree with Wilson. My Grandmothers' stories are the essential core of my being. The stories are cultural, traditional, educational, spiritual, and political. Nana's stories point to the land where she was raised, that special place where she held memories of her ancestors—her Mother, Father, Grandparents—and siblings. But also, identifying this land as traditional Songhees territory is crucial as the Songhees Band is currently negotiating their treaty through the B.C. Treaty Commission. The land that Nana identified is no longer a part of Songhees territory, although she was born there.

Grama tells me about the cultural and traditional rights that I inherited through my family. I have the inherent right to have Sxwaixwe, or masked dancers, at all dances our family hosts. This is our most sacred ceremony, which is passed down through familial rights. Grama also asks what names were given. Behind a name is history—it brings forward with it the Ancestors of the past who shared that name, where they were from; they may bring songs, dances, or masks and other important messages. These teachings are passed along to the ones who today carry those names.

Amma's stories teach about conservation—taking, using, and throwing out only what is necessary. She taught me about taking care of Mother Earth long before anyone else. As well, she taught me about recycling and composting before these things were trendy.

These stories include important teachings that pass down historical facts, share culture and traditions, and life lessons. Traditionally, stories and storytelling were used for the same reasons—to teach values, beliefs, morals, history, and life skills to youth and adults. Wilson claims that:

> Stories in the oral tradition have served some important functions for Native people: The historical and mythological stories provide moral guidelines by which one should live. They teach the young and remind the old what behavior is appropriate and inappropriate in our cultures; they provide a sense of identity and belonging, situating community members within their lineage and establishing their relationship to the rest of the natural world. (Wilson, 1998a, p. 24)

Storytelling also taught us about resistance to colonialism—our people have resisted even when legislation attempted to assimilate our children. All stories have something to teach us. What is most important is to learn to listen, not simply hear, the words that storytellers have to share. Many stories from First Nations tell a counter-story to that of the documented history of First Nations in Canada. For example, Alex's story is not the "Canadian" story of residential schools—the story of education and Christianity. In fact, his is a story of abuse, survival, and resistance—how he fought to survive in a system that abused him and how he resisted this abuse as a means of healing. He lived to tell his story and to share it with all those who needed support to begin their healing journeys. His story, and the stories of the three storytellers in my thesis research, are very important because they give us teachings that allow us to continue to hear and document those counter-stories—our truths. A mentor of mine, Delmar Johnnie, once said that it is such a shame that every time someone who went to residential school dies without telling his or her stories, our government and the churches look more innocent. Telling these stories is a form of resistance to colonization. As one storyteller told me, despite all of the government and churches' attempts, I am still here. I am Indian and I am proud. These stories simply must be told.

Most First Nations peoples traditionally come from an oral society. A storytelling methodology honours that tradition and the Ancestors. As storytelling was traditionally done orally and in a different language, we are compelled to listen and document stories in the spirit of the Ancestors. In other words, I feel that storytelling enables us to keep the teachings of our Ancestors, culture, and tradition alive throughout the entire research process. Silko (1998) believes that "storytelling can procure fleeting moments to experience who they were and how life felt long ago" (p. 42). As we share stories from long ago, we are given an opportunity to go back to that time. What an honour to bring to life a moment from years ago.

But for me, there is always the fear of documenting our stories. Will the voices be heard? Will the voices of the storytellers be edited? Documenting, in and of itself, is a foreign concept. When I began to transcribe the tapes, I even wondered if they are contradictory, the oral and the written. But as with everything, times change and in order for First Nations peoples to have their voices heard, they have had to adapt and write down their experiences, while at the same time trying to maintain their stories. Again I am talking about counter-stories—the stories that have never been told by our own People. Storytelling in this sense is an act of resistance. The stories in my thesis are written as they were told and experienced, not edited to parallel the Canadian story; they give voice to a story that has not been fully told. Certainly the stories of residential schools tell the other story—the story of colonization and genocide—but so do many other stories that First Nations have to tell: The stories of land dispossession; the stories of the sixties' scoop. These are all resistance stories because they validate the lives and times of our People. They tell stories that have been inaccurately documented in a new way.

The beauty of storytelling is that it allows storytellers to use their own voices and tell their own stories on their own terms. Cruickshank (1990) states that her work, *Life Lived Like a Story*, is "based on the premise that life-history investigation provides a model for research" (p. 1). In the past, life stories (storytelling) have been viewed as supplementary material to support other forms of research. However, as

Cruickshank states, this view is changing, and I believe this view must change. All that is written and researched is someone's interpretation of what happened. In her book *The Social Life of Stories: Narrative and Knowledge in the Yukon Territory*, Cruickshank questions the dominant voices of history by asking whose voices are included and whose are left out.

> Contesting the legitimacy of the dominant discourse is not new, of course. Certainly a concern that many voices are systematically erased from written history has been recognized for a long time now in northern aboriginal communities. As feminists have pointed out, enlarging discourse involves much more than adding and stirring in additional voices, there are fundamental methodological problems involved in rethinking familiar genres of historical narratives. (Cruickshank, 1998, p. 116)

Storytelling is often deemed illegitimate because it is subjective and therefore biased. However, we must consider that in some communities there were little, if any, written records. How else were our communities to record our histories? Our history often includes a counter-history, such as the impact that legislation like the Indian Act has and continues to have on our communities. Why is it that our only means of recording histories—by oral tradition—must be validated by a more "legitimate" research methodology? When we search, we will find that, in fact, in our communities (the Coast Salish) we had and continue to have very sophisticated traditional ways of documenting important events in our communities. I will give you an example.

In 1998 I was given my traditional name, Qwul'sih'yah'maht. This was my Grandmother's name and originated from the Snux'ney'muxw people. Prior to receiving my traditional name, our family was required to go to the eldest surviving female of my Grandmother's family and ensure that it was acceptable for me to be given this name.

At the naming ceremony, we have a system of paying "witnesses," representatives from different communities who are called upon to witness the event. Witnessing is a huge responsibility because you are asked to pay attention to all the details of the evening (what the name was, where it originated, and the protocol that was followed to ensure that I had the right to use this name, as well as other details). In the Big House, visitors are seated in sections according to the community they are from. Witnesses are selected from every community that is present.

This way, the information is shared throughout Coast Salish territory. If there were concerns or questions about what took place, what my name was, or where it was from, we could ask any of the witnesses. They will know this information because it was their responsibility to pay attention to all the details. This highly sophisticated process of witnessing continues to be central to our traditional ceremonies.

All major events that took place in our community were documented. However, "documentation" in traditional research arenas seems to refer only to the written. I am suggesting that the level of complexity and sophistication in which major events were witnessed in our communities demands that these oral histories and stories be reconceptualized and viewed as primary sources. These events are our Department of Vital Statistics—they record births, marriages, and deaths, to name a few. Storytelling creates space for the "Other," or those voices that have been excluded or erased, to be included in the dominant discourse. Storytelling fills the gaps in the present documentation of the lives of First Nations peoples.

Storytelling provides an opportunity for First Nations to have their histories documented and included in the written records. In other words, storytelling revises history by naming and including their experience. Life stories "take seriously what people say about their lives rather than treating their words simply as an illustration of some other process" (Cruickshank, 1990, p. 1). Furniss (1992), in *Victims of Benevolence: The Dark Legacy of the Williams Lake Residential School*, states that "it is critical for these and other stories to continue to be told, and to be heard with an open heart and mind, if we are to prevent the tragedies of history from being repeated" (p. 120). When we listen with open hearts and open minds, we respect and honour the storytellers. I find this process incredibly comforting and respectful. I believe that storytelling respects and honours people while simultaneously documenting their reality.

Gluck and Patai (1991) describe oral histories as a "way of recovering the voices of suppressed groups" (p. 9). Of particular value is the possibility that life stories can share a perspective that is in conflict with another perspective. For example, the residential school perspective from the voices of those who attended these institutions is in conflict with the perspective of residential schools held by the dominant society (Gluck and Patai, 1991, p. 11). This conflict is highlighted these days as many groups of former residential school students seek justice from the church and Canada for the injustices committed in those institutions.

Storytelling has a holistic nature as how the story is told is up to the storytellers—they will tell the story the way they want. Storytellers may opt to share their culture and tradition (spiritual), how events made them feel (emotional), what things looked like, or how they physically felt (physical), or how this affected their ways of knowing and being (mental). Oral histories or life stories "generally range over a wide range of topics, perhaps the person's life from birth to the present" (Reinharz, 1992, p. 130). Because the process of telling the stories is in the hands of the storytellers, they have the opportunity to include in their stories that which they wish, that which they perceive as important, that which they want documented. Storytellers hold the power in this research methodology—they are in control of the story, and the "researcher" becomes the listener or facilitator. Cruickshank (1998) refers to this process as the "open ended possibilities" of oral history because the researcher does not enter the relationship with any preconceived directions that the research will take (p. 72).

Storytelling uncovers new ways of knowing. First Nations peoples have ways of knowing, but for the most part these ways of knowing and being were stripped from us through the process of colonization. Residential schools are but one example. First Nations students were forced to speak English and practise Christianity. Our ways of knowing and being were not permitted, and storytelling is a means through which these ways of knowing and being can be uncovered or reclaimed (Yow, 1994). Gluck and Patai (1991) state: "oral history interviews provide an invaluable means of generating new insights about women's experiences of themselves in their world" (p. 11). I too see storytelling as providing an opportunity for the generation of new insights into the experiences of First Nations peoples.

Yow (1994) believes that oral histories, as a form of qualitative research, allow the researcher to "learn about a way of life by studying the people who live it and asking them how they think about their experience" (p. 7). This is not about studying that which the researcher deems important, but being open to hear what the storytellers deem as important about their experience. In order for me to hear what the storytellers wanted to share, I met with them and had coffee or tea and they shared many stories. Some might call this interviewing, but even the word "interview" does not seem appropriate as it denotes structuring from the researcher. I knew that if I asked specific questions,

I would get specific answers. What would happen if I asked the wrong questions? What would my research look like? It would answer only the questions I asked and as such I would be structuring the process. I was not the expert; the storytellers were and I was the learner, listener, recorder, and facilitator.

The use of informal conversations, Patton (1980) claims, "is the phenomenological approach to interviewing" (p. 198). Unstructured interviews are useful when the research has "no presuppositions about what of importance may be learned ... " (Patton, 1980, p. 198). It was crucial for me to enter my research with no presuppositions about the experience of attending Kuper Island Indian Industrial School. Maintaining maximum flexibility allowed the information to be gathered in whatever direction the conversation went.

Authenticity was a concern for me from the time I started my research. I wanted to authentically tell another's story. That is, I was concerned about how I could tell someone else's story when I was the researcher (both the listener and the writer). How could I ensure that it was their story in their words, not mine? What worked best for me were series of dialogues. By this I mean that each time we met, the process was more storytelling in nature and interactive than questions and answers. The dialogues actually came to be only a part of the process. The relationship that transpired between the storytellers and me became very fluid. The storytellers would contact me either over the phone or in person and say "I just remembered another story," or tell me how they felt after the interviews, or how they felt when something else happened. I strongly believe that the relationship that developed was possible because of the nature of dialogue—storytelling:

> One of the most trenchant observations of contemporary anthropology is that meaning is not fixed, that it must be studied in practice—in the small interactions of everyday life. Such practice is more likely to emerge in dialogue than in a formal interview. (Cruickshank, 1998, p. 41)

To facilitate my desire to capture the essence of experience, I chose to conduct multiple dialogic interviews. However, there were many conversations during which I recorded and listened to the various stories of particular storytellers with little interaction other than the occasional "ahh," "really," "wow," "ha ha ha," and looks (I am sure) of disbelief. Mostly, the dialogues took place before and after the actual recording.

There was no need for me to question during the stories. Conversations took place over tea or coffee at either the storytellers' homes or mine. The storytellers decided where they wanted to meet. The interviews were tape-recorded and at the same time I would take brief notes. These notes often included my observations of the storytellers' physical reactions to their process and of my own reactions to the stories. After each conversation, I would listen to the tapes and re-read my notes. If I did not understand something that was recorded, I would ask for clarification at the next meeting. The process of clarification was brief, and then the stories would begin. The unstructured dialogical nature of the interviews enhanced the collection of stories.

I found it an interesting process to watch how the storytellers set their boundaries. Initially, storytellers openly shared the "easy" parts of their stories—that is, the parts of their stories that they felt safe discussing. Then, at each of the subsequent interviews, the storytellers returned to where they left off, and set out on their journey into the more dangerous, less explored territory of their experience at Kuper. It was after the second interview that the fluid nature of the process began. After beginning the exploration into the unexplored territory, the storytellers were often inundated with memory, feelings, thoughts, etc. At this point I began to receive phone calls at home. On one occasion, a storyteller phoned and asked me to come over that evening and tape-record; he was ready to tell more stories. I received phone calls from them saying things like "I remembered more about that time ...." I strongly believe that the flexible and personal nature of my research supported the storytellers during their process of sharing.

As my research focused on former students of Kuper Island Residential School, the participants were specifically selected. Also, they needed to feel safe and strong enough to share intimate parts of their lives in such an open and vulnerable way. Patton (1990) describes this process of selection as purposeful sampling. Purposeful sampling is a method of selecting "information-rich cases whose study will illuminate the questions under study" (Patton, 1990, p. 169). For the purposes of my research, I selected experts in the field of residential school. Specifically, the storytellers selected had first-hand experience from Kuper Island Indian Industrial School. Unquestionably, these former students were the experts because they have special skills and knowledge about this experience. Freire (1970) claims, "who are better prepared than the oppressed to understand the terrible significance of an oppressive society" (p. 27)?

Prior to any interviewing or recording, I met with each of the storytellers individually and explained the purpose, nature, and intended outcome of the research. We read through the informed consent form and they signed the form on that first meeting. From this point on, the storytellers took the lead role. I met with them when and where they wanted and for the length of time they determined.

As I had chosen storytelling as my methodology, how the stories were perceived, documented, and written was a crucial point. It was imperative that the stories remained the storytellers' stories and did not become mine. My story needed to remain separate. I had realized early on that as the researcher, I had such incredible power to shape the final work that I was doing. For example, had I decided to use interview questions for the most part, the thesis would have covered the areas that I deemed important enough to ask a question about. Another source of power to shape the work occurred once the interviews had been completed. I could have taken the transcriptions, wrote the stories myself, and finished the work necessary to complete my thesis. But I was determined to authentically represent the voices of the storytellers.

When the storytellers told me they were finished, I transcribed the tapes. The written transcription was given to the storytellers and I asked them to ensure that what was transcribed was accurate, encouraging them to add, delete, or edit what was written. Only then did I begin to formulate stories. As I drafted the stories, these too were passed back and forth between the storytellers and me.

The stories had to speak in the voices of the storytellers, not mine. This process was incredibly difficult as the transcription was not a single story told from beginning to end, but the many stories that had shaped their lives. I spent hours listening to the tapes and then relistening to their voices. As I wrote, I would ask myself how they would say this. My task was to compile all the stories into one story while at the same time not losing the intent of the many stories. I had to, in fact, find the story to tell.

How would they begin this story? I would listen and read the interviews over and over again, looking and listening for themes. Was there a phrase or topic that came up consistently that I could form a story around? This process of finding the story was more difficult than I ever anticipated. Well, actually, I was not really that sure what to anticipate as storytelling was brand new to me.

What words would they use to transition from one thought to another? As much as possible, throughout the story-writing process, I used the words of the storytellers directly from the transcripts. When I had to write a transition statement or statements, I would ask myself what words they use when they make a transition. These were areas in the stories that I would highlight and ask them to pay particular attention to. The first time I did this with one of the storytellers, he laughed and said, "Robina, this sounds so much like you!" So we rewrote that section! Really listening to their words and their voices was the only way that I could authentically present the voices of the storytellers. How might they end this story? Again, I listened and relistened. Did they have some closing statements that they might like to say? This was probably the easiest task in the storytelling process. Each of the storytellers naturally had words of wisdom that he or she wanted to share. Each had his or her own way and particular audience to address. The storytellers edited the stories into the format in which they were presented in my final thesis.

A final struggle that I want to share about editing is determining what to include and exclude. It was very difficult to make the decision to cut a piece of the transcript from the story. This too was done in consultation with the storytellers, but it was still tough. Even though I strove for authentic voice representation, how influential was I in shaping the story by including some things and excluding others? I have not completely resolved this yet. It should be a struggle—as researchers, we have the power to shape the lives of the storytellers and this issue should be taken seriously.

The notion of how to do this work right (some might call this ethics) was of utmost concern for me. How could I do this work with a good mind and a good heart or, to use the Hul'qumi'num word, uy'skwuluwun? In this story I will begin to touch on some aspects of this subject. A part of ethics for me as a Lyackson woman relates to my responsibility to the storytellers. I was "witness" to their stories, and as such was responsible for ensuring that the work done respected uy'skwuluwun—that is, that I had paid attention to their words, their lives. Over my life, I have been taught that when you ask people to share their wisdom, you must respect and honour their teachings. This was the most important ethical responsibility that I had. I had to ensure that while I was storytelling, I simultaneously respected and honoured the storytellers.

Prior to beginning my research, I believed that informed consent and confidentiality would be the most important ethical concerns. As each of my storytellers had agreed prior to my research that they wanted to be involved, informed consent was established prior to beginning the work. All the storytellers knew they were going to share their lived experience. There was no room for deception. The participants were involved in all stages of the research, including data analysis, editing, and participating at my thesis defence.

As for confidentiality, two of the storytellers had already publicly identified themselves as having attended Kuper Island. They did not want to be anonymous for the purpose of this research. Lipson (1993) claims that researchers "should do everything in their power to protect the physical, social and psychological welfare of informants and to honor their dignity and privacy" (p. 335) unless they want to be identified. The three participants were Belvie Berber, Delmar Johnnie, and Herman Thomas. Originally, one storyteller wanted to use an alias to protect himself and his family. However, once we had finished interviewing and writing the story, he said that he wanted to use his own name—this was his story.

Punch (1994), when discussing ethics, states: "in essence, most concern revolves around issues of harm, consent, deception, privacy, and confidentiality of data" (p. 89). While I certainly agree with these issues, what I experienced was not quite that simple. There were ethical issues that I had not anticipated, and I now call these the Spirit of Ethics. I believed, when I began this work, that I was prepared. I had read every book, article, and story that I could get my hands on pertaining to residential schools. I had talked to nearly everyone I knew that had attended one of those institutions. But, I was far from prepared. I had no idea what obstacles lay ahead on my path.

When I began my research, I thought about working from a place of uy'skwuluwun while at the same time being involved in a community where I am well known. What I failed to consider was the emotional impact of listening and sharing stories when the characters are family. Many of the stories included family members. At times, listening to stories of my family caused me much sadness. Here I was, as a part of my thesis, learning about my family. Some of the stories were funny, but others were so sad and tragic. And this was my family too.

However, had I not been there, I would not have had the opportunity to learn. Here I was, listening to stories of the past, about my Ancestors, my Grandparents, Aunts, Uncles, and Cousins. I was given the gift of knowledge that I otherwise would not have had.

As the storytellers were family, there was little choice but to be a part of the research. Again, being so intimately involved in the research was emotionally draining. Interview after interview I would leave physically, mentally, spiritually, and emotionally exhausted. I thought that I would do an interview a day, but I never thought about how much time would be needed between interviews to feel balanced and prepared for the next interview.

One day I drove northward on Vancouver Island to interview one of the storytellers. The night before, I had interviewed for about five hours. I was thinking about the interview and began to cry. I almost had to pull over because I was completely overwhelmed with grief. I learned to pay particular attention to the time necessary to heal between interviews and then to prepare for the next.

On the same day as that I was overcome with grief, I wondered about uy'skwuluwun. Was asking people to participate in this research and share this grief working from a good mind and heart? I now knew how painful it was for the storytellers to relive those times. I had heard and seen the pain, agony, sadness, and grief that the storytellers endured while sharing their stories. For the sake of research, should I continue? Here I was falling apart, but it was their lives. At this time I needed to consult as many people as I could. Should I continue? Was this ethical? Is there another way of doing this project?

My conflict was quickly resolved when two storytellers contacted me after really difficult interviews. Both of them shared the agony they had gone through with the interview, but also the lightness they felt after going back to that place and telling about what really happened. So the research would go on.

With the storytellers acknowledging the healing nature of sharing, I knew the stories would continue. But I also knew that I needed to be aware of my own Spirit. During one interview, the storyteller was sharing an incident of sexual abuse. As I sat and listened, I started feeling physically numb. I had to consciously say to my Spirit, "You must move over here beside me." This needed to be a mental process because the pain and grief of this story were too harsh for my soul. I would leave and pray to the Creator to make sense of this stuff that I was hearing and feeling.

Just as I felt this responsibility to the storytellers, I also felt a responsibility to the Ancestors—my Grandmothers, Grandfathers, and all those residential school students who had gone to the other side. And, I wondered, what does it really mean to say that the reason I have chosen storytelling as my research methodology is because it honours the oral traditions of my Ancestors?

I have come to realize, more through my inability to write my thesis than through the writing of it, that this process must be real. I was unable to use words such as "honour," "tradition," and "Ancestors" only as token words that glorify or romanticize my academic process of producing a thesis. There was a point in the research when I was unable to write. I wondered why. As I closely examined the work, I realized that I had, on one hand, the stories—the words that honoured the traditional teachings of my Ancestors. Then, on the other hand, a traditional academic process was shaping the remainder of the thesis. I felt that I was not a part of either. The traditional academic words did not have life; they were not a part of me—of my identity—nor was this work in anyway respecting uy'skwuluwun.

As I mentioned above, in 1998 I received my traditional name, Qwul'sih'yah'maht. Aunty Helen wanted me to have a name so that I would always remain grounded in where I am from—a Coast Salish woman, partner, mother, daughter, sister, granddaughter, aunt, friend, etc. With this name came the responsibility of walking in a good way that honours and respects my Grandmother, Lavina Wyse Prest.

The message I received from the Creator and my Ancestors was that I was not to use words that justified an academic process of meeting my thesis requirements, but to believe in and use the integrity of a storytelling approach throughout the thesis. As such, my final thesis was many interconnected stories—no beginning and no end, but rich with teachings and gifts.

Storytelling traditionally was, and still is, a teaching tool. As such, the stories that are told in research too will be teaching tools. Sharing stories validates the various experiences of the storytellers, but also has the ability to give others with similar stories the strength, encouragement, and support they need to tell their stories. For example, as more and more former students are coming forward in quest of justice for the crimes of the residential school system, stories shared about others' experiences at residential schools can support them as they tell their own stories. As such, storytelling is also a tool of resistance. This research begins to uncover the genocidal characteristics of residential schools.

Many of us have stories in our families that have never been shared. This in part is another impact of colonization. Stories and legends were our culture and tradition, and over the years these rituals were banned through legislation and then enforced and entrenched through residential schools. We need to go back and collect these stories and share them with our families, friends, and communities. Consequently, another significant gift of storytelling is the ability to share and document missing pieces of our history and pass these teachings on to our future generations. As stories continue to be told, we continue to build the strength and capacity to continue our resistance to colonization and assimilation.

I never dreamed of learning what I learned. I never dreamed of learning to listen in such a powerful way. Storytelling, despite all the struggles, enabled me to respect and honour the Ancestors and the storytellers while at the same time sharing tragic, traumatic, inhumanly unbelievable truths that our people had lived. It was this level of integrity that was essential to storytelling.

I am not a storytelling expert. No, I see myself as a storyteller-in-training. Having used storytelling as my methodology for my thesis, I will continue the rigorous path required to train as I see the countless gifts and teaching that storytelling has to offer each of us. When we make personal what we teach, as I see storytelling doing, we touch people in a different and more profound way. As I end my storytelling story, I want to thank each of you for being witness to my story.

It's December as I write this conclusion, and again I find myself thinking about fish. What is the connection between fish and stories, you might ask. Simple—they are both soul food—they feed my spirit. Stories continue to do what they always have—teach. Through these teachings we continue to pass on values and beliefs, morals, history, and instil a sense of pride in our young people. Recently, I had the honour of sitting in on two lectures given by Dovie Thomason, a Lakota and Kiowa Apache storyteller. Thomason shared the importance of storytelling and stated that there are things going on in our communities today that we never had stories for. These stories need to be created and told. And, we can see how important stories are—they bring the past, the future, and present together for now and for the next seven generations.

References

Berber, Belvie. Mentor.

Cruikshank, J. (1990). *Life lived like a story: Life stories of three Yukon Native elders in collaboration with Angela Sidney, Kitty Smith & Annie Ned.* Vancouver: UBC Press.

Cruickshank, J. (1998). *The social life of stories: Narrative and knowledge in the Yukon Territory.* Vancouver: UBC Press.

Freire, P. (1970). *Pedagogy of the oppressed.* New York: Continuum Publishing Company.

Furniss, E. (1992). *Victims of benevolence: The dark legacy of the Williams Lake residential school.* Vancouver: Arsenal Pulp Press.

Gluck, S., and Patai, D. (Eds.). (1991). *Women's words: The feminist practice of oral history.* New York: Routledge.

Johnnie, Delmar. Mentor.

Josephson, Val. Grandmother.

Lipson, J. (1993). Ethical issues in ethnography. In J.M. Morse (Ed.), *Critical issues in qualitative research methods.* Newbury Park: Sage.

Maxwell, J. (1996). *Qualitative research design: An interactive approach.* Thousand Oaks: Sage.

Mihesuah, D. (Ed.). (1998). *Natives and academics: Researching and writing about American Indians.* Lincoln: University of Nebraska Press.

Moody, Mary. Grandmother.

Nelson, Alex. Mentor.

Patton, M. (1980). *Qualitative evaluation methods.* Beverly Hills: Sage.

Patton, M. (1990). *Qualitative evaluation and research methods.* Thousand Oaks: Sage.

Prest, Lavina. Grandmother.

Punch, M. (1994). Politics and ethics in qualitative research. In N.K. Denzin and Y.S. Lincoln (Eds.), *Handbook of qualitative research,* 83–97. Thousand Oaks: Sage.

Reinharz, S. (1992). *Feminist methods in social research.* New York: Oxford University Press, Inc.

Silko, L. (1998). *Yellow woman and a beauty of the spirit: Essays on Native American life today.* New York: Touchstone.

Thomas, Herman. Mentor.

Wilson, A. (1998a). American Indian history or non-Indian perceptions of American Indian history? In D. Mihesuah (Ed.), *Natives and academics: Researching and writing about American Indians,* pp. 23–26. Lincoln: University of Nebraska Press.

Wilson, A. (1998b). Grandmother to granddaughter: Generations of oral history in a Dakota family. In D. Mihesuah (Ed.), *Natives and academics: Researching and writing about American Indians,* pp. 27–36. Lincoln: University of Nebraska Press.

Yow, V. (1994). *Recording oral history: A practical guide for social scientists.* Thousand Oaks: Sage.

CHAPTER TEN

BECOMING AN
ANTI-OPPRESSIVE RESEARCHER

Karen Potts and Leslie Brown[1]

Beginning with Choices, Assumptions, and Tenets

Given a simple choice between being an oppressive and an anti-oppressive researcher, hopefully we would all choose the latter. However, the choice is not really that simple or straightforward. Committing ourselves to anti-oppressive work means committing to social change and to taking an active role in that change. Being an anti-oppressive researcher means that there is political purpose and action to your research work. Whether that purpose is on a broad societal level or about personal growth, by choosing to be an anti-oppressive researcher, one is making an explicit, personal commitment to social justice. Anti-oppressive research involves making explicit the political practices of creating knowledge. It means making a commitment to the people you are working with personally and professionally in order to mutually foster conditions for social justice and research. It is about paying attention to, and shifting, how power relations work in and through the processes of doing research.

The purpose of this chapter is to explain more about this concept of "anti-oppressive research" in a way that we hope will be helpful to all researchers, and to research students in particular. We do this first by outlining key principles or tenets, then discussing how anti-oppressive research may look in the process. We provide one student researcher's example of how she applied anti-oppressive research, and finish with a few closing thoughts. We tried to keep the research jargon to a minimum and offer some definitions via endnotes when a term seemed important to further understanding.

A Bit about Us

Before we go too far, for purposes of transparency and context, it's important for us to explain where we as authors have come from and hope to go to in becoming anti-oppressive researchers. Both of us are social workers whose field practices used research as a method of working toward social justice goals, Karen as a community development worker and social economist, and Leslie as an academic researcher with First Nations communities. We met when we were both teaching an undergraduate social work research class at the University of Victoria. When the School of Social Work began to develop its mission focusing on anti-oppressive theory and practice in the late 1990s, we realized we wanted to articulate a research approach more consistent with anti-oppressive work.

Both of us had already been struggling in our field practice and as academics with the assumptions underlying traditional, positivist research, and both of us had looked at and experimented with many alternative methodologies. With our research attempts we had run into the same problem that perplexed Lather: how is it that "our very efforts to liberate (through our research) perpetuate the relations of dominance" (Lather, 1991, p. 16)? We found that part of this problem was because qualitative research, as a general category, was still often laden with positivist assumptions about epistemology.[2]

Initially, Karen was very committed to participatory action research, but began to see the difficulties in applying this methodology within institutional constraints. Participatory action research seemed to have been co-opted by mainstream researchers, that is, academic researchers claimed that their research was "participatory," but the locus of power and initiation of the research remained firmly grounded in the hands of the academics, not the "participants."[3] Leslie was a feminist researcher who found this approach was insufficient when working with First Nations communities. We found that empowerment approaches spoke to the process of the research, but still often fell short of our goals of social change and justice. We were also concerned that the newest trend, currently called "community-based research," did not really ground itself in the community control that we felt strongly about. Therefore, our interest in articulating something we are calling "anti-oppressive research" is not only to be consistent with the school's emerging mission statement, but also for our own personal and practice values.

We first began to write this chapter five years ago as an introductory article for the 175 students who take our curriculum's research course each year. In our struggle to articulate an "anti-oppressive research approach," it was soon apparent that this truly was an act of "becoming." We found ourselves rewriting this paper every year to reflect our emerging ideas and critical[4] reflections, and no doubt we will continue to do so. What has remained constant is our assumed audience for this chapter—student researchers who we hope will take up research[5] as a tool for their anti-oppressive practice. In their feedback on drafts of this chapter, our academic colleagues have said, "What about us?!" So, yes, we hope that the experienced researcher will find this chapter useful as well, but we remain committed to speaking directly to our primary audience—students of research, who want to make research part of their daily social justice practice.

So, a Bit about You, Our Assumed Reader

In our work as instructors we have seen research students approach research as everything from frightening, to boring, to mystifying, and many points in between. We want to argue that research can be emancipating, community building, a catalyst for social change, and a starting point for some serious self-discovery. So since we will probably talk about research in a very different way than you are used to, for this chapter to make sense, and for it to make an impact on the type of work you do, we are going to ask for some "leaps of faith" from you, our readers.

First, we want you to consider that even if you are a beginning researcher or an experienced researcher, you have already done research. By research, we want you to think of the poll you took of friends and family about your first relationship, or how you decided on a place to live the last time you moved. We need you to set aside the idea of research being only something that "experts," usually men in white lab coats with rats and statistics, engage in. Some social research texts encourage the myth of the elite, expert researcher; that research is something only to be dreamt about by the "un-credentialed." For example, one book describes itself as "permitting" students to "put a toe in the water, so to speak, to give beginning social work students a taste of what it might be like to swim" (Williams, Unrau, and Grinnell, 1998, p. vi). We believe that anti-oppressive research—the art of asking questions, building relationships, seeking answers, and coming up with

257

more questions—is in the art of daily life. All of us can swim and have been doing so most of our lives.

Secondly, we need you to see yourself as potentially both oppressor and oppressed. We ask that you believe in your capacity for "agency"—that is, your capacity to act and alter the relations of oppression in your own world. Most of us can recognize oppression when it occurs or when we are being oppressed ourselves, but can we also recognize the complicity that each of us has in creating and sustaining oppression over others? This is often harder, especially for all of us who are well-meaning people. For White, middle-class, able-bodied, heterosexual people, this is our most important work in anti-oppressive practice—recognizing our own privilege and working to dismantle the unjust systems that keep us in that privileged space. The key in recognizing oppression is seeing the oppression that occurs through the various activities, social relations, and social practices we engage in with others. One such activity is the research process, even when as a student researcher you feel like the least powerful person in the world.

Third, we want you to consider that anti-oppressive social work, including research, is not contingent upon physical or political location. It can be done anywhere by everyone. The political nature of our environment is important to recognize and work with, but we do not have to have a job description that says "anti-oppressive researcher" (good luck waiting for that one!) before we can do anti-oppressive research. As social workers we are located everywhere, including dominant institutions such as government departments, schools, and hospitals. Anti-oppressive research is more than critique; it is something do-able. We want you to consider that doing anti-oppressive research is a commitment to a set of principles, values, and ways of working, and that you can carry out these principles anywhere—it's a matter of choice amid various constraints.

Fourth, we would like you to see anti-oppressive research as a method of social work practice. We therefore will argue that anti-oppressive research is not just something you do when you have been asked to conduct a research project, but that anti-oppressive research is also a strategy you could use when you are doing community building, economic development, policy analysis, counselling work, etc. If anti-oppressive research can truly be a tool of emancipation and social justice, as well as a method of inquiry, then it should also be seen as a method of intervention.

This brings us to the last "leap of faith" or assumption we are asking you to make. We would like you to consider the power of epistemic privilege[6] and agency. Communities, those we label as "clients" who are the lived experts in issues under study, have their own capacity to recover knowledge. We believe that all of us have "agency," that ability to act which separates us as subjects from objects. Often when we label ourselves as "clients" or have been labelled as "clients" (or students), and have been treated as objects for so long, our "agency" is a bit rusty and needs a bit of nurturing. Therefore, we argue that those people who have experienced an issue are perhaps the best people to research that issue. However, seeing the value in epistemic privilege and realizing agency is not always straightforward or easy.

A Bit about Theory

Anti-oppressive theories are emergent and people take these up in many different ways. Therefore, it is important that we situate ourselves, and this chapter, in relation to theory. For the purpose of this paper, we see anti-oppressive theory[7] as an extension of Marxist, feminist, and most predominantly critical theory.[8] Critical theory informs our conception and practice of anti-oppressive social work and research. In addition, poststructural and postcolonial thought, feminist, Indigenous, queer, and anti-racist theories have contributed to our understanding of anti-oppressive approaches. Our theoretical stance is evident in the tenets we propose for anti-oppressive research. Our theoretical "baggage" shows by virtue of the language we use and the concepts we focus on in our emerging tenets for anti-oppressive research. For example, social justice is most often linked to critical theory. The idea that knowledge is socially constructed is often associated with Marxism and feminism.

Three Emerging Tenets of Anti-oppressive Research

We propose three tenets of anti-oppressive research. These are not discrete; rather, they are fully interrelated and our articulation of them reflects how they inform one another. When we want to reflect on whether our research work is actually anti-oppressive research, we refer to these principles to assess our topic, our methods, our relationships, our analysis, our action, and the overall evaluation of our research work.

Anti-oppressive Research Is Social Justice and Resistance in Process and in Outcome

Research can be a powerful tool for social change. It also can, and has been, just as powerful in maintaining the status quo and supporting the evolution of societies that reward some people and inhibit others. Research can be used to suppress ideas, people, and social justice just as easily—maybe even more easily—than it can be used to respect, empower, and liberate. Good intentions are never enough to produce anti-oppressive processes or outcomes.

Choosing to be an anti-oppressive researcher is not for the faint of heart. Being a dedicated social worker or a competent researcher is not enough. As anti-oppressive workers, we are social justice[9] activists, not only in the placard-waving sense, but also in the sense of making a personal commitment to action, of purposefully working to make change for individuals, communities, and institutions. As anti-oppressive researchers, we recognize that usually the first target of change is ourselves.

Many research endeavours have a social justice outcome in mind. However, this chapter is not about research such as the social justice statistical work of the Canadian Centre for Policy Alternatives, which publishes important research on poverty, alternative budgets, and so on. We laud this work, but it is important to recognize that there is an epistemological difference between such social justice research, grounded in reclaiming positivism, and what we are describing here as anti-oppressive research.

Choosing to be an anti-oppressive researcher means choosing to do research and support research that challenges the status quo in its *processes* as well as its outcomes. It seeks to resist oppression embedded in our selves, our work, and our world. bell hooks talks about the challenges of "teaching to transgress," of creating an environment in which we continually reflect on our processes in order to transform the enterprise of teaching and learning (hooks, 1994). Similarly, anti-oppressive researchers have the challenge of continually reflecting, critiquing, challenging, and supporting their own and others' efforts in the process of research and knowledge production to transform the enterprise of research, social work, and ultimately the world in which we live.

Anti-oppressive Research Recognizes That All Knowledge Is Socially Constructed[10] and Political

> Science and empiricism offer no more an "objective" explanation of the world and reality than, for example, ancient myths. (Chambon, Irving, and Epstein, 1999, p. 34)

So how do we know what we know? This is a question of epistemology, and it is key for understanding an anti-oppressive approach to research. From an anti-oppressive perspective, knowledge does not exist in and of itself, isolated from people. Rather, it is produced through the interactions of people, and as all people are socially located (in their race, gender, ability, class identities, and so on) with biases, privileges, and differing power relations, so too is the creation of knowledge socially located, socially constructed. Recognizing that knowledge is socially constructed means understanding that knowledge doesn't exist "out there" but is embedded in people and the power relations between us. It recognizes that "truth" is a verb; it is created, it is multiple: truth does not exist, it is made. Therefore, in anti-oppressive research, we are not looking for a "truth"; we are looking for meaning, for understanding, for the power to change.

Having accepted that there are many "truths," each socially constructed, whose knowledge is constructed through our research projects? Knowledge has become a commodity in the new "knowledge economy." Patents and copyrights protect the elite ownership of knowledge and such ownership can then be bought and sold. This puts the power of knowledge into the hands of the elite, the wealthy, and the privileged. Anti-oppressive research puts the ownership of knowledge back into the hands of those who experience it, who need it.

Picking up on the notion of how power and knowledge are inherently interrelated, anti-oppressive researchers recognize that knowledge is political; it is not benign as it is created in the power relations between people. Knowledge can be oppressive in how it is constructed and utilized and/or it can be a means of resistance. Often, it is a complex combination of both. Anti-oppressive practice is about resistance and therefore research processes can also become acts of resistance.

Anti-oppressive researchers are aware of the dynamics involved in the social construction of knowledge, and use this awareness to further the goals of social justice. Therefore, anti-oppressive research is not a process to discover knowledge, but a political process to co-create and rediscover knowledge. Through anti-oppressive research, we construct emancipatory, liberatory knowledge that can be acted on, by, and in the interests of the marginalized and oppressed.

The Anti-oppressive Research Process Is All about Power and Relationships

> If power is cunning and pervasive enough, it will co-opt freedom; if freedom is resistant and persistent enough, it will cause power to tremble. (Caputo, 2000, p. 33)

So what is power and what does it have to do with the research process? Power is a concept that has been taken up in many different ways by many different theorists. For the purposes of this chapter, we use a conceptualization proposed by Elias:

> Instead of power being a "thing" which persons, groups, or institutions possess to a greater or lesser degree, Elias argued that we should think in terms of power relations, with ever-changing "balances" or "ratios" of power between individuals and social units … and that all human relationships are essentially relations of power. (van Krieken, 2003, p. 118)

To apply Elias's idea of power relations, consider the relationship in positivist research between the researcher and those being "researched." In positivism, the researcher is the expert and is seen as the primary, and often only, person with the power and ability to create knowledge, to act on that knowledge, and to profit from its "creation." Those who are being studied, although they are not necessarily treated badly, are nevertheless objects; they are acted upon and have no input or real involvement or control in the process. In positivist research, those being researched rarely have any interpersonal relationship with the researcher, and there is usually no recognition of these hierarchical and distant power relations or any attempt to change them.

Even in many qualitative or what are termed "empowerment"[11] approaches to research, the relationship between researchers and the researched is often paternalistic. "Participatory" approaches often have members of the researched group conducting interviews or surveys, but with little substantive control over the research process. "Giving" people voice and hearing their stories can be exploitative/paternalistic or empowering or a confusing mix of power relations. Attending to issues of power in the relationships between people involved in research is complex.

In anti-oppressive research, a number of key relationships and power relations are foregrounded; that is, relations between:

- the knower and known
- groups of knowers
- knowers and any outside researchers
- researchers and external institutions and ideological paradigms

In anti-oppressive research, constant attention is given to these relations, and care is taken to shift power from those removed from what is trying to be "known" to those closest to it—that is, those people with epistemic privilege or lived experience of the issue under study. In anti-oppressive research, we say that "we do not begin to collect data in a community until all the dogs know us," which is our way of saying "no research without relationships." We do not approach relationships as time-specific, beginning and ending, throw-away relationships. Rather, we approach them as if we may be in relationship with people for life.

Rethinking the Researching Process: Anti-oppressive Practice in the Process of Inquiry

Anti-oppressive research requires an attitude that accepts ambivalence and uncertainty, thereby enabling us to question that which appears "normal" and taken for granted to (re)negotiate processes and create spaces for ourselves and others who are commonly excluded from the creation of knowledge. We have found that the work of becoming anti-oppressive researchers has challenged us to reflect upon our sense of self, history, our context(s), and our actions with others. It has highlighted the need for skills in thinking critically, listening carefully, and analyzing relations of power of which we are a part so that we can identify and unpack assumptions, unearth patterns of thinking and acting, and recognize their effects.

In most social research texts, the research process is described as a problem-solving process. You are likely familiar with this linear process: (1) pose a question; (2) design a plan to study it; (3) collect some information; (4) analyze the information; (5) draw some conclusions and pose new questions. We contend that research is not as linear as this model implies. In fact, this linear problem-solving model reproduces the dominant Western scientific method(ology) of constructing knowledge. As well this model leaves out some key research processes, like taking action on the knowledge that our work constructs.

While we question the linearity commonly associated with conducting research, we acknowledge that the dominant discourse of social work remains grounded in the linear scientific method. One of our main purposes in writing this chapter is to show how there are alternative ways of interpreting and engaging within the (research) process that is produced by and reproduces power relations that do not oppress anyone or reinforce relations of domination. Therefore, we decided to organize our discussion of rethinking the research process within this problematic problem-solving structure—not to reinscribe the model but to demonstrate our epistemological assumption that we work from where we are, not from where we would rather be.

Questioning

> Learning is really remembering, found by asking the right questions
>
> —Plato

Questioning is the "mess-finding" stage in the research process as well as the one that opens us up to possibilities. What are the issues? What do we know already? What is our relationship to the issues and questions? What do other people know about it? What do we want to find out?

Anti-oppressive research involves paying attention to power relations, beginning with asking, "Who says this is a question that needs to be studied anyway?" We also find ourselves constantly negotiating our position along a continuum of insider/outsider relations. On the insider pole of the continuum is epistemic privilege; that is, the privilege insiders have since they have lived experience of the issue under study. The outsider end of the continuum is a more traditional, positivist researcher role. You position yourself as outside the situation and in a position of studying "Others." Most of us on the journey of becoming anti-oppressive researchers find ourselves somewhere in the middle of the continuum. In practice, negotiating and positioning ourselves as researchers is seldom as simple as declaring which position we hold. In some instances, we may think we are insiders only to find that others involved in the project (especially those providing data) see us as set apart, as outsiders. There are insider/outsider tensions in all research relationships. Linda Tuhiwai Smith (1999) talks about her experience as a Maori woman doing research in her own community.

> I was an insider as a Maori mother and an advocate of the language revitalization movement, and I shared in the activities of fund raising and organizing. Through my different tribal relationships I had close links to some of the mothers and to the woman who was the main organizer .... When I began the discussions and negotiations over my research, however, I became much more aware of the things which made me an outsider. I was attending university as a graduate student; I had worked for several years as a teacher and had a professional income; I had a husband; and we owned a car which was second-hand but actually registered. As I became more involved in the project, interviewing the women about their own education stories, and as I visited them in their own homes, these differences became much more marked .... An interview with a researcher is formal. (Tuhiwai Smith, 1999, p. 138)

Therefore, as Tuhiwai Smith illustrates, outsider relations are established in the very declaration that a question is "research" with all its formal connotations. There is an inherent power in naming the issue to be studied and why it is worthy of study. The research topic and question(s) guide the research by articulating what is, and therefore what isn't, to be explored. Anti-oppressive researchers pay attention to the ways a research topic is produced and pose various questions to ascertain what is happening and uncover assumptions. Who is involved in shaping the topic? What is and what is not explored? Anti-oppressive researchers continually wrestle with whose interests are being served (and not being served) by the study of this question.

For example, consider these questions in analyzing the politics of the research question: Is there funding available for certain topics? Who determines those topics and why? Is an issue "hot" because it is topical in the newspaper? If so, who decides what gets to be newsworthy and why? Is an agency requesting the research? If so, what are their reasons, explicit and implicit, for doing so? Is it to justify future funding? Is it to rationalize actions already committed to? Is it for reflecting on practice in order to change processes? Has an instructor requested it? Is it developed by participants and, if so, why? It is important to acknowledge who is involved, or to be involved, in any way in the research. There are a myriad of reasons and interests to be served in any piece of research.

A topic may be readily converted into a research question with little regard for the political and epistemological implications of posing such a question in a particular way. In anti-oppressive research, we closely examine our process of creating topics and questions. We work to avoid jumping thoughtlessly from what "we" interpret is happening to the development of a topic, and then to a question. Instead, we contemplate the possible effects of asking a particular question as opposed to other questions, and strive to unearth our assumptions about people, relationship, power, and knowledge that are embedded in each of the ways that we might construct the question. As our individual perspectives are limited, we do so in concert with others. Then we can make more informed choices about which topic and question we really want to pursue.

For instance, we may ask: What relations of domination might be reinscribed by the questions we pose? The way a question is posed may embed the research(er) in a particular epistemology that may not be well suited for this particular research. Often in conventional practice, questions of epistemology are not asked and researchers assume the dominant discourse as a given. As noted earlier, in anti-oppressive research we pay attention to the ways we construct knowledge, who is a knower, and what can be known.

This initial stage of questioning involves finding out what others know about the topic. Traditionally, this means checking the academic literature. Being an anti-oppressive researcher means critically reading existing knowledge to understand how it was constructed, by whom and for whose benefit, and therefore how it will affect our construction of research about the issue. Anti-oppressive researchers recognize "knowledge" other than what is published in academic books and articles. For instance, lived experience of self and others can also provide a valid point of departure for a research topic. Popular knowledge found in magazines and on TV may also supplement data. We each have to ask ourselves how we determine the trustworthiness or validity of knowledge. Are we more persuaded by what our professor says or what our mom says about our topic? Critical assessment of the

266

various sources of knowledge on a topic and the authority each source brings to that knowledge is part of an anti-oppressive approach to the first stage of the research process.

As important as it is to have a clear starting place, the initial clarity of the research question is tenuously held. When it comes down to it, finding "the question" is seldom that simple. Sometimes the question finds us. Sometimes questions are more like hunches, experienced tensions, or disjunctures sensed in our own lives. Going from clarity to fuzziness can be okay. Questions usually change as the inquiry proceeds. And sometimes the question that was answered is not clearly revealed until the end of the process. We have often found that throughout the process, we learn more about what it was we really wanted to know. The art of the question is in the re-researching, the willingness to look again.

Designing and Redesigning a Plan to Study the Questions

Anti-oppressive research must be anti-oppressive in terms of both purpose and process. More often than not, social work research strives to be anti-oppressive in terms of purpose; that is, the desired outcomes are consistent with goals of social change. But this focus alone can result in the objectifying study of "the oppressed." Because of this, we argue that we need to push the boundaries of good intentions and power relations beyond the ultimate outcome to the research process as well. Significant thought and relationship building are integral to the designing and planning of emancipatory methods. The research journey must be purposeful (goals) and intentional (process).

When you are on a planned road trip, you often run across opportunities and obstacles that didn't exist on your map. Modifications to the plan are made within the context of your purpose, who is on the trip, how much time and money you have, and so on. Similarly, a research design is a dynamic plan that gets tweaked and altered along the way. The process is shaped by the design, which reflects the goals of the research. The intention or purpose of the research is interrogated and made clearer as one considers the topic and question. It is revisited throughout the research journey. As the topic, questions, and purpose become clearer, ideas about data, data sources, and ways to gather and think about data begin to emerge. This feeds the development of a research design.

There are many questions that an anti-oppressive researcher asks in the ongoing process of articulating a design. These questions arise out of an epistemological understanding of the nature of the relationship between the researcher and the researched. Who has an interest or stake in the research? Who are we going to involve, and how? What are the ethical considerations in the research? How are we going to collect data and, once collected, how are we going to interpret it? Who owns the data? What constraints are there to the research design? What criteria will we use to judge the quality of our research? Exploring these questions is integral to the process of designing a research study.

The first question posed asks us to consider how the various interests/power relations construct the research process. Just as there are stakeholders in the construction of the research question, there are stakeholders in the research design, and they may not be the same people. For example, if perchance we are doing a research project as part of a university course, then we have to be aware of how the requirements of the assignment and the ethical review processes of the university construct the research and constrain the possibilities. Or, if our purpose is to secure future funding for an addictions support program and we know that the funders want to know the extent of the problem, who needs to be served, and what alternative programs cost, we would not likely design a research project that interviewed one client in great depth about her experience as a drug user. If we happened to be receiving pay from a government department, we also have to recognize how the interests of government will affect our relations with participants we may be working with in the research. Conversely, if we didn't have external funding but were working collectively with others to explore an issue common to all of us all, we would want to ensure that our design included the collective participation of everyone in the group rather than being controlled by one designated researcher. Regardless of the project, there are always interests that shape the conduct of the research and ultimately the construction of knowledge produced.

There are also interests that will affect the utility of the research. It is therefore useful to develop relationships with our potential audience and with those whom we are targeting for change. Politically, we have to consider when is the best time to engage this stakeholder group. There may be some merit to engaging this group throughout the research process in order to build rapport and possible support. There are a variety of ways one might consider, from developing an advisory group made up of representatives of all stakeholders to connecting the marginalized with the dominant through the actual research processes. Touraine, for example, achieved change in an organization through the process of putting labour and management representatives together in the same focus group in order to "reproduce social relationships in a research context, bringing together dominant and contesting actors in the same research groups" (McDonald, 2003, p. 248). Whatever the approach, the intention is that the actual process of the research becomes an intervention for change rather than relying only on the impact of the research outcome, or product.

At some points decisions will need to be made regarding who to involve in some or all of the research process. This is what positivist researchers may call developing a "sampling strategy." However, the goals for anti-oppressive research are very different as involving people is done more for community building, empowerment, and a better understanding than for goals of representativeness or validity. "Sampling" in anti-oppressive research is seldom random. Sampling is a power-laden decision and seen as one of many political acts in research. In this, ideally, an outsider researcher is never the sole source of invitations to participate. Ideally it is a community of participants/ insider researchers who do the inviting/including.

Ethical questions affect every research design. The ethics of anti-oppressive research reflect a commitment to and respect for people and relationships as well as for action and social justice. The use of "informed consent" is one example. Constant renegotiation regarding a process of informed consent is important as this highlights our commitments to the community, about our relationship to them, the data, and the process. Although most "informed consent" processes have become institutionalized for purposes of avoiding liability, we have reclaimed the concept of "informed consent" to be a formal contract of our obligations to research participants, and a declaration of their ownership of the data, their right to a transparent research process, and their right to as much involvement or control as they choose. Certainly this way of working has led to some interesting situations for us (e.g., a community deciding to withdraw its data toward the end of a study) and as logistically difficult as these situations have and can be, revisiting the ethics of anti-oppressive research guides one's decision making.

Respecting people and relationships also guide our response to questions of the ownership of data. The term "data" in its origins means "gift." From an anti-oppressive perspective, we see data as a gift that participants bestow and we work to respect those gifts and treat them ethically. This means we must ask who owns the data, and what does ownership mean? If "we" (researchers) agree that participants own the data, and if after the research is completed the participants decide they don't like what we, the researchers, have said, what happens then?[12] Or if we hear the story of a participant that is compelling but filled with tangential comments and expressions that we feel are distracting to what the research is saying, do we have the right to edit their story? Once edited, whose story is it? There are at least three voices in interpreting data: the participant who gives the story, the writer/researcher who records and retells it, and the reader who interprets it (Marcotte, 1995). "How are all these voices attended to?" is a question we ask ourselves. Developing and attending to relationships, including those to data and data sources, is critical in anti-oppressive research.

Identifying the constraints to any design is important so that an anti-oppressive researcher can then identify the spaces within those constraints that can make the research less oppressive in its process, and ultimately in its outcome. The types of constraints you will encounter will differ and change in every inquiry. However, there are some constraints that you can usually anticipate, such as time, resources, and institutional/organizational structures. For example, if your research is connected with a university, you will be expected to submit your study for approval to an ethics review committee. In general, the policies of these committees have been designed to address the issues of ethics in positivist research. Therefore, you might anticipate having to mould your presentation of an anti-oppressive research design to fit these institutional regulations. In another example, suppose you have been asked by government to do some research. You will likely have a limited time frame and budget and may face the constraints of having the research questions predetermined, and possibly the design as well. Just because we may be confined to doing a standardized survey questionnaire doesn't mean that we can't think about how to involve participants in the research, its process, and its outcome. Rather than designing the questionnaire yourself in isolation, it is possible to give up or share control with those being "researched" to design the questions and the process. Rather than administer a questionnaire "to" participants, for example, we could complete it "with" participants. This should be more than just semantics; this shift in language produces a different relationship among the people involved in the research. It is also important that we never ask questions of others that we are not willing to answer and share ourselves. Whatever the challenges and constraints, we have a responsibility to work with what we have, to not give up.

We wondered whether a partial solution to responding to the constraints we face is to place what we really want to know within what we are permitted to ask. To illustrate, Leslie conducted some research for the Royal Commission on Aboriginal Peoples where there were particular research questions posed by the Commission that she was charged with researching. Within these overriding interests, communities involved in the research each developed their own research questions, and subsequently unique research designs, that would respond to the particular needs of their community. The challenge was to make the research useful for each participating community while still attending to the goals (constraints) of the Royal Commission.

Within the design, it is also important to be clear about the criteria by which we want the quality of our research work to be evaluated so that we can ensure that there are methods in place to achieve them. It is the operationalization of "quality" that will make your research credible, publishable, actionable, and worth listening to. Without quality assurance strategies, research can be dismissed as an opinion essay with no relevance for being acted upon. So what criteria are appropriate to judge the quality of anti-oppressive research? And who gets to decide this? Figuring this out requires attention to the perspectives of those who have an interest in the research, all within the framework of tenets and ethics of anti-oppressive research. So, for example, you may know that statistical data will be important for having your research taken seriously by a certain policy maker, so you will need "valid and reliable" data-gathering and analysis procedures. Yet, you will also be cognizant that such procedures are designed to be consistent with the tenets and ethics of anti-oppressive research.

Collecting Data: Seeking, Listening, Learning

In a perfect world, everything we have planned in our design goes exactly as predicted. However, we live in an imperfect world. Collecting data is not a process in the research journey that is isolated from the other processes. As anti-oppressive researchers, we strive to be perceptive, to pay attention to what we are in the midst of. By paying attention, we gradually enhance our abilities to perceive, describe, analyze, and assess our reality. This increased perceptivity produces expanded experience and enables us to recognize and respond to opportunities as they arise throughout the research process.

In order to undertake the work of collecting data, we have to develop our listening and critical reflecting skills. By paying attention, a unique approach to listening emerges, one that we call political listening. We listen not for what we expected to hear or for what fits with what we already think, but for assumptions made both by ourselves as listeners and by speakers while attending to the dance of power. It involves being open and perceptive, interpreting, and judging. Too often social workers work hard to develop their interviewing practice skills and neglect the development of their perceptivity and interpretation skills. Through political listening, one becomes aware of the construction of multiple interpretations and multiple truths. Listening not only affects the relationship between researcher and participant, but facilitates analysis and the opportunities for anti-oppressive actions. By listening to participants, we begin to interpret the data, refine our research question, and rethink our design. By articulating their experience and thoughts, the participants make meaning of their lives. By paying attention and listening, we become increasingly aware of contexts, histories, and social dynamics. We can discover new opportunities for acting that we had not foreseen or planned, and come to know only through critical and detailed reflection on practice. Through paying attention and listening, research is reconceptualized and becomes an emergent, unfolding process rather than a trip to a predetermined destination.

This responsive and attentive way of doing research involves being open to shifts and shape changes in the research design, including the topic and question(s). This openness to uncertainty and emergence carries into the way that we attend to relationships as well. Interpersonal relationships are constantly open to renegotiation and change. Staying on top of the ebb and flow of relating is a time-consuming and challenging part of doing anti-oppressive research. We can't assume that we or anyone else can anticipate or control all that goes on between people during a research project. Instead, we position ourselves to respond well.

Making Meaning

Making meaning is often thought of as "analyzing data." When doing anti-oppressive research, we assume that meaning making is not restricted to any one part of the research process but happens throughout the research process. As such, we pay attention to our processes of interpretation, reflection, and construction of meaning as the research journey unfolds.

While meaning making is ongoing, we do have "data" to compile and make sense of, which is the focus of this next part of the discussion. In practice, we have found that it is useful, as we begin to review our data, to revisit our research questions and design and consider how they have evolved and shifted from the original plan. By rearticulating our research design, we can open ourselves to understanding more specifically what we want to know and thus ask of the data. We also can become more aware of the kinds of data and data sources we have and our positioning in relation to the data. This clarity grounds our interpretations and analysis of the data. Our way of gathering and working with data has probably been modified as the research process unfolds. All these shifts and changes influence and determine what data we actually have and how we make sense of the data.

There are a number of questions that we reflect upon as we plan for and engage in making meaning. These include issues of power and who does the analysis as well as issues of what concepts frame the analysis, who benefits from the meaning making, and what analytic tools are appropriate.

Power lurks in all our reflections and decisions. Just figuring out who gets the privilege of making meaning is laden with issues of power. For us, research is a social process and therefore the more positivist notion of one or two designated researchers who are responsible for analyzing the data is not our reality. Yet, even though we work collaboratively with participant-researchers, potential users of the research, and others in making meaning of our data, we are often challenged with the underlying hierarchy inherent in our relationships. The analysis stage presents an opportunity for the social construction of knowledge to be facilitated in an intentionally liberatory way. Some people in the process are seen as experts in the topic of study while others are seen as experts in particular data analysis techniques or in the lived experience of the data. Our collaborative meaning-making processes are influenced by the perceived and exercised power that we each bring to the process. These differences often become visible when there are disagreements about meanings or the importance of meanings. Further, while it may be ideal to have everyone possible involved in the meaning making, the reality often is that not everyone has the time or interest in participating. Figuring out how to enable individuals to participate as they would wish is challenging.

Another point of reflection in planning and engaging in meaning making concerns the conceptual framework that informs the research. Kirby and McKenna (1989) challenge us to articulate our "conceptual baggage" — that is, the concepts, beliefs, metaphors, and frameworks that inform our perspective on, and relationship to, the research topic. The term "baggage" has somewhat of a negative connotation, so we like to think about our "luggage." We carry our framework, which is not inherently good or bad, around with us and it is through this framework that we view the data. Making visible the luggage is an individual and collective process. Ensuring that everyone has had the opportunity to discuss the concepts that inform our perspectives helps to alleviate conflicts that can arise during the analysis of different perceptions of meaning and can expose contradictions in helpful ways. The conceptual framework that informed the project at the outset evolves during the project and new or additional concepts, metaphors, and frameworks emerge. Winnowing through minutes of meetings about the topic or trying to explain to your friends what the research is about are often fruitful ways to discern the emergent frameworks. Discussing these frameworks with research-participants can illuminate contradictions in concepts that may be held. It is illuminating to consider how different concepts, metaphors, and frameworks produce different meanings and the production of different knowledge. Such discussions often bring up questions about which interpretation(s) is seen as more valuable or believable than another and why.

As researchers we have found it particularly helpful to revisit the topic and questions to think through the fit between our approaches to analysis with what we really want to know. This revisiting is vital and informs the ability to make meaning and to extend the findings into conclusions and action.

The other point of reflection in the meaning-making process is thinking about who benefits from the chosen research process. What (whose) purpose does the research serve? There is an old saying that "figures don't lie, but liars can figure." The techniques of analysis, of making meaning of data, contribute to the meaning made. What is the intended outcome, and how is the data analysis, whether statistical or not, being constructed? What data are included in the analysis and what are left out? Why? If using interview data, who decides which quotes from participants to include and who to exclude? Again, knowledge is constructed, and paying attention to why and how it is constructed is an ongoing challenge for anti-oppressive researchers.

One of the strategies that Kirby and McKenna suggest as part of analyzing data is that one should "live with the data," meaning distancing oneself from the analysis in order to reflect on it (Kirby and McKenna, 1989). While we have found that being connected with and reflecting upon the data is critical in every stage of a research project and that it needs to be shared with co-researchers/participants, it is a particularly useful task to incorporate in the meaning-making process. This means that the participant-researcher(s) have to step back from the analysis for a while in order to reflect upon the data, the analysis, and the destination of the research. Once again, this illustrates that research is about relationships. Researchers develop an intimate relationship with data. Understanding that relationship (as articulated by the earlier questions posed in this section), and reflecting on the data in light of that relationship, is what analysis is about.

What kind of approach should be taken? Some options include involving participants or those ultimately affected by the research (who may not be the participants) in analyzing the data. What about having an advisory group for our research and having them conduct the analysis? Or finding a way to involve the people who will be responsible for making change as a result of the research? Whichever approach is used, consider how it will affect the "results" of the research and how those results could be used.

Posing Conclusions and New Questions, and Taking More Action

One continuously thinks about new questions, new realizations, and applications of ideas as one travels through the research process. Yet at some point along the journey, there is the time to capture them as "conclusions" to the trip. Tied to these conclusions are new questions as any research study usually raises more questions than answers. This circular process, a research process, reflects the lifelong learning process we are all in.

Conclusions have a particular power because they are the construction of knowledge that leads to recommendations and actions. As well, the conclusions are often the "sound bites" in the research that an audience listens for. Sometimes these consumers of our research are interested in our trip, in the story of our process, but more often they are interested in what we have "found." How conclusions are constructed, therefore, has particular impact on how consumers will take up the research in their own lives. We have found it challenging to construct conclusions that give the context of our journey to our findings. We have had to remind ourselves that posing conclusions is useful for us individually and collectively as researchers, as well as other potential audiences. Once again, questions regarding who gets to articulate the conclusions and questions and how this is done arise for us. These ideas may guide future research studies, so we ask ourselves whose interests are, or may be, served in these questions.

The manner and form in which we present our conclusions and questions also affects how they may be taken up. Formal written report form is commonplace and although useful, it is almost inherently classist, exclusionary, and appropriative in that it requires translating marginal knowledges into the language of the elite. A written report may be appropriate for our purpose, but as the way we present our research contributes to the meaning and significance attached to conclusions, other options are worthy of consideration. Brainstorming with co-researchers for options that could facilitate goals of empowerment and social justice then becomes a key part of the work. For instance, would it be better to hold a community workshop to discuss the research, or produce a journal article, or write a letter to the editor, or put the findings into a popular theatre presentation, or convene a session of strategic planning, or produce a video or a web site? Whose interests are served by each of the options available?

As we have noted throughout this chapter, research happens in relationships between people. It is a site for practising democracy. Recognizing our "agency," our ability to make a choice in how something will be done, enables us to be purposeful in our anti-oppressive actions. Reframing research as practice that produces radical democracy has helped us as researchers to move beyond the trap of oppositional thinking within anti-oppressive research. How we pose conclusions and devise actions is yet another opportunity to practise democracy and thereby make real our beliefs about power relations and social justice. Posing conclusions brings us to ask the critical question, so what? How will the research be used, and by whom? Who else could make use of it, and how? What uses could it have that were not intended? Remember that producing a product that sits on a shelf does not mean that the research, or the research report, does not fill a purpose. Too often research is used to delay decision making or distract attention from an issue. What is the professional obligation of the researcher in ensuring that the research is used for social change, not only throughout the process of conducting the research but after the research is concluded? We have found that by returning to our original discussions about the issues and what we wanted to know, we discover many possibilities about what to do with the findings and who will use them and how they will or could be used. Anti-oppressive action in the research process means taking up the processes and tools of research in ways that are congruent with the principles and values of empowerment and social justice wherever and whenever possible.

Credibility, Action-Ability, and Trustworthiness: Reclaiming Reliability and Validity

Assessing how well we did, how we know if our research is credible, actionable, and trustworthy, is important in anti-oppressive research. However, in contrast to most positivist work, this assessment is a theoretical, principled question as opposed to a technical concern. Anti-oppressive research is not so much concerned with the ability of our research instruments to "measure" accurately; rather, our concerns relate to whether we adhered to our research principles.

Some of the questions we ask include: Can participants see themselves in the study? Does the analysis "ring true" to participants? "Yes" answers to both these questions are most easily assured by having the participants of any research study determine the questions and do the analysis. We ask ourselves if we can see our own limitations as researchers and participants. Can we see where our conceptual luggage and our biases affected the process and outcome? We ask if we have been transparent in our biases and in the power relations and decisions that were made regarding the research process. Did we make any effort to include multiple perspectives? Did we take enough time for authentic relationships to be built and did we give people the time and respect to be truly honest? Finally, did we just skim the surface or did we strive for a critical understanding of an issue—that is, does our research have "soul"? And, we ask, did this research matter? Did it leave participants better off?

Putting the Tenets to Work: One Student's Experience

As mentioned at the beginning of this chapter, the University of Victoria School of Social Work requires students in their third-year BSW class, "Research for Social Change," to design and carry out an anti-oppressive research project. Christine, a student in this class, and Charles, an interviewer in Christine's project, agreed to let us share their experience of anti-oppressive research with you.

Initially Christine really struggled with grasping anti-oppressive research principles discussed in the course. She did not do very well on her research proposal assignment for the class, but she had good intentions. She worked with mentally challenged people and was concerned about how they were treated by professionals in the community (police, health workers, etc.). But in her initial research design, she proposed having other professionals talk on behalf of people with mental disabilities. In her next attempt, she then switched and proposed surveying the "clients" herself, so that the "clients" at least got to tell their own stories. But she, as the researcher, was still in control. All of her initial designs were loaded with "power over" relations where she was going to benefit (getting course credit, learning how to do research, developing relationships) by using marginalized people and their stories for her direct benefit.

Then one day, as Christine describes it, it came to her what anti-oppressive research was all about. She asked the people labelled as "clients" in the day home where she worked if any of them would like to be researchers into why professionals sometimes treat them so badly. Several said yes. She helped them learn about research, design their own interview questions, and they chose the professionals whom they would interview ("researching up" on the power ladder). It was an amazing process in which they interviewed professionals about their attitudes and training toward people with mental illnesses and cognitive disabilities, and at the end of the interview they revealed that they were living with mental illness/disability. The professionals were shocked, and change happened through the *process* of the research interviews. These participants (now called "interviewers," not "clients") have gone on with Christine to present at research conferences and write in newsletters, and have been truly empowered to become advocates in their own lives. This is what anti-oppressive research can be for marginalized people with the support of an "outsider."

278

In Christine's Words:

One of the first things I facilitated in this "learning" journey was a "team meeting" with the interviewers and myself. The conversation in the room that day was profound. On November 6, 2000, I met with the interviewers. The excitement and electricity that was in that room was indescribable. The interviewers were so excited that they were going to have "tactical advantage" and the "power of having the professionals come to them." For me as a facilitator, it was exciting to realize that I have had a positive impact on this marginalized group. The fact that I have simply provided these people with the environment to share their stories with the goal of educating people about mental illness has resulted in individual change with the interviewers and with [myself] the facilitator. I feel that my process was very empowering of the marginalized mental health clients. The fact that they were equal team players in each step of the research empowered them. They were involved in who was going to be interviewed, how the interviews were going to take place, where the interview was going to be, what type of questions were going to be asked, who they wanted to interview, how the information was going to be documented, and if they wanted to disclose their mental illness. This empowerment increased their self-esteem, their self-worth, their self-confidence, and their importance to society. I often see mentally ill people being labelled as incompetent citizens of society and this research process challenges this label of mentally ill people.

In addition, for me in hindsight, I realized that I have developed a respectful relationship with each interviewer. In realizing that, I listened attentively to them and took their advice, resulting in developing a sincere relationship with people, which all reiterates the fact that mentally ill people are valuable citizens. I am very proud of the [research-facilitating] work I did, and even though I have helped many mentally ill people in the past, I now know what it means to facilitate "power and freedom," which should be the true goal of social workers. I am thankful that I experienced such a wonderful transformation of attitudes with the clients/the interviewers, the professional people interviewed, and, most importantly, with myself. (Christine, electronic communication, October 2, 2001)

Christine also went on to support the co-researchers' presentation of their research at a conference. One researcher was Charles, and this is how he described the experience:

It all started when Christine asked me if I was interested in participating in a school project she was doing .... Intrigued, I immediately asked to interview a police officer. I thought to myself that this could be quite exciting; the shoe on the other foot type [of] thing .... We sat down together and discussed the interview. She [Christine] let me help in the formulation of the questions for the interview. This boosted my self-confidence quite a bit, having someone show interest in my ideas and suggestions. This way, I did not feel like a mindless test subject, and I was determined to do the interview to the best of my ability.

Charles goes on to describe his interview with the police officer regarding their attitudes and training about mental illness.

In our discourse, I was informed that there was no real training provided about the mentally ill in the RCMP infrastructure. She [the officer] said her department left days open for various training seminars. Upon learning that their training was on the streets, I understood why, when I was ill, various officers treated me so differently. This opened my eyes to the humanness of the police in general. As we were talking, the officer asked me if I was a student, like Christine. When I told her I suffered from mental illness, she was quite surprised. When I told her my diagnosis, she found it hard to believe. I felt surprised and delighted, for here was a police officer, a 10-year veteran on the force, dead wrong about my illness. I thought to myself that these people are heavily trained in psychology and human nature. Her surprised reaction broke the stereotype I felt about myself.

We conversed further, and then the ice broke. She relaxed suddenly, leaning forward and sideways, at the same time easing her arms up a little. Instead of her steely gaze of authority, her eyes were much warmer and friendly. In return I lowered my guard a little more and, in my perspective, we developed what could be defined as a good rapport. I think we both learned something. Her, the experience of talking with someone who is mentally ill, in a rational state of mind, and me, I learned that a police officer could casually chitchat, in a friendly manner, with the public, while on duty. It was a nice experience—I will always remember it. (Charles, personal writing, March 10, 2001)

The three tenets of anti-oppressive research that we outlined at the beginning of this chapter are very much present in the above story. The research project turned power on its head; it was all about relationships, it recognized that knowledge is socially constructed, and in its process and in its outcome, it was clearly focused toward social justice.

Foes and Allies: Relating Other Approaches to Anti-oppressive Research

By now you may be wondering if there is a distinctive anti-oppressive method of inquiry. In a word, no. There is no fixed or bona fide set of methods or methodologies that are inherently anti-oppressive. And yet, there are some alternative research methodologies that share similar political agendas and attend to relationships with the goal of empowerment and emancipation. These methodologies may help to inform our processes of designing an anti-oppressive research project.

Various emancipatory and critical social science research methodologies, such as feminist research and Freirian emancipatory or participatory research, are potential "allies" in doing anti-oppressive research. Participatory action research (PAR) is feasible and appropriate in only certain situations, and yet the term "participatory action" has become quite popular in community and government groups in the past few years. With this popularity has come co-optation. What passes for participatory action research in some instances is neither participatory (in that the research question has not come from the group but rather has been laid on or "sold to a group" by a researcher) nor action (in that any knowledge created through the research process is not owned and acted upon by the participants for their growth and transformation). In some cases the research process is quite prescriptive and yet labelled PAR. Social justice, the goal of emancipatory research, is truly realized only through participation, not prescription. As anti-oppressive researchers, we must learn to discern when principles of participation and social action are being misused, and to be careful about how we use these methods in our work.

Indigenous paradigms[13] also provide an approach to research and knowledge that goes beyond the positivism of Western science. Such methodologies are openly critical of and oppose the status quo and are committed to a transformative agenda to build a more just society. Such research methodologies call for critical inquirers to practise in their empirical endeavours what they preach in their theoretical formulations. The concept of Indigenous research methodology can be attractive to both Aboriginal and non-Aboriginal scholars and practitioners. Cora Weber-Pillwax poses several principles that underlay such a methodology. These include:

> (a) the interconnectedness of all living things, (b) the impact of motives and intentions on person and community, (c) the foundation of research as lived indigenous experience, (d) the groundedness of theories in indigenous epistemology, (e) the transformative nature of research, (f) the sacredness and responsibility of maintaining personal and community integrity, and (g) the recognition of languages and cultures as living processes. (Weber-Pillwax, 1999, p. 31)

Much interest currently exists for exploring the anti-oppressive and empowering possibilities of qualitative methodologies. Mehmoona Moosa-Mitha, in an earlier chapter in this book, for example, comments that she has found narrative approaches potentially compatible with anti-oppressive principles. Other chapters in this book pick up on ethnography and other approaches. Such qualitative methods, however, are not inherently anti-oppressive, so critical consideration of ethnographic methods, heuristic methods, grounded theory methods, phenomenological methods, narrative methods, discourse analysis, and so on are necessary. As anti-oppressive researchers, we do not necessarily dismiss these methods as inappropriate, but work with them to reconceptualize/retool how we may use the general approaches in ways that are in keeping with our values and purposes.

Other alternative methodologies that you may want to explore include critical ethnography, life histories, narratives, and autobiography. Becoming a vigilant reader of emancipatory and critical social science is one way to become conversant with the ongoing quest for methodologies that may be useful in doing anti-oppressive research. Several social work journals, such as *Journal of Progressive Human Services, Affilia,* and *Critical Social Work* (on-line journal) are great places to browse. In addition the references cited in this article may introduce you to some ways of rethinking research and becoming an anti-oppressive researcher.

The point is that many methodologies touch on some but not necessarily all of the tenets that we are trying to foreground in anti-oppressive research. If anything, we are arguing that anti-oppressive research is not methodologically distinctive, but epistemologically

282

distinctive. We have come to believe that if we are to transform research into an anti-oppressive practice, then it is the epistemological underpinnings (e.g., relationships of the knower, the known, and those who want to know) that are key. Therefore, while a piece of research may use anti-oppressive or positivist jargon, the words are irrelevant. It is the principles/tenets put into practice that are important to consider. And it is these principles (e.g., social justice, shifting power to insiders, community building, working for change) that we need to look for in our critical reading of research. A number of emergent methodologies have lost their principles in their bid for institutional acceptance, and in this sense we cannot rely on labels alone to reveal their anti-oppressive/ oppressive positioning. We must continually be vigilant in assessing the tenets at work as we uncover methodological foes and allies.

A Few Concluding Thoughts ... for Now

Part of the concept of agency that we have talked about is the ability to change one's self. This requires constant reflection and critique. In proposing the idea of "anti-oppressive research," we do not want to create another dogma. Horkheimer, in later life, critiqued the arrogance of any revolutionary tradition that in itself can turn around and be oppressive (Ray, 2003, p. 164). Always being reflective about yourself and your work is not easy. Just when we think we're getting it right, we realize we're only getting it better. Becoming anti-oppressive is not a comfortable place to be. It means constantly reflecting on how one is being constructed and how one is constructing one's world. This chapter is part of our becoming. We hope it helps you in your research journey as well.

Notes

1. We want to acknowledge the support and hard work contributed by Pat Rasmussen, who collaborated on early versions of this paper. We also acknowledge the Social Work 301 students who have been with us on this journey to anti-oppressive research, with special thanks to Christine and Andrea for their unique contributions.
2. Definitions of epistemology: "The philosophical theory of knowledge—of how we know what we know" (Marshall, 1998, p. 197). "That branch

of philosophy which deals with the theory, nature, scope and basis of knowledge, or which investigates the possibility of knowledge itself .... The critical study of the principles, hypotheses and findings of the various sciences" (Macey, 2001, p. 114).

3. One of the first articles to look at co-option of Freirian methodology was R. Kidd and K. Kumar, Co-opting Freire: A critical analysis of pseudo-Freirian adult education. *Economic and Political Weekly* 16 (1/2) (1981), 27–36.

4. Critical: By using the term "critical," we want to point to a connection with critical theory as associated with the Frankfurt School thinkers. This is not to be confused with use of "critical thinking," etc., as found in liberalism, or "criticism" as found in literature, film studies, etc.

5. Research: We define research as to re-search, to look again, in a careful and considered manner.

6. Epistemic privilege: "The claim of 'epistemic privilege' amounts to claiming that members of an oppressed group have a more immediate, subtle and critical knowledge about the nature of their oppression than people who are non-members of the oppressed group" (Narayan, 1988, p. 35).

7. For a more thorough discussion of anti-oppressive theories, please see the earlier chapter by Mehmoona Moosa-Mitha in this book.

8. Critical theory: "Critical theory springs from an assumption that we live amid a world of pain, that much can be done to alleviate that pain, and that theory has a crucial role to play in that process" (Poster as quoted in Lather, 1991, p. 3).

9. For us, social justice means transforming the way resources and relationships are produced and distributed so that all people can live dignified lives in a way that is ecologically sustainable. Our critical view of social justice includes social sustainability, intergenerational equity, global justice, and eco-centric justice (Ife, 2002, pp. 75–78). It takes direct aim at the sources that reproduce structural disadvantage, whether those are through institutions, like income security, or through human relations, such as racism. It is also about creating new ways of thinking and being, not only criticizing the status quo. Social justice means acting from a standpoint of those who have the least power and influence, relying on the wisdom of the oppressed (Ife, 2002, p. 88).

10. Social constructionism speaks to theories that relate to the socially created nature of life. These theories are first associated with the 1966 book, *The Social Construction of Reality* (Berger and Luckmann, 1966).

11. "Empowerment" is a problematic term because it is often used with varied meanings. In this chapter, when "empowerment" appears in quotations, it is being contested as a term that often implies a feeling without real

power, upward mobility, individual self-confidence, or it is an illusion of real power. When we as authors speak of real empowerment, we are using the term as Lather does, "drawing on Gramsci's (1971) ideas of counter-hegemony ... empowerment to mean analyzing ideas about the causes of powerlessness, recognizing systemic oppressive forces, and acting both individually and collectively to change the conditions of our lives" (Lather, 1991, pp. 3–4).

12. Cultivating co-researchers is one way that many who try to be more anti-oppressive in their research engage the tenets of anti-oppressive work. As knowledge is socially constructed and what is created through coming together as knowers is more than what each co-researcher knew before coming together, co-researching can become a way of producing knowledge and producing knowers. Yet such an approach is not without its own power issues. Too often, we have seen projects where insiders are co-researchers who are marginalized or given a token position within the research design. It begs the question, to what extent can research truly be anti-oppressive unless the people experiencing the issue under study *are* the researchers and are in control of the research decisions?

13. We use "Indigenous" rather than "First Nations" to acknowledge the work being done around the world by Indigenous peoples to resist oppression, particularly oppressive research.

References

Berger, P., and Luckmann, T. (1966). *The social construction of reality*. Toronto: Random House.

Caputo, J.D. (2000). *More radical hermeneutics: On not knowing who we are*. Bloomington: Indiana University Press.

Chambon, A.S., Irving, A., and Epstein, L. (1999). *Reading Foucault for social work*. New York: Columbia University Press.

hooks, b. (1994). *Teaching to transgress: Education as the practice of freedom*. New York: Routledge.

Ife, J. (2002). *Community development: Community-based alternatives in an age of globalization* (2nd edition). Frenchs Forest, NSW: Pearson Education Australia.

Kirby, S.L., and McKenna, K. (1989). *Experience research social change: Methods from the margins*. Toronto: Garamond Press.

Lather, P. (1991). *Getting smart: Feminist research and pedagogy with/in the postmodern*. New York: Routledge.

Macey, D. (2001). *The Penguin dictionary of critical theory*. London: Penguin Books.

Marcotte, G. (1995). Métis c'est may nation. "Your Own People," comme on dit: Life histories from Eva, Evelyn, Priscilla, and Jennifer Richard. Paper prepared for the Royal Commission on Aboriginal Peoples.

Marshall, G. (Ed.). (1998). *A dictionary of sociology* (2nd edition). Oxford: Oxford University Press.

McDonald, K. (2003). Alain Touraine. In A. Elliott and L. Ray (Eds.), *Key contemporary social theorists*. Oxford: Blackwell.

Narayan, U. (1988). Working together across difference: Some considerations on emotions and political practice. *Hypatia* 3 (2), 31–47.

Ray, L. (2003). Max Horkheimer. In A. Elliott and L. Ray (Eds.), *Key contemporary social theorists*. Oxford: Blackwell Publishing.

Tuhiwai Smith, L. (1999). *Decolonizing methodologies: Research and Indigenous peoples*. London: Zed Books.

van Krieken, R. (2003). Norbert Elias. In A. Elliott and L. Ray (Eds.), *Key contemporary social theorists*. Oxford: Blackwell.

Weber-Pillwax, C. (1999). Indigenous research methodology: Exploratory discussion of an elusive subject. *The Journal of Educational Thought* 3 (1), 31–45.

Williams, M., Unrau, Y., and Grinnell, R. (1998). *Introduction to social work research*. Itasca: F.E. Peacock Publishers, Inc.

CONTRIBUTOR BIOGRAPHIES

Kathy Absolon is Anishnabe kwe with British ancestry, a sister in the Marten clan, and a member of Flying Post First Nation. She is also first-degree Midewiwin of the Three Fires Society. Kathy is an assistant professor of Indigenous Studies at the First Nations University of Canada in Regina, Saskatchewan. She teaches courses in history, Indigenous women, and research. Kathy is currently working on her doctoral degree at the Ontario Institute for Studies in Education with an emphasis in Indigenous epistemology and Indigenous research methodology. Kathy strives to seek balance in her traditional and contemporary research and education.

April Barlow is a former youth in care and a founding coordinator of the Victoria Youth in Care Network. She has a background in working with youth and young mothers.

Erinn Brown is a former youth in care and has an interest in working with youth and children. She has been a research assistant and a workshop co-facilitator with the project for more than four years.

Leslie Brown is the director of the School of Social Work, University of Victoria. She enthusiastically teaches and learns about research and knowing in undergraduate and graduate programs in social work, Indigenous governance, and human and social development. She just as enthusiastically engages in community-based and anti-oppressive research projects whenever invitations and curiosities present innovative possibilities.

Fairn herising is currently a graduate student at the University of Victoria, School of Social Work. She attempts to engage life, love, and work as strangely and queerly as possible. She is profoundly aware that her ability to do so is woven from the beautiful fabric of partners in struggle. She offers her thanks to these many partners of the past and present.

Carol Hubberstey is a community-based researcher and consultant with a particular focus on practices and policies affecting children, youth, and families. She has participated in several social development projects that explored opportunities to create change in people's lives through program and policy development.

Sally Kimpson is a doctoral student in nursing and education at the University of Victoria. She has research interests in women with disabilities and the barriers to health, such as poverty and inequality, that they face.

Maggie Kovach is Saulteaux from southern Saskatchewan. She is an assistant professor at the School of Social Work, University of Victoria, and is currently working on her Ph.D. in Interdisciplinary Studies (Social Work and Education). Her research interests include the application of Indigenous theory(s) and Indigenous research design within interdisciplinary contexts. She has also worked extensively in the field of First Nations curriculum development (academic and community based) with a particular focus on distance education and community-based course development and facilitation for Indigenous peoples.

Rena Miller has worked in clinical practice since 1985 at Island Family Counselling Centre, and has been a social work educator at University of Victoria since 1994, focusing on practice-oriented courses. She has taught for the School of Child and Youth Care at UVic and for City University, as well as providing training and supervision for many community social service agencies and consumer groups. Rena's MSW thesis, from which her chapter is adapted, was featured in Dr. Marie Campbell's recent text on institutional ethnography. Rena is currently acquiring more lived experience on southern Vancouver Island.

Mehmoona Moosa-Mitha teaches at the School of Social Work at the University of Victoria. Her research interests are in the areas of anti-racist feminist theorizations of citizenship rights, particularly children's citizenship rights, as well as those of marginalized communities. She is also interested in social theory, particularly anti-oppressive theories, as it is taught and conceived both in the academy through teaching and in the community as an activist.

Karen Potts is from Saskatchewan and holds degrees in economics and social work. She currently is a Ph.D. candidate at the University of Victoria where she also teaches courses in anti-oppressive research, community development, and social justice economics.

Deborah Rutman is an adjunct assistant professor with the University of Victoria School of Social Work, and a research associate with the Research Initiatives for Social Change unit. Her most recent projects focus on support issues for adults and youth affected by fetal alcohol spectrum disorder, substance use during pregnancy, and young people's transitions from care.

Susan Strega has been an activist in feminist, anti-racist, and sex worker organizations for many years. She is currently an assistant professor in the Faculty of Social Work at the University of Manitoba. Her research interests include violence against women, child welfare, sex work, and ethics. She believes that anti-oppressive practice is both necessary and possible.

Robina Thomas, Qwul'sih'yah'maht, is Lyackson of the Coast Salish Nation. She is an assistant professor at the School of Social Work, University of Victoria, and is working on her doctorate in Indigenous governance. One of her main topics of research interest is residential schools.

Cam Willett is an assistant professor of Indigenous Education at the First Nations University of Canada in Regina, Saskatchewan. With over 14 years of experience in Aboriginal education as a classroom teacher, researcher, and administrator, his teaching and research focuses on the retention of Aboriginal students in postsecondary education, Aboriginal research methodology, and postcolonial theory. He is currently a doctoral student in the department of Adult Education and Educational Psychology at the Ontario Institute for Studies in Education at the University of Toronto.

INDEX

multiple differences, 64
multiplicity, 63
not-knowing stance, emphasis on, 60
ontological assumptions, 64–66
oppression, analysis and conceptualization of, 63
postmodern theories, 56–61
praxis, notion of, 67
social constructionist, 49
social identity theories, 61–64
Anzaldúa, Gloria, 144, 145
"apologetic addendum," 137–138
The Archaeology of Knowledge (Foucault), 217
asymmetrical research, 132
authenticity, 246
autobiographical narratives
    androcentric bias, challenge to, 74
    biases, 84, 89
    conclusion, 91–92
    cultural themes, 84, 86–87
    described, 73–74
    ethnographic intentions, 79–82
    feminist research, 74–76
    first person, use of, 76–77
    initial approach, 78–79
    margin, movement from, to centre, 88
    "place," 82–83
    power, representation, and research, 83–86
    as powerful tool, 75–76
    self-reflexivity, 74–75, 90
    storytelling, 76–77
    study method, choice of, 79–82
    support for, 90
    time, 82–83
    topic, choice of, 79–82

B

Barlow, April, 14, 153–178
B.C. Federation of Youth in Care Networks, 175–176
B.C. Health Research Foundation, 160, 162
Blood, Bread, and Poetry (Rich), 133
borderland, 145
Braidotti, Rosi, 133, 139
Brookes, Anne-Louise, 87
Brown, Erinn, 14, 153–178
Brown, Leslie, 1–15, 15, 255–283
Bryson, Mary, 138
BSN students, 79–80
Butler, Judith, 140–141

C

Campbell, Marie, 183, 196
care. *See* Supporting Young People's Transitions
choices, 255, 260
Chow, Rey, 144
collective underpinning of Indigenous methodology, 30–31
collectivist research principles, 28
Collins, Patricia Hill, 144
colonialism, understanding of, 120
colonization, 117, 121, 252–253
communitarian liberals, 40–41, 43
community-based researchers, 160
complicity, 230–231
conceptual framework, 274
conclusions, posing, 275–277
conscientization, 221
contextual validation, location as, 122–124
credibility, 277
crisis of representation, 2–3
critical race theory
    discourse, 217